INSIDE THE GAMBLER'S MIND

BOOKS BY DAVID SPANIER

Europe, Our Europe

Total Poker

The Gambler's Pocket Book

Total Chess

Welcome to the Pleasuredome: Inside Las Vegas

Inside the Gambler's Mind

INSIDE
THE GAMBLER'S
MIND

DAVID SPANIER

UNIVERSITY OF NEVADA PRESS

RENO   LAS VEGAS   LONDON

THE GAMBLING STUDIES SERIES
Series Editor: William R. Eadington

Inside the Gambler's Mind by David Spanier was first published in Great
Britain in 1987 by Martin Secker & Warburg Ltd. under the title *Easy Money:
Inside the Gambler's Mind* and was reprinted in Great Britain in 1988 by
Penguin Books. The 1994 University of Nevada Press edition reproduces the
original except for a new title, the front matter, which has been modified to
reflect the new publisher, and minor changes to the text made by the author.

The paper used in this book meets the requirements of American
National Standard for Information Sciences—Permanence of Paper for
Printed Library Materials, ANSI Z39.48-1984. Binding
materials were selected for strength and durability.

LIBRARY OF CONGRESS CATALOGING-IN-PUBLICATION DATA

Spanier, David.
Inside the gambler's mind / David Spanier.
p.   cm.   — (The Gambling studies series)
Revision of: Easy money. 1987.
"With minor changes throughout text made by the author"—T.p. verso.
Includes index.
ISBN 0-87417-242-X (paper : acid-free paper)
1. Gambling.   2. Gamblers—Psychology.   I. Spanier, David. Easy
money.   II. Title.   III. Series.
HV6713.S63   1994
616.85'227—dc20   94-8704
CIP

University of Nevada Press, Reno, Nevada 89557 USA
Copyright © 1987, 1994 by David Spanier
All rights reserved
Cover design by Heather Goulding
Cover illustration by Ian Miller
Printed in the United States of America

2 4 6 8 9 7 5 3 1

For
Bill and Margaret Eadington,
good spirits of Lake Tahoe

CONTENTS

FOREWORD

Gambling is good for you. That's my thesis, and I don't feel I need to apologize for saying it straight out.

Any activity such as gambling, which the human race has pursued since man first began to walk upright, and perhaps even before then, which has been popular in virtually all societies throughout history, and which is so prevalent in nearly every country in the modern world, has got to have a lot going for it.

I believe that human instinct is to be trusted here, against all the mass and weight down the ages of reformers, moralists, legislators and assorted do-gooders who think that gambling is bad for people, and have tried to curtail it. On the contrary, I happen to believe that people should be allowed to do what they want to do, provided it does not upset other people, or do too much harm to themselves.

I confess that while I gambled away most of my allowance as a young man, nowadays my gambling – apart from poker, which is a game of skill – is limited to the occasional good bet when I think the odds are in my favour. So I am not a gambler myself, really; I am a student *of* gambling, which is rather different.

As the text makes clear, my thanks are due to very many people who talked to me about this subject, in all its aspects. The insights into gambling and gamblers in my book are a tribute to their experience and their views: the misjudgements (like bad bets) are my own.

Oh God, let me break even tonight
GAMBLER'S PRAYER

I
WINNERS & LOSERS

1

THE DAY OF THE LAMB

The big thrill came from learning
things nobody else in the world
had ever known.
                    Edward O. Thorp

He was tall, thin, wore rimless spectacles and looked just like
what he was, a young assistant professor of maths on a weekend
trip to the bright lights of Reno. What's more his play was irri-
tatingly slow. He paused for thought and stared at all the cards
dealt. 'Another system player' was the unspoken comment of
the blackjack dealer. She was particularly unfriendly to this slow-
witted hick, dragging out her time with one-dollar bets at five
goddam a.m. in the graveyard shift. When he asked if he could
play two hands at a time, she refused. It was house policy, she
told him with a derisive little snort, that he had to bet two dollars
per hand if he wanted to play two hands. He was tired and
irritable, already down a hundred on the night, and there was a
sharp exchange of words. Pert in her buckskin shirt and string
tie, she retaliated by dealing out as fast as she could.

The prof stolidly continued to play his one hand, won, raised
his stake to four dollars, won, raised his stake to eight dollars, and
won again. He let the sixteen dollars ride and won that hand too.
'Guess it's time to take a small profit,' he told the infuriated
dealer. He stacked up twenty dollars in chips on the table and
continued to bet in units of twenty. By the end of the deck he
had recouped his hundred loss and a few dollars extra. He picked
up his pile of chips and, sandy-eyed and stiff, stumbled off to bed.

Two nights later at a casino in Lake Tahoe he was betting in
units of a hundred dollars. His maladroit fumbling had been
honed to a streamlined accuracy. Within thirty minutes of sitting
down the prof and a companion had emptied the table's money

tray, which is the blackjack equivalent of breaking the bank. The dealer began to panic. One of the girls sent an SOS to her boyfriend higher up in the casino. 'Oh, help me! Please, help me!' The pit boss who had welcomed the high rollers with dinner and expansive smiles looked apprehensive.

In a couple of hours the pair broke the bank again. The huge pile of chips in front of them stood at over $17,000. By now the professor was feeling the after-effects of dinner and, tiring rapidly, decided to cash in. As he threaded his way over to the cashier's cage he was surprised to observe three or four very pretty, scantily clad girls wandering back and forth across his path, flashing him inviting looks. 'If you've got the money, honey . . . I've got the time.' Weaving his way back between the ladies, like Ulysses sailing home, he was horrified to see his friend at the blackjack table (now that his mentor was no longer at his elbow) hell-bent on hurling his profits back whence they had come. Despite all pleas, despite his losses, the man wouldn't budge. He hung onto the table yelling, 'I . . . WILL . . . NOT . . . LEAVE . . . THIS . . . PLACE!' He kept shouting the cards were hot. It took forty-five minutes and several thousand dollars down the chute to prise him out.

Yes, the prof was a system player all right. He had discovered a system which reversed the laws of gambling. It was soon to up-end Nevada. The petulant blackjack dealer, if she had but known it, was participating in an experiment which changed the face of the industry. Its repercussions are still being felt in every casino, every night, in every resort worldwide.

Edward O. Thorp was not, is not, a gambler. But since childhood he had always been excited by scientific experiment. Son of a Los Angeles security guard, he loved shrill noises and loud bangs. His most bizarre test was when he filled a war-surplus balloon with stove gas and floated it 800 feet into the air, tethered by a blackened cord invisible in the night. A few minutes later the young Thorp watched in delight as a parachute flare suspended from the balloon automatically activated itself, illuminating a good section of LA with an eerie white glare. The mysterious UFO was never explained.

A mysterious light might well have manifested itself over the casino that night when he first tested his blackjack theory. As he told me, he believes he could have made an income of three hundred thousand a year at the game. (In practice, one must doubt that claim because he would have had to contend, in the process, with being cheated out of every cent he had, if he had tried: apart from a few casual trips he never played blackjack seriously again.) No, Thorp was a mathematician. Instead of playing blackjack, he went away and wrote a book about it, *Beat The Dealer* (1962), which has become a classic of gambling literature. It stands in relation to gambling rather as Einstein's theory of relativity does to physics – it changed perception of reality. It has sold in hardback alone over 100,000 copies and has gone on selling every year. It has been followed by commentaries and further studies and deeper analysis, spawning a whole sub-culture of blackjack.

Blackjack is the American name for the homely card game of 21, pontoon as it is known in England when played around the kitchen table, or vingt-et-un, to give it its French title. It is an entertaining game, first of all because each player is in control of his own hand (unlike the impersonal mechanical spin of a roulette wheel). Secondly, it can be quite a sociable game during which there is time to chat to friends or other players at the table, sharing the ups and downs of fortune; alternatively, if you feel like unwinding by yourself, you can play blackjack all night without uttering a word to anyone. And third, the game offers enough of a mental challenge to make it continually interesting, to experts and novices alike. (I set out the basic rules of the game on the following page.)

In 1987 blackjack accounted for more than half of Nevada casinos' gross 'win' of $1·5 billion from table games. In Britain, though it was only 18 per cent of the drop (roulette is more popular), it nevertheless produced around £60 million in profit. It's the only casino game that really tempts me, though like Professor Thorp (but I am no mathematician at all) I do not pursue it seriously: my idea is 40 minutes' relaxation at the table after dinner sometimes . . . and if I get five units ahead, I streak for the exit. As you can see from the figures, blackjack is very big business indeed. The casinos, notwithstanding Thorp

THE RULES OF BLACKJACK

The dealer deals out two cards to each player around the table and two to himself: the point of the game being to get nearer than the dealer to a total of 21. Cards are counted at their face value, with court cards counting 10 and aces either 1 or 11.

Each player in turn either stands pat on his hand or draws additional cards, to try and get closer to 21. But when the player (who has to act before the dealer) goes over a total of 21, his hand is busted and he loses his stake.

On his side, the dealer must stand on totals of 17 and over, and must draw on hands below 17. He shows only one card, concealing the other, until all the players have acted, so they do not know in advance what he holds.

Winning hands are paid off at even money. Ties are a stand off. A blackjack (ace and a 10-card) is paid out $1\frac{1}{2}$ times to the lucky player.

From this it will be seen that, whereas the player has several options open to him, the dealer has to play according to a fixed formula, without any skill or variation. (Ergo, it is very silly to lose your temper or otherwise abuse the dealer.)

The player may stand pat on a stiff (12 to 16) to avoid the risk of busting, if the dealer is also showing a bad up-card. Other player options include splitting pairs so as to play two hands at once, or doubling down so as to double the stake on a good hand.

A dealer blackjack wins only the player's stake (not $1\frac{1}{2}$ times): when the dealer is showing an ace up, the player may take insurance which pays out 2–1 against a dealer ace-ten. In a single-deck game a blackjack will be dealt on average every 25 hands.

There are many sub-variations to the above rules, which vary from casino to casino. Thus, in some places doubling down is permitted on any total; in London it is allowed only on totals of 9, 10 or 11; in some places any pair may be split, in London not 4s, 5s and 10s.

It is just as well to spend a couple of minutes reading the casino's rules – which are either on display or available if you ask the dealer before actually sitting down at the blackjack table.

Caveat emptor!

and his followers and all their arcane calculations, will never give it up.

Some time before the earnest young man's experiment took place, he had had a preliminary run. During a Christmas school vacation, when he and his wife decided to take a break from teaching at the University of California at Los Angeles by spending a few days in Las Vegas, a colleague had called Thorp's attention to an article in the *Journal of the American Statistical Association*, describing a strategy for playing blackjack. It claimed that, following the strategy given, the house's advantage was limited to the tiny edge of 0.62 per cent. This allowed the player an almost even break. ('Almost' of course is not enough: as explained in chapter six, that percentage will wipe out a gambler's capital in the long run, as surely as night follows day.) Thorp purchased ten silver dollars and tried out the strategy as recommended. After many vicissitudes, up and down, he lost eight-and-a-half bucks, and quit. No gambler he! But the experience intrigued him, especially the evidence before his eyes that most players hadn't a clue about the fundamentals of the game or how to play their hands correctly. (In my experience, this still holds true today.) The visit implanted a seed in his mind. When he got back home he studied the article ('The Optimum Strategy in Blackjack', Baldwin, Cantey, Maisel and McDermott). Then came the quantum jump, the moment – Eureka! – that Thorp changed the world. 'In a flash of mathematical insight I realized it must be possible for the player to beat the game.'

His idea, as he described it, was this. The basic strategy by Baldwin *et al.* was a complete set of instructions for the player, advising him how to play his cards according to the hand he was dealt and the dealer's upcard. But to simplify the calculations, this analysis assumed that the deck always contained its average composition, that is that all the hands were dealt from a complete shuffled deck. Yet that is not the case in actual play! (It would be like coming upon a large area of the earth and expecting to find it completely flat.) After the first card is dealt out, the deck is in a marginally different composition, and after the first half-dozen hands are dealt, the deck is likely to be in quite a radically different composition. Suppose, to take an extreme case, that all four aces have been dealt out – you cannot get a blackjack. Or again, take a very extreme case, that the deck has been dealt out all the way to the last six cards and they consist of two sevens and four eights. How should you bet? The answer, as Thorp explains, is the maximum – borrow from the bank if you like because you cannot lose. You stand pat on your two cards and when the dealer looks at his hand he finds either (7,7), (7,8) or (8,8). Being below 17 he has to draw – and whatever card he draws busts his hand.

This will never happen in practice, maybe. But in general the proportion of cards left in the deck, after the first cards come out, will not be the same as in a complete deck, and the casino/player advantage will fluctuate. Mathematical considerations suggested to Thorp that this fluctuation would often be larger than 0.62 per cent, and further, that the player would frequently have the advantage himself. 'If the player were to bet very heavily when he held the advantage and very lightly when he had the disadvantage, he would not need to have the advantage very often in order to make a handsome profit.' This was Thorp's great insight. Obvious when you see how, isn't it?

So Thorp, now an assistant professor of maths at M.I.T., set about determining when the player did have an advantage and how large it would be. A deck of cards is a complicated affair. There are 34 million different ways of removing cards from a deck as they might be removed by a dealer. The Baldwin calculations had taken four capable young men a total of twelve man-years of off-duty army time, working with the aid of desk calculators. Thorp's first step was to master every detail of these calculations; his next to analyse the effect on casino advantage when changes were made in the proportions of various cards in the deck. The serious disadvantage to the player if all the aces are out I mentioned above. Because greater precision was required, it was necessary to extend the Baldwin calculations many times and since ten thousand man-years at desk calculators were required, the problem could only be cracked with the aid of a computer. Thorp had access to an IBM 704. It was a long and tricky business writing out the program. When he had finished it took the computer seven hours to print out the answers, enough numbers to fill an average exercise book.

The answers he got amazed Thorp. The typical casino advantage over a player using the best complete strategy, now known everywhere as basic strategy, he found to be only 0.21 per cent. If various groups of cards were used up in play, the advantage surged wildly back and forth between casino and player (blackjack players knew this empirically but they had no idea why – winning and losing to them was just 'luck'.) The biggest swing was caused by the four fives. When they were out of the deck the player had an edge of more than 3.3 per cent. The next most important group was the four aces; with them out the casino advantage rose to about 2.7 per cent. The effect of variations in the 16 cards of ten-value (king, queen, jack, ten) was even more dramatic. The player or house advantage sometimes swung to plus ten per cent, occasionally much more. (What this means, putting it in a simple way, is that when there are lots of tens in the deck, the house is likely to go bust drawing on 'stiffs', small hands of 12 to 16, whereas the player can stick.)

Thorp developed a detailed system of play which involved keeping count of the number of ten-value cards remaining to be played. This technique is known – dreaded word for the casinos! – as counting.

The essence of it is that low cards are counted as $+1$ and high cards as -1. (If the cards are dealt out in the order A,2,3,4,5,6,7,8,9,10, the point values would be A (-1), 2 $(+1)$, 3 $(+1)$, 4 $(+1)$, 5 $(+1)$, 6 $(+1)$, 7 (0), 8 (0), 9 (0), 10 (-1), giving a running total of $+3$. Modern systems are much more elaborate.) The casinos hate counters. If they detect you counting, anywhere in the world today, even playing for very small stakes like a couple of bucks a hand, the dealer and the pit boss will be on their guard. If you look like an expert, they will usually intervene to take preventive action, quite often barring you straight away. 'OK fella, you're so smart, go count the spots on the dice!'

When Thorp emerged from his back room into the light of day, he was hailed, to his astonishment, as a mathematical wizard, a man who had discovered the philosopher's stone which could turn dross into gold. What happened was that he decided to give a little talk to the annual meeting of the American Mathematical Society in Washington DC on a simplified version of his strategy based on counting fives; a few days before the meeting, the society, as is usual in academic get-togethers, published abstracts of the two hundred or so papers that were to be delivered. Included was his short abstract titled 'Fortune's Formula: A Winning Strategy for Blackjack'. After his talk he was asked to give a press conference; then he was televised by a major network and interviewed on a number of radio programmes. Over the next few days and weeks he received literally hundreds of letters and long-distance phone calls, requesting more information, and several offers to back him in a casino test of the new system. The amounts proffered ranged from a few thousands to as much as $100,000. He had unwittingly touched a deep, probably universal, chord in the public's subconscious, the desire to get rich quick at the expense of the casinos: easy money.

As I explained, Thorp is not a gambler, he is a mathematician. He is not against making money; he later developed, as I shall relate, a 'system' for beating the stock market which is probably the most successful method ever developed, which he has employed, consistently, with spectacular success, to become a millionaire many times over. All this was in the future. For the moment, the question was whether to go to Nevada and put his theories to the test. He finally decided to go: what may have clinched matters, as he confessed in the *Atlantic Monthly* (June 1962) were the scoffs and boasts from casinos themselves that his claims were ridiculous. Their arrogance was succinctly summed up by a casino operator who was asked on a nationwide television programme if the customers ever walked away winners. The man replied, in a memorable formulation: 'When a lamb goes to the slaughter, the lamb might kill the butcher. But we always bet on the butcher.'

Thorp took up the most attractive of the many offers pouring in, from two New York millionaires, both large-scale gamblers. There were two approaches possible: a 'wild' method of playing which involved betting the casino limit whenever the advantage to the player exceeded, say, one per cent; and a conservative method of progressively increasing the stakes, as the advantage in any particular deck grew bigger. The former method could produce the greatest gain in the shortest time, but in the run of a few days the fluctuations in the player's capital could be violent. His sponsors were prepared to back him beyond $100,000 if necessary, but Thorp did not know how he would be affected if he found himself betting more each minute than his monthly salary. Besides, his objective wasn't to make big money for his backers, but to conduct a serious experiment. Accordingly, he favoured the second approach, of being certain of a moderate win. His staking method – which has become the basis of all counting techniques at blackjack in the years since then – was to double his basic stake when the player advantage was one per cent, increase it to four times when the advantage was two per cent, levelling off at ten times when the advantage increased to five per cent or more. If his bets ranged from $50 to $500, six or seven thousand capital would probably suffice; to be on the safe side they took $10,000.

Is it any wonder when the cutey-pie dealers at Reno saw this earnest gangling young fellow at the table, with his tedious way of peering around at all the cards, that they marked him down as another nut – and got irritated at his play? It's all very different nowadays, if you ever get invited behind the scenes in a modern casino. Up in the 'eye in the sky', in the tangle of cables and switches behind the one-way mirrors, you will find a space-age scene: a bank of TV cameras tracking every blackjack table in the house, monitored by a card-counting expert, capable of recording on video tape every hand that is played out night and day. What they are looking for, apart from checking on the dealers' honesty, are Thorp's heirs and successors.

A couple of things rapidly happened to Thorp on this field trip which are still typical of management behaviour. First, when it became clear, whether he was a nut or just lucky or whatever, that he could beat the game, the casinos took preventive action. Their most simple resource was shuffling up the deck. If the cards are re-shuffled early on in the deal, there is less scope for the player to pick up variations in the composition of the deck, which naturally show up more markedly as the deck is reduced to the last few cards. The casinos did not know what

Thorp was really up to; this was simply a device to change the flow, break the pattern in some way. He also detected cheating. Secondly, as soon as Thorp and his companions changed gear, to play at the high-stakes tables, the managers would arrive, wreathed in smiles. High rollers are the jam on the bread-and-butter of the regular small-time punters, and each casino wants as much of the pot as it can get its sticky fingers on. Thorp and his friends were playing $500 maximum. Many pleasantries and politenesses would be exchanged and hospitality proffered. But the deck was shuffled up even earlier, 15 cards from the end, 25 cards from the end and finally 42 cards from the end! Note that Thorp was not doing anything wrong whatever. He was playing by the rules of the game. But he was using his expertise to beat the game, and that, to put it plainly, was not acceptable. *Rien ne va plus.*

Next day, when they returned to the first casino where they had played, where Thorp had upset the dealer, they found they were banned. The casino would be happy – another typical user-friendly touch – to pick up their tab for dinner. Thorp called the pit boss and asked him what it was all about. He explained, in a very courteous way, that they were puzzled at his winning the day before at a rate which was large for his bet size, and had decided some sort of system was involved. (Thorp had merely recouped a $100 loss and made a small profit, but small profits to the players are not what casinos are in business for.) Word travels fast in the green felt jungle. He was then informed he was banned from playing at the hotel they were staying at, and this went for his two friends as well and any other friends he might have. However, re-visiting another casino where they had played and won the night before, he was warmly welcomed as the high roller who had been down but somehow wriggled off the hook. They were invited to dine, courtesy of the house, and did themselves well – baked oysters on the half shell, twice, plus all the trimmings. Long hours of blackjack give you a he-man's appetite.

Approaching the end of their long weekend, Thorp and his friends drove out to Lake Tahoe where, just inside the Nevadan border with northern California, sits an incongruous complex of tower block casino-hotels, like a Lego model on the ski slopes. The place they chose was jammed wall-to-wall and he was barely able to find a seat at a blackjack table. But as soon as he plonked down a couple of thousand dollars worth of chips the scene changed. A pit boss almost drooling in anticipation rushed over to invite him to dinner and the show. Thorp asked if his two companions could be included. No problem, step this way, Gen'lmen. The champagne and filet mignon were to cost them $11,000.

As I described at the start of this story, after dinner the trio broke the bank (emptied the dealer's tray) not once, but twice. Feeling the after-effects of it all, Thorp prudently cashed in. But the temptation to pick up what looked like money for nothing was far too strong for one of his New York friends to resist, and while Thorp was away from the table, he plunged. As they say on Wall Street, there's no such thing as a free lunch.

On their last day they returned to one of the casinos where Thorp had started out by betting in one dollar units. This time he bought $1,000 dollars in chips and began winning. He was now so proficient he could play up to seven hands at a time faster than the best dealers could deal the cards. Whenever he varied the number of hands, the dealer shuffled up at once. Finally he happened to scratch his nose, and the dealer shuffled up. Incredulous, he asked her whether she would shuffle each time he scratched his nose: she said she would. A few more scratches convinced him she meant what she said. When he asked for larger denomination chips, as all he had were twenties, the owner of the casino himself stepped forward to refuse. This man then sent for a new deck of cards and ordered them spread out face down, and then face up. The dealer explained they thought that Thorp had unusually acute vision and could distinguish tiny blemishes on the backs of the cards which enabled him to tell in advance what was going to be dealt. Thorp scoffed but the owner brought in four new decks in five minutes.

In spite of the new cards he continued to play as before, so in heavy whispers they changed their theory. The dealer claimed he could count every card as it was played, so that he knew exactly which cards had not been played at each and every instant. Thorp challenged her by rashly claiming that no one in the world could watch thirty-eight cards dealt quickly off a pack and then tell him how many of each type remained. She claimed her pit boss could do just that. Thorp offered five dollars for a demonstration. No reply. He raised the offer to $50. Still no takers. Finally one of the New Yorkers threw down $500 for the pit boss to put his money where his mouth was. Sheepish silence.

Thorp had proved his system. In thirty man-hours of medium and large-scale play they had built $10,000 into $21,000 (despite the haemorrhage of $11,000 gambled back in Thorp's absence). At no point did they have to go into their original capital further than $1,300. 'Our experiment was a success, and my system performed in practice just as theory predicted,' Thorp concluded. He added: 'The day of the lamb had come.'

Or so it seemed. The casinos were not convinced. Another guy with a system, a goddam professor, they thought. If he's so smart, why ain't he rich? The casinos were sceptical, insofar as they noticed Thorp's book at all. Indeed you can walk into any casino lobby in Nevada today and find arrayed on the shelves of the drug store a score of books and brochures telling you how to win, how to make a fortune at gambling. Virtually all of them are worthless. But this time it was different. As the weeks went by the book was read by hundreds and thousands of people, blackjack experts and novices alike. They all had the same thought – El Dorado! Could anything in this whole world be sweeter than to walk into a gambling hall and be sure of winning? That's how it seemed to all those bedazzled people as they pored over Thorp's tables and dealt out the cards to themselves on the dining-room table. Go for it!

The casinos began to have second thoughts. These guys knew something. They were winning. Actually, casinos don't think in those neutral terms. What they think, to this day, is that counters are stealing from them. That is not too strong a word. Casinos don't mind winners *per se*, they welcome winners because it's essential for gambling to have winners – provided only that the winners keep on coming back. But winners who are guaranteed winners with an edge in their favour are something else. That spells ruin. As a spokesman for the Las

Vegas Resort Hotel Association was to put it, 'In the last 15 years there hasn't been one plane that landed without at least one person in possession of a system. This guy (Thorp) is the first in Las Vegas history to have a system that works.'

So the casinos changed the rules. There were several ways in which the game of blackjack could be adjusted to cut out some of the more favourable options for counters. A fraction of a per cent here and there – it all adds up. Forbidding the splitting of aces and restricting doubling down, which was the Association's initial promulgation, served to reduce the basic strategy player's advantage by roughly one per cent. It was an electrifying decision, the first time in history, according to Thorp, that the rules of a major casino gambling game had been significantly altered because people were winning at it.

The trouble was the new ruling did not work as intended. Overnight, it turned off all the other blackjack players, the mass of ordinary gamblers and junketeers, the so-called 'recreational' players who like to play the game for fun. The change aroused nothing but resentment. There were protests and recriminations. Turnover slumped. After three weeks, the casinos threw in the towel and reverted to the old rules. 'Casino employees, whose income depends in large part on the number of tips they receive, began screaming that the new blackjack rules were a bane to the industry,' explained an acute report in the *National Observer*. 'First one casino, then another, quietly scuttled the new rules. They admitted they'd rather have all the business back, even if it meant putting up with the system players.'

This decision by the casinos to stick to the original game, in the greater interest of overall profit, despite the threat from the new breed of counters, had, and still has, far-reaching implications. It ushered in the cat-and-mouse game between dealers and counters which characterizes every blackjack deal, wherever the game is played, all over the world. As a casual night-out-on-the-town sort of player you might never notice what is going on. But this cat-and-mouse game is for real. It has caused litigation and blood.

Consider, for a moment, the case as the casinos might put it: Here we are, a billion dollar industry, the entertainment heartland of the Old West, now transformed into a modern enterprise, responsible to our shareholders, paying big taxes, conforming to extremely strict codes of conduct, employing many thousands of people, giving our customers, Mr and Mrs Middle America, a square deal and a good time. We are a part of the entertainment industry. We offer the public, in the chance to gamble and have fun, superb facilities, glittering floor shows, fine hotels, service around the clock, all at low, low prices – in a word, Value. Many players win a fortune, many others go home winners, the chances are fair and the same for everyone. You can bet a million bucks or nickels and dimes, it's up to you. It's our pleasure to give anyone who walks into a casino the excitement of gambling, regardless of age or class or colour or anything else. As the road signs say on the way out from Las Vegas, 'Bet you had fun!'

There's just one little thing we need in our industry. We've got to have an edge, to pay for everything above and make a profit. Like any other business in the country, you might say.

Yes, Sir! Right, Ma'am! And there's more to it than that. Casinos are not a public place like a federal bureau of employment or a railway terminus. Casinos are open to the public subject to certain rules, which is a very different thing. We have the right, under law, to refuse admission to anyone whom we consider is not acting in the true interests of our establishment and our business practice. That is the law of the State of Nevada, which in its wisdom has set up an elaborate regulatory agency to control gambling. We know our business and we are in the best position to judge what is in our interest and what is not in our interest. You know what counters are doing? Bleeding us to death.

I shall return to this conflict of interest, which has preoccupied the courts in Nevada and New Jersey at such length. For Professor Thorp was not the end of the affair, he was merely the beginning. A stream of experts, would-be millionaires, followed in his wake. Thorp's calculations were refined, as the variety of rules in the different casinos was compared and analysed, and the probabilities evaluated in computer programs; other methods and systems were devised and marketed; and blackjack began to produce its own folk heroes and its own folklore. The game became, at one level, a kind of minor discipline of mathematics. It was and continues to be discussed by academic experts as a branch of game theory. At another level it remains the greatest challenge in gambling to all the professional counters up and down the state of Nevada and in Atlantic City, as well as in London and other gambling resorts. These people are trying to earn their living by using their wits to outsmart the casinos. And the corollary is that blackjack for the casino managements is a continual source of friction, at one and the same time a great money-earner and a great headache.

Why didn't the present author, you may at this point inquire, set about becoming a counter too? After all, wouldn't I have made a helluva lot more money than trying to write about it here? Maybe so, maybe not. Of course I read Thorp's book and one or two others, and I could no doubt have sweated through the hours of memory and practice. But being a successful counter is not just a matter of learning the tables. It is a life-time's occupation. As I wrote in a guide to casino games a while back (*The Gambler's Pocket Book*, 1980) to make a living at blackjack probably takes as much time and effort as working fulltime in any other profession. It seemed to me that one could spend the time and mental effort required more productively in a regular job, as a doctor or dentist, butcher or baker, with a rather more satisfying role in society than dodging the casino authorities. So, no, I am not a blackjack millionaire myself.

I have met one or two guys who are millionaires, or getting on that way, thanks to their skill and application at blackjack, though. They do not have an easy life. Only a tiny proportion of counters ever succeed in making it. Not because they cannot count a deck of cards or six decks of cards absolutely accurately, but for psychological reasons. The heat is always on. It has been estimated that one out of every 20,000 players is a counter and of these only about one out of twenty is a winner. There is no way of knowing exactly but the ratio is certainly extreme. Counters may crack up because they cannot stand a long losing sequence, which in the nature of things may last for several weeks, and burn up their capital. They may crack under the continual hassle from pit bosses and the psychological pressures of evading surveillance and retaliation. They simply may not possess the character to keep their game together.

The doyen of card counters was Ken Uston. When he turned up at one of the academic get-togethers on the strategy of blackjack, everyone wanted to listen. He was indeed a star of the game but a star who found it increasingly difficult to exercise his talent. Banned, warned off, cheated, mugged, number one in the casinos' little black book of undesirable players, plaintiff in the courts, Uston has become a legend in the business. He made a lot of money at blackjack and also from his books on the game – which depict him in manifold disguises, dodging the management out to detect him and his 'teams' and sling him out.

Born into a comfortable middle class family, Uston had a college education, served a spell in the army, proceeding to Yale and Harvard Business School, and then to a job with the Pacific Stock Exchange, where he rose to the rank of senior vice-president. In those days he was a clean-cut young executive in a three-piece suit, who spent his time with bankers. There was always something of the showman in him, or as he would say, the ham. 'I guess the real reason I was originally drawn to blackjack was because of the mathematical challenge and the "Mission Impossible" aspects of being able to use skill and imagination in beating the casinos at their own game,' he has written. He first joined a group of blackjack players while vice-president of the stock exchange and when the team disbanded he wrote a book about the experience, *The Big Player* (1977).

His experience in running a team of players at Atlantic City is instructive. A team comprises several players who work together by pooling their capital and their winnings, but play separately, as individuals, to avoid for as long as possible being picked up by the management and barred. Barred what for? For winning. The edge which an expert counter enjoys is very, very small. Uston describes it as follows: Imagine a game in which you have three jars filled with white and black beans. If the player pulls out a white bean he wins. If he pulls out a black bean he loses. One jar has 51 black beans and 49 white beans. When a player pulls beans out of this jar (one third of the time) he bets $10. The second jar has 50 white beans and 50 black beans. When the player pulls beans out of this jar, which constitutes a dead-even game, he bets $20. The third jar has 51 white beans and 49 black beans, decidedly favouring the player, who accordingly bets $100 when he pulls from this jar. In this three jars game the player has an edge over the house of just under 1.4 per cent. This essentially describes the game of blackjack as played by the counter.

Not exactly lucrative, is it? If the player makes 300 pulls from the jars (100 from each) as Uston outlines, on average he should win $180. The total amount bet is $13,000, so his edge is $180/$13,000, or 1.38 per cent. If the game averages 45 hands per hour, 300 pulls would require six hours forty minutes play, or earnings of $27 an hour. What's more, there can be wide fluctuations round the average. In fact in four out of ten 300-pull sessions, on average, the player would lose; in six out of ten he should win. The advantage of playing as a team is that it helps even out the bad swings – when a player hits a long run of black beans – and thus to equalize the psychological pressures. As Thorp noted the first time he tried out his system at the tables, heavy losing runs may be mixed with lucky streaks of the most dazzling brilliance.

In January, 1979, an ideal situation, a unique opportunity, arose for Uston to take a team to Atlantic City, because the only casino then open, Resorts International, was operating on a provisional licence, waiting for its full licence to be approved. In such a situation, being on its best behaviour, the casino was likely to treat professional card counters with the kind of courtesy the pit bosses in Las Vegas would suppose existed only in fairy stories, if they ever read fairy stories. The Atlantic City game was different in some respects from the Vegas game but judged to be favourable. Organizing a team is not like whistling up a tennis foursome. Uston took out second mortgages on his property and was only too well aware of the financial risks he was running, in getting into debt in order to gamble. Assembling a team of players who were both expert and trustworthy was also a major task. Resorts itself was doing fantastic business, up to

$650,000 a day, despite the fact that, unlike the 24-hours-a-day gaming in Nevada, the casino was open only from ten to 4 a.m. The desperate droves of gamblers, bussed in from New York and New Jersey and Philadelphia, were actually lining up – a most un-American habit – at the tables, waiting to get in and blow their money.

Uston's team hit town and checked into a cheap hotel. The objective was to win a million dollars. Ever-suspicious, Uston donned one of his stock disguises, a ratty old grey wig, smelly white paint spray for his beard and moustache, and coke-bottle glasses. Within a few minutes word got around to the other counters working the blackjack tables that Kenny was there, and people sidled up to the table to smile or wink; finally the pit boss caught on. Next day he thought the hell with it and went in undisguised. The day-shift manager came over but, instead of giving him heat, the boss was all smiles. Atlantic City, he confirmed, had a 'no barring' policy. Uston was amazed. 'It seemed so unreal and so pleasant. I wondered if blackjack could ever be like this; where skill would be respected, instead of feared; where a counter wouldn't be forced to feel like a quasi-criminal.' What's more a member of the Casino Control Commission was right there stationed on the floor of the casino.

Uston's team got to work but without making any profits. The hourly 'expected value' was only about $50, which multiplied by four or five players working an eight-hour day would yield only $11,000 a week. Another high-rolling team was scooping all the money, and there was a number of freelance counters around, too. Uston's team did not have sufficient capital to risk betting at high stakes. The atmosphere in the casino seemed to take on a bit of a chill. After weighing up the prospects Uston decided they might as well raise their stakes while the going was good and 'go for the gusto'.

And the results were exciting. In four days of intensive play, raising their stake levels as their working capital increased, the team got ahead $51,000. That might not seem like such a big number, viewed from this distance; at the time, when everyone concerned had had to strain their financial resources to the utmost to get a bank together, it seemed sensational. Uston was hoping and praying that the Resorts' licence hearings would run on and on, so that they could continue to play in these ideal conditions for another three or four weeks. In the past his teams had endured many long losing spells, when they would try to console themselves – 'We do have the advantage ... (pause) ... but they have the money!' When the team reached $75,000, the players split their winnings and formed a new bank worth $100,000, which meant that their top bet on a hand could go up to $1,000.

Not surprisingly, Resorts had begun to take counter-measures, notably by installing six-deck shoes at all the bigger games, which made counting less productive. Although the casino was jam-packed with gamblers morning, noon and night, the 'counters' convention', as one dealer termed it, was evidently putting a crimp in the management's bottom line. Even so, as the only casino then open, Resorts was still doing unbelievable business. 'This joint,' one of the bosses confided, 'is a money machine.' The team continued to pull ahead.

During one session, Uston's Mom and Dad dropped in, to watch their boy play. But it was not a family game, as the technique involved in playing a six-deck shoe shows.

When it was time to bet, I would note the 'running count' and the number of aces, as indicated by the position of my feet. I'd calculate the 'adjusted running count' by adding '4' for every ace rich [remaining] in the remaining cards, or deducting '4' for every ace poor in the deck. I would then estimate the number of half-decks remaining in the shoe by eyeballing the discard pile. Dividing the 'adjusted running count' by the number of half-decks gave me the 'betting true count', which I multiplied by 1.5. Then I added $150. That is the amount I would bet, rounded to the nearest $100 ...

When it was time to play the hand, I went through a similar process. Sometimes playing decisions were required ... there were about 140 numbers on which we had to have nearly instant recall.

In short, it was more like being a human computer than playing a game, except that at the same time as playing, it was necessary to be nice to the dealer, josh around with the pit bosses and act pleasantly to all the other players at the table. Uston relished the challenge. He prided himself on his accuracy, eliminating his inner feelings while playing, and avoiding mistakes (which cost money). The team continued to pull ahead. Then came Black Tuesday.

Word flashed round that the casino was going to bar counters that night at 8 p.m. The atmosphere was weird. Counters kept coming up to the table where Uston sat, retailing the latest rumours. Meanwhile the tables were virtually unsupervised by floor personnel, as if the management was standing back, watching from the 'eye in the sky'. The rumours continued, the barring would be at 9 p.m., then 10 p.m. Uston felt a sinking feeling in his stomach, it became impossible to count correctly. He decided to leave the casino and joined some of the others up in their hotel room. Like some affluent hippie crash-pad, the room was a jumble of bedclothes and laundry, strewn with betting chips and banknotes. It was their ninth day in town. $181,600 was scattered around, of which the win from the second Atlantic City Bank was $65,000. Uston feared more than a barring – reprisals might follow. He was, admittedly, paranoiac, having been slugged in the jaw by a security guard in Reno a while back in a little 'accident', and was still undergoing dental surgery. They reviewed the alternatives and decided to cash out. If the barring was only a rumour, they could return. The emergency 'get-out-of-the-casino-immediately' signal (right fist pounding on the chest) was given to the rest of the team.

Uston loaded $25,000 worth of $500 chips in a chip rack and stuffed a few thousand more in assorted denominations into a laundry bag, and went down to the cashier's cage. The casino seemed calm. He opened the laundry bag and gradually piled up his chips. There was a commotion behind him. He turned and saw an entourage approaching, led by an official-looking grey-haired man in a business suit. He was followed by three plain-clothes security guards. The official was wearing an 'A' badge, the top designation in the Resorts administration. 'What's your name?' Ken told him. 'Address? Phone number? Date of birth? Social security number?' The information was written down on a clipboard, then the official uncovered a tiny 3-by-5-inch card from his board and read it out:

I represent the landlord of the premises. I am informing you that you are considered to be a professional card-counter, and you are not allowed to gamble at any blackjack table in this casino. If you attempt to gamble at a blackjack table, you will be considered to be a disorderly person and will be evicted from the casino. If you are evicted from the casino and return, I will have you arrested for trespassing. If you refrain from gambling at a blackjack table you are welcome to participate in any other game offered by the casino.

All right, they had it coming to them. Uston was naïve, you may say. But note that he wasn't going in for any kind of sharp practice, let alone cheating. He was simply playing the game according to the rules. He was playing the game better than the casino, he knew much, much more about blackjack than the casino. Indeed most counters know more about the game than the casinos do. Uston took up his barring with the Control Commission. His proposal was for a kind of fair deal for both sides in blackjack, which he termed, in a memo on the subject, an 'Open Environment' for blackjack in New Jersey. So far this has not come to pass and one must doubt that it ever will.*

For the sake of basic sanity as distinct from basic strategy it was essential to inject some humour into blackjack, and it came from a very funny man, Arnold Snyder. He was a counter like all the rest, but also held down a job as a postman in a small town in California. Perhaps it was on his delivery rounds that the revelation came to him that the cult of blackjack was really a form of religion. It had that intensity of belief and commitment about it. At the National Conference on Gambling and Risk Taking in 1981, one of the heavy-weight gatherings of specialists from across academe and the gaming industry, Snyder promulgated his First Church of Blackjack, ordaining himself Bishop.

My people. I have a vision. I see the dawning of the age of Blackjack. I see a world with a casino on every street from Atlantic City to L.A.,

* Ken Uston's untimely death at 52 occurred while on vacation in Paris, in October 1987. He was found in bed in his hotel room, propped up against the pillows, hands behind his head as if in deep reflection.

New York–Chicago, Your Town–My Town. I see a world where dealers make house calls!

Welcome, My People To Blackjack Heaven!

I see a world where pit bosses direct traffic on the green felt streets and towering stacks of multi-coloured chips line the side-walks like so many lawn ornaments! Lucky bucks in every pocket! A cocktail waitress in every garage!

Welcome, My People To Blackjack Heaven!

I see a world where insurance pays 3-to-1 and everyone counts and no one gets barred. Where all the games are dealt from a single deck and all 52 cards are dealt because no cards are burned!

Welcome, My People To Blackjack Heaven!

Enjoining his congregation, 'Learn ye to count these cards and thou shalt take from Caesar the chips that are Caesar's', Snyder set out his Commandments:

Blackjack is thy game. Thou shalt have no other game before it . . . Thou shalt not overbet thy bankroll . . . Thou shalt not lose thy count . . . Thou shalt not imbibe intoxicating beverages while playing . . . Thou shalt remain cool in the face of heat . . . Thou shalt not obviously study thy neighbour's cards . . .

Snyder edited for some while a little blackjack magazine which circulated among the faithful, mixing sharp and ironic advice with reviews of the latest developments in technique. In the sub-culture of blackjack it had the status of a mock-serious devotional in which all the editorials were signed simply 'Bishop'.

There was much truth in Snyder's jesting. At the academic conferences it had become standard practice for casino executives to discuss their campaign against counters. Bart Carter, a pit boss at Caesar's in Atlantic City, has good humouredly described the avoidance ploys of card counters as a subtle game of espionage; it had forced casino personnel to achieve the same kind of expertise and sophistication as the counters had. He started out as a counter himself, he confided to the 1984 gambling conference, but over-bet his bankroll – a common mistake which leads to instant ruin.

There are three levels of expertise, as he explained it. The average counter knows how to play but his betting is overly systematic and his behaviour pattern easily detectable; even betting at low limits attracts heat these days. The good counter is better at counting and playing, understands money management and knows how to avoid give-away signals in his style of play. The professional counter carries these traits one step further. In addition to his technical mastery, he will have developed an 'act' to avoid detection – either by looking and sounding like another face in the crowd, a tourist or junketeer, or by the opposite device of standing out as a flashy player, a high roller demanding instant attention – 'Howdy folks, I'm Billy Williams from Dallas, my friends call me Tex!' Many very clever variations on these two basic themes are acted out by expert counters, such as coming into the tables in a bus driver's uniform – 'Ain't got nuthin' to do till the ol' bus pulls out tonight ... Jeez, if I could only get me back to evens.' But the best disguise of all is to be a woman.

According to Carter there is an industry-wide prejudice that men are better players, a view shared even by women supervisors. Many top professional counters are women under the guise of a dumb blonde image. 'If you come in with blonde hair and wear a low-cut dress, and seem to be drinking ... then you've got it made, they won't even watch you play. You can bet almost anything.' Many card counters take along a pretty woman as a decoy at the table, a woman who in reality either knows how to count well enough herself or can follow his signals. 'Now, honey, whaddaya wanna make that play for ... splittin' nines ... Hey, is this one lucky lady!'

It is harder being a man. Whatever role a professional counter chooses, he must act it out. No need to worry about the supervisors if they are thinking, 'Oh, that's Joe, he's a dentist from Philadelphia, he's here every weekend.' But a counter in disguise must not become known as a tough player or a lucky player. Once he gets the reputation of being too tough or too lucky, the heat comes around. It's time to move to another pit or another casino. The best cover is being a losing player. Obviously if a guy is losing at the table, he can't be counting ... pit bosses believe all counters win, that is why they are afraid of them. I asked Bart Carter why he gave up the life of a counter himself and joined the ranks of the casino. His answer, which applies to many such people in the industry, is the security of a steady job. Instead of having to weave and bob through the net of supervisors and pit bosses, seeking to snare him, it was far preferable – and just as much of a challenge – to work on the other side of the line.

In the game of espionage, the counters have developed still subtler methods to avoid detection. One of the best is table hopping, also known as back counting or shadow counting, or 'Wonging' (after the recommendation of another expert, Stanford Wong). The idea is to count the cards at a distance, while strolling through the blackjack pit, or to have a confederate at the table give a signal when the count is good. The table hopper then jumps in to make a few quick high stakes bets while the count is plus, before vanishing to repeat the trick somewhere else. In team play, several players may play for low stakes at different tables, waiting to signal the big player – hair is brushed back or an ear is scratched. Arriving at the table the big player then picks up a second signal, giving him the count, and bets it up until the advantage changes.

Sometimes casinos make mistakes and jump on harmless little old ladies in sneakers. The supervisors are especially sensitive to changes in the betting pattern, which is the easiest way of picking up counters. To take one bizarre instance, an elderly gentleman, flush from a run at roulette, joined his wife at the blackjack table where she was playing dollar bets. In exuberant mood from his previous winning, he plonked down $500 on his wife's bet. The pit boss rushed over, scooped up the bet and with dire warnings and imprecations, slung the couple out. The real counters sitting at the table continued playing, undisturbed.

The point is that the casino staff are under terrific heat themselves, from their bosses, to catch counters. They are often so frightened of losing their jobs they will over-react. Competition for jobs in Las Vegas, where there is no other ready means of employment, and the choice is to work or starve, is very fierce.

Dealers have no trade union, no job security and no way of protecting themselves. Everything depends on 'juice' – an expressive term meaning 'influence', deriving from the bad old days when crooked operators employed an electro-magnetic current to control the roulette wheel. Juice in this instance is having a friend or knowing someone who will give them work when a vacancy comes up.

'Dummy up and deal!' is the dealer's self-mocking work slogan. It means keep your mouth shut, your eyes on the layout and the cards flying. The game must go on, no matter what. Actions which threaten a dealer's job include unnecessary talking to players, openly soliciting for tokes (tips), irritation, rudeness or impatience towards players, losing streaks, emotionalism at the table or major errors (as explained in *Dummy Up and Deal* by Lee Solkey, 1980). Casinos, this resumé of dealers' experiences observes, would rather replace a dealer than lose a player.

I have been talking here about counting and the measures taken by the casinos to prevent it. Everything the counters do in their play is perfectly legal and according to the rules. I have not been talking about cheating. Perhaps you think casinos do not cheat, or only a few incorrigible bad hats? Well, cheating and gambling go together: cheats are drawn to gambling (on both sides of the tables) like kids to candy. So, yes, virtually all experienced card counters have encountered cheating. As strong card players, they can usually detect it rapidly. The forms of cheating are many and varied, the sleight of hand often extraordinary, and new cheating methods continue to be invented. In Thorp's experience, even the most experienced cheat spotters miss some of the moves, only becoming alerted to what hit them after a run of losses that is statistically so improbable as to defy credibility. Ordinary players must take their chance. The only advice one can offer is that if you are losing very rapidly, walk away. It's a good rule in any case.

Thorp made several trips to investigate cheating. Originally he supposed that, although skilful dealers could cheat if they so desired, they did not cheat. The argument is that, as casinos enjoy a natural advantage in the game, they will win anyhow, so why risk exposure and bad publicity? In the great majority of blackjack games, Thorp concluded, there was no cheating; but the average player would face a cheat perhaps five or ten per cent of the time, which was enough to make it a serious problem. He played at most of the major casinos in Vegas and Reno on his field trips for periods ranging from a few minutes to several hours, with bets ranging from $1 to $125. He found there was cheating at large plush casinos as well as small out-of-the-way places. And there was cheating at all betting levels, even for twenty-five cents! All this was a few years ago, so perhaps things have now changed. Perhaps the industry has cleaned itself up from top to bottom. Perhaps human nature has undergone a magical transformation in the interval. What do you think?

Marking cards, peeking at the top card, dealing seconds (holding the top card of the deck for himself, and dealing out a bad second card for the player), stacking the deck – there are a thousand ways of separating the mug from his money. I am certainly not suggesting cheating is a one-sided affair. Players cheat too; always have done, always will. The commonest form of cheating among blackjack players is to peek at the dealer's hole card, known as 'spooking'; sometimes it can be done by a confederate standing behind the table and sending signals to the player; most easily by collusion between dealer and player. Some cardsharps are so adroit that in cutting the deck they can place a sequence of cards where they want, or identify a particular card to gain a quick advantage. As soon as one trick is exposed, another slips in. That is why the casinos have such elaborate supervision of the games from the 'eye in the sky'. For all the easy-going, open style of modern casinos, it pays to be watchful, inside, and out. Thorp was never careless: if on his own, he avoided vacant men's rooms, never ventured into a shadowy parking lot, always kept close to other pedestrians. Paranoiac? No, the word is street-wise.

The doyen of the theoreticians who followed the first wave of blackjack innovators was Peter Griffin, a professor of maths at California State University, Sacramento. Although he took the subject itself seriously, he brought a light-hearted approach to blackjack, which is refreshing, depicting himself on the back cover of his book disguised as a happy-go-lucky monkey, reaching out for a beer as the dealer pushes another stack of winning chips in his direction. Scenes such as this, Griffin averred, had struck terror into the hearts of Nevada casino bosses for the last ten years – 'His winnings are rumoured to run into hundreds. At the present time Hollywood has no plans for a movie about his life.'

Griffin debunked a lot of the hucksters and plagiarists who followed Thorp, and in the foreword to his book *The Theory of Blackjack* (1979) quoted Senator Eugene McCarthy on the similarity between politicians and football coaches: 'You have to be smart enough to understand the game and dumb enough to think it matters.'

The interesting thing about Griffin is that he does not claim to be a winner at blackjack – on the contrary. I spent a night on the town with him in Las Vegas and was able to observe his approach to gambling – both amused and amusing – at first hand. He first encountered the game when he was preparing to give a course to a class of maths majors on the mathematics of gambling. It occurred to him that he had absolutely no gambling experience at all. Whenever travelling through Nevada with friends he had always stayed outside in the casino parking lot, 'to avoid the embarrassment of witnessing their foolishness'. At first he had no interest in card counting but after totalling up his losses on his brief initiation in the game, he vowed revenge. 'Short of armed robbery or counterfeiting chips (and I had considered these), there was only one way to get my money back.' He anted up for Thorp's book and soon recouped his losses. But then the pendulum swung the other way again.

Typical of this experience, indeed the weirdest experience Griffin ever had, was a certain memorable trip through Reno. During the first six days he won a hundred a day. After this, no matter where he went, no matter how he tried, he could not win. His continuous losses were devastating – not least to his self-esteem. As a mathematician he could not understand it. He re-analysed his game and checked his calculations. Everything was correct. Yet he had now lost 30 sessions in a row. This was equivalent, so he estimated, to $\frac{1}{2}^{30}$ or about 1,000,000,000 to 1 odds against losing in an even game. He was not playing an even game, he actually had the advantage. So how on earth could this happen? It simply wasn't credible. He went to new places, drove out to Tahoe, everywhere it was the same. He lost back all the money he had won, $4,000. He had no emotional problems, he says, no evidence of cheating, and is still groping for an explanation. I recounted this little tale to Thorp, who did not hesitate for a split second. 'He was cheated. Once they've marked you down, they'll get you. One casino will warn the others no matter where you go.'

Griffin candidly admits in the introduction to his book (which by the way is more of a mathematical treatise than an easy guide to blackjack) that he can offer no encouragement to those who hope to profit from casino blackjack. 'Today I find myself farther behind in the game than I was after my original odyssey . . . My emotions have run the gamut from the inebriated elation following a big win which induced me to pound out a chorus of celebration on the top of an occupied Reno police car to the frustrated depths of biting a hole through a card after picking up what seemed my 23rd consecutive stiff hand against the dealer's ten card up.' The deeper he delved into the mysteries of the game, the more he lost! He can console himself by reflecting that he is acknowledged as the mathematical authority on the game he can't beat.

On our night out in Vegas, Griffin treated gambling as a form of farce. The idea was to get as much out of the casino, for free, as we could, but at a very low level. Thus, on checking in, hotel guests are customarily issued with a booklet of vouchers entitling them to a free cocktail, or a half-price hamburger, or sucker come-ons like the offer of a dollar bonus on your first one-dollar bet at blackjack if it wins. Some gamblers indeed make a serious practice of going around collecting vouchers and expect to gross up to twenty bucks a day at it, I was told.

Griffin and the others in the party rushed around using up our vouchers in a spirit of carnival, the climax coming with the one bet you can't lose, at dice. With the bonus of an extra dollar paid out on your first bet if it wins, one player puts his dollar on the pass line and the other player puts his dollar on the don't pass line. The result is that while one player will lose, the other must win two bucks – net profit one silver dollar! Except of course if the dice roll double one, 'snake eyes', in which case one player loses and the other merely breaks even. Griffin and I put our silver dollars down full of confidence . . . and up came a double one. 'That,' said the professor ruminatively, 'has never happened before.' This particular casino was rumoured to be going broke. It was very careful indeed. Griffin's companion Lydia put down three bucks for a bet at blackjack, let her winnings stand, and the dealer shuffled up. 'Lydia bets because I don't want to lose. When I lose it crushes me – Lydia has more heart, she just shoves it out.' Griffin's addiction to blackjack has nothing to do with the game, it's a fascination with how far the human mind can be pushed, a gaming equivalent to running the four-minute mile.

Thus he despises 'spooking' and thinks blackjack experts who go in for that kind of cheapo advantage are unworthy of their maths. A prime motive for cheating from the dealer's side of the table, he believes, is psychological rather than financial, in the boredom that dealers have to endure. Instead of acting like automata, they may choose to assert their own will by interfering with the random distribution of the cards. Indeed it is perfectly understandable that dealers do not warm to people who can beat them at their own game. The reversal of roles, whereby the customer becomes the casino, grinding out his percentage, and the casino becomes the sucker, is most unwelcome.

We moved on, coupon winners to the triumphant tune of $4.50 a head. Griffin still finds the single-deck game intellectually fascinating, but trying to beat the four-deck games, he says, (quoting Thorp) is like breaking rocks. As for playing without counting, he has described it, in a lapidary phrase, as 'missionary blackjack'.

Uston has pursued a long, circuitous and exhausting campaign in the courts. As so often happens in litigation on issues of principle it is not easy to see who the winners are – apart from the lawyers, of course. His complaints to the Casino Control Commission about the conduct of Resorts in Atlantic City were not upheld. Uston's lawyers then appealed the decision to bar card-counters to the New Jersey Appellate Court, petitioning for his right to play blackjack. It took almost a year and a half before the Court of Appeals ruled unanimously that casinos may not bar counters and issued an order to Resorts to allow him (and other counters) to play. The same day Resorts, accompanied by the Commission, filed for a stay of this order pending a decision by the Supreme Court as to whether they would hear the case. After many ups and downs, Uston also won that appeal. 'You should have seen the casino people there,' Uston recalled. 'They were there in droves. They had a half-a-million dollar, maybe a one-million-dollar-show. They had helicopters and limousines . . . All these casino people there, and there was nobody to testify for the counters. It was so funny. They had this vast report, and here I'd stayed up the night before – I was out partying – and I took a look at this thing and I said, "If they're going to have limousines I'm going to have a limousine, too." It was so ridiculous. I took a little portable typewriter that just about types . . . I typed a list of proposals outside the men's room of the Howard Johnson's. I'd put the typewriter on a high chair . . . I really thought we'd lost that one, but I think we won because I got up on the stand and I came out objectively.' The Supreme Court decision was largely an exposition on the evolving law relating to the exclusion of individuals from public places. The question was whether Uston would then seek the same ruling in Nevada.

He felt ambivalent about the enervating effort and hustle involved. Then an incident happened at Lake Tahoe which made up his mind. On a skiing vacation with a girlfriend in early 1984, Ken couldn't resist playing a little blackjack. Naturally he got barred. The scene at Harvey's Inn was typical. After playing for about two hours, he was offered dinner on the house. The party proceeded to the cocktail lounge where after a few minutes a security guard approached the table and in a loud gruff voice said: 'You can't play here no more.' Uston replied: 'Yessir.' The guard repeated his ultimatum several times in a threatening voice and Uston left. The same sort of thing happened, if slightly more politely, in the other places. So he decided to file a complaint with the Nevada State Gaming Control Board asking for a hearing on whether he and other skilled blackjack players may be arbitrarily excluded from playing blackjack by Nevada casino managements.

It is no fun being pulled up by casino security people for counting. Being asked to leave nicely is one thing. But in many cases the unfortunate player is marched out to a back room, photographed and finger-printed and generally given a rough time. This sort of infringement of civil liberties is not legal, though very few counters have had the pluck to fight back and seek redress in the courts.

One player who did was an English acquaintance of mine – he went even further and sued for damages. The security people had jumped on him when he was winning at blackjack and accused him of cheating, by marking the tens. He was used to being hassled, but this charge was preposterous. This particular individual was a pro who knew more about the theory of blackjack than any half-dozen pit bosses put together – besides there was not a tittle of evidence to substantiate the accusations. But the casino chose to charge him formally with cheating. Perhaps they thought he would run out of town rather than stand up and face charges in a Federal Court in Las Vegas.

On the contrary, this man was an awkward sort of customer. He was ready to defend himself, however long the case might take. He had been playing in the company of another young Englishman, a bespectacled young chap with a round, schoolboy face, whom any jury could see was not a heavy gambling type. When it came to the crucial hearing this fellow donned his best Yorkshire tweed suit (the outside temperature was the usual 105 degrees) and managed to find an old school tie. In court he looked the perfect English gentleman, or a fair imitation of one. On the stand the casino lawyers thought they were going to turn him inside out. They threw a lot of questions at him about his friend cheating and finally demanded, 'Okay, you say he didn't count tens but don't you think he could have found a way of cheating if he'd wanted to?' – a leading question if you like. Drawing himself up like an envoy presenting his letters of appointment to the Queen, the witness turned to face the judge. 'Your honour, I'm really awf'ly sorry, but I simply don't understand the question.' There was a moment's stunned silence as this mannered

English drawl sliced through the cross-examination. The judge banged his gavel down and told the smart-ass lawyer to stand the witness down.

The plaintiff was awarded a total of $48,000 in damages for the treatment he'd suffered, plus loss of interest on his confiscated winnings. After lawyer's fees it still came to over forty grand, but it took a long time to prise the money out of the cashier's cage. Bob Stupak of Vegas World threatened to dump the whole lot on him in nickels. Some while later, when they happened to meet socially, Stupak took his defeat fairly well. 'Ya know, you were winnin' all night, the guys thought ya must be fixin' the cards, or sump'n.' It is because counters have not got the nerve, or the time and energy, to uphold their rights that Uston wanted to have an established code of conduct, to enable the best players to play without being harassed.

The majority of executives in the casino industry are grossly misinformed about the fundamentals of card counting and the dangers posed by counters. Anthony Curtis, a professional counter who has also edited a gambling magazine, recalls how casino people continually asked him how much money he made per hour. Some believed that a counter could win over 75 per cent of his bets, which would be a money-making machine indeed. In reality not even computers can win at rates of ten per cent. The best card counters in the world reckon on an advantage of $1 - 1\frac{1}{2}$ per cent. Moreover, the casino managements are wrong in assuming that everyone who counts cards is a winning player. According to Curtis, most players make half-attempts to master the intricacies of the game, and lack the self-discipline required to be successful. The resulting equation ($\frac{1}{2}$ diligence + $\frac{1}{4}$ knowledge) $\times$ (any size bankroll) = money in the bank for the casinos. But casino personnel, from dealers on up, are terrified of low returns from their tables. Everyone feels heat from the guy above, all the way up to the top. And when jobs are on the line, the easiest thing to do, if it looks like someone is a counter, is to give him heat, first.

The professional learns how to avoid heat. Curtis compares the situation of the expert counter to that of a finely tuned athlete who is allowed to perform to his true ability only during training.

When game time arrives, he must conceal his talent to the point of appearing a beginner or a sucker. This ego-deflating trait, Curtis suggests, explains why so many blackjack experts have given up playing and turned to writing and lecturing about the game. In reality, the industry has gained enormously from all the publicity about blackjack, from the knowledge, that has certainly taken hold among 'recreational' players, that the game can be beaten. In that sense casinos ought positively to promote card counting.

The idea of removing human error by introducing a portable computer into play was the final step. Nicknamed 'George', this device was strapped to the player's leg and operated, believe it or not, by his toes. As it was explained to me by Robert, a dedicated but fairly low-level counter (he took the sensible precaution of holding down a job as a sales clerk in downtown Vegas), it was not as difficult to operate as it sounds. The user had to learn two movements of each big toe: right toe up counted 1 and down 2, left toe up 4 and down 8. This enabled each card dealt to be entered into the computer – for instance a ten-value card would be down with both toes, a seven would be right toe up and down, left toe up. A signal was then given to the player under the arch of his foot – da or dadaaa – whether to hit or stand. George originally sold at $10,000 but came down to less than half that price as demand waned. Most operators, according to my informant, suffered anguished fantasies of being caught. But George was very effective, in theory. John Gwynn, professor of computer science at California State, Sacramento, who ran some 20 million hands through a pocket computer, described its power as 'rather awesome'. His results indicated that with flat stakes betting, a blackjack computer could yield a player an advantage of 1.26 per cent under Vegas rules, and with a 1 – 2 betting ratio, 2.88 per cent. So perhaps the casinos were right to be alarmed.

In the summer of 1985 the casino industry – ever quick to over-react – persuaded the Nevada legislature to ban the use of such computers at blackjack. 'The people of the State of Nevada, represented in Senate and Assembly, do enact as follows . . . It is unlawful for any person at a licensed gaming establishment to use, or possess with intent to use, in a game played with cards any device to assist . . . 1. In projecting the outcome of the game; 2. In keeping track of the cards played; 3. In analysing the probability of the occurrence of an event relating to the game; or 4. In analysing the strategy for playing or betting to be used in the game.' Punishment for first offence imprisonment in the state prison for not less than 1 year nor more than 10 years, or by a fine of not more than $10,000, or by both fine and imprisonment. (It's probably just as well for the counters that the Nevada legislature meets only every other year.)

A point which Robert emphasized, in explaining the counter's life and hard times to me, was the misery – and he kept repeating the word – the misery of bad losing runs, when you can't talk to anyone about it. The gulf between mathematical theory and the reality, as he found it, was so wide. The counter says to himself, 'How come I'm losing when I do everything right, and the guy next to me, who is a complete idiot, is winning a fortune?' The solo counter has no friends at the table, he can't confide in anybody. He may pace the full length of Caesar's and back again at one in the morning, trying to find a seat in a good game, then hoof it two blocks down the strip to another place, and the same thing happens; and then when he does get a game, one of those freak runs come up, which wipe him out. Playing off a bankroll of $1,000, and betting a range of $5 to $20, Robert reckons that one in 20 times he'll go broke; the answer is to treat the winning runs with great caution. As he put it, the counter has to learn: 'What goes around, comes around.'

How would it be, though, to be able to bet both hands and win, the dealer's hand and the player's hand, and still be sure of showing a profit? Not possible, obviously. But that, in essence, is Professor Thorp's strategy for the stock market. Making bets on stocks and shares in such a way that it doesn't matter whether the market goes up or the market goes down – if the dealer wins or the player wins. Either way the investment should still show a profit. Alchemy? No, just scientific method.

One summer afternoon Ed Thorp was sitting under a tree (like Isaac Newton) in the New Mexico sunshine when a powerful thought struck him. He was reading a little book about warrants, which are options to buy common stock. He read of undreamed-of profits mixed with the cruellest losses. The question which Thorp pondered was: could there be a way to realize some of the enormous profit potential of warrants and yet be safe from the losses? What is the relation between the price of a warrant and its associated common stock? He set himself the task of finding the 'laws' connecting the two prices.

Thorp saw the stock market as the ultimate game for applying the mathematical skills he had developed from learning about gambling, games and probabilities. 'Hedging' – a stock market term meaning covering the risk on one investment by another investment in parallel – was not a new idea, but he investigated it as a scientist, writing an elaborate series of computer programs to test his theories out. To put it simply, when a warrant seemed over-priced he would sell it short and when it seemed under-priced he would buy it. The formulae he devised are explained in *Beat The Market* (1967), written with Sheen Kassouf, a like-minded colleague he met at the University of California at Irvine. (Since those days the market and the technical opportunities for hedging have changed and the game has become tougher as other players discovered the opportunities; Thorp is now planning a revised edition.) Since a warrant and its underlying stock tend to move up and down together, he would reduce or hedge the risk in his warrant position by taking an offsetting position in the stock. His personal experience in investing with this technique and success in maintaining roughly a 25 per cent a year return led Thorp to create a limited partnership, in 1969. Since that date, his hedge fund – run for about 70 friends and private clients – has kept going at a growth rate of nearly 20 per cent a year. Thorp terms his approach 'getting rich slowly'. In good times and in bad, Thorp told me with satisfaction, the fund has never faltered. It has shown a profit in each of the 76 consecutive quarters in which it has been operating; in the process it has out-performed the best of the mutual funds on Wall Street by quite a clear margin.

The methods that he has used in the hedge fund owe much to the things he learned from casino blackjack. First the fund sought high return with low risk. He and his partners have expanded their original warrant hedging technique so that they hedge many pairs of related securities. 'We often don't know what the right price of either security is, but we often have computerized formulae for comparing the value of the two securities. If one is comparatively over-priced, we sell it short and hedge the risk by buying the comparatively under-priced security. If the comparative mispricing disappears, we capture an excess profit.' At any given time the fund may have as many as a hundred hedged positions in its portfolio (playing a hundred hands at once!). This diversification protects it against the occasional situation which works out badly. The fund uses a pair of advanced computers (DEC VAX 11–785) to read the ticker tape live, calculate option values and put the best option trades on the screens of the fund's traders within a couple of seconds.

Thorp participated in the largest dollar value block ever traded on the New York stock exchange on December 1, 1983, a five million share trade in old American Telephone and Telegraph versus five million when-issued shares of the new AT&T and five hundred thousand shares of each of the seven regional holding companies. The market value of Thorp's part of each side was about a third of a billion dollars. When AT&T broke up, small price discrepancies appeared between the price of one old share and the sum of the prices of the various new shares that were traded on a 'when-issued' basis. Overall, the operation produced a profit of $2,400,000 of which $800,000 represented the cost of capital. Not all that much, considering the huge figures involved? Well, perhaps you know how to make a million dollars in a day. I have to confess I've never done it.

Thorp grew up poor and as an academic he stayed poor. It's all rather different now. He uses his means to lead a free-wheeling, free-thinking way of life with his family in Newport, California. He likes walking trails and running marathons, looking at birds and animals, and thinking about mathematical ideas. In 1986, for example, he took time off to fly to Australia, as the best place from which to observe Halley's comet. Behind his desk is a picture of a rattlesnake and another of a horned owl and chalked across the blackboard facing him, as likely as not, a string of algebraic equations. A new system in the making, perhaps.

Ironically, one of Thorp's most spectacular deals concerned Resorts International. If Ken Uston had but known it, instead of getting so involved in litigation with Resorts he could have made a fortune trading the company's stock, rather than trying to beat its blackjack games. Back in 1972, Resorts stock was down to 8 and the warrants, entitling the holder to buy the stock at 40, were 27 cents. Thorp's calculations, weighing the length of time to expiration, expected interest rates and the volatility of the stock, indicated that the warrants were worth $4. He bought all he could, 10,800, for a total outlay of $3,200. But rather than risk even so modest a sum, he sold 800 shares of the common stock short to hedge his bet. (The episode is described by journalist Andrew Tobias in *Money Angles*, 1984.) A few months later the stock fell to $1\frac{1}{2}$ so Thorp covered his short for a profit that more than paid for the warrants. Years passed and around 1978 he began getting calls from people who wanted to buy his warrants. They were offering $3 to $4, not bad for a 27 cents outlay. By then Resorts was trading around 15. Thorp's model told him the warrants were now worth $7 to $8. So he bought more and again began shorting the stock to cover his risk. Ultimately he sold his original 10,000 warrants for $100 apiece. 'The arbitrager's approach,' as Tobias put it, 'consists of finding wonderful little lapses of logic in the prices of related securities and exploiting the bejesus out of them.'

Blackjack continues to flourish as a major gambling game, but the dilemma at the heart of it remains. The counters will try to extract their marginal edge, the casinos will strive to cut them out. The recreational players will lose their money – fairly slowly but very surely – in effect paying for both sides. What better epilogue to the blackjack story than 'Bishop' Arnold Snyder's stirring hymn?

> Onward Blackjack Soldiers
> Counting down the deck
> Never be a loser
> You can win your bet

You can Beat the Dealer
Leave him in disgrace
You can make the pit boss wish
  he'd never seen your face.

2

OH NO, NOT THE RITZ

> I am a gambler, I have always
> been a gambler, and I will always
> to a certain extent gamble.
>
> John Aspinall

One dark night in January, 1958, Inspector Samuel Herbert of Scotland Yard found himself hanging 'almost by the eyebrows' from the grille of a window outside a flat in Mayfair, trying to see what was going on inside. The flat was rented by Lady Osborne, wife of the 16th baronet, mother of John Aspinall, then aged 31. What Inspector Herbert managed to see, from his precarious position on the fire escape, was 'a table covered with green baize cloth, people sitting round the table and someone dealing from a dealing shoe'. Earlier in the day the police had observed a trailer drawn by a Rolls-Royce transporting chairs, boxes and other paraphernalia from Aspinall's home over to the flat. The same kind of move had been observed two weeks before. At about 10 or 11 in the evening things became quite active; people were seen to arrive at the flat in cars and on foot; later others came out.

Shortly before 1 a.m. the police, who had been waiting and watching outside, went in. 'Anyone would think we were a crowd of criminals!' Lady Osborne protested. 'Why don't you catch some real criminals? There are plenty.'

The police brought summonses against Lady Osborne and Mr Aspinall and a friend, John Burke, under the Gaming Act, charging them with conducting unlawful gaming: chemin-de-fer.

The game itself was not illegal: conducting chemin-de-fer on a regular or habitual basis, as in a gaming house, which was what the prosecution alleged, was illegal. The case, because of its aristocratic connections, was an immediate *cause célèbre*. All three defendants pleaded not guilty.

Inspector Herbert told the court he went into the dining room and saw a large table, covered by a green cloth, sub-divided into numbers from 1 to 10. At position number 10 was John Aspinall. Just in front of him was a wooden box containing counters marked in different denominations, a dealing shoe and packs of playing cards. Most of the people around the table had counters in front of them. There were also two wooden 'card scoops'.

After the order authorizing entry had been read, Inspector Herbert said he asked Aspinall what they had been playing and he replied, 'You know what it is.' He asked him the value of the bank and Aspinall made no reply. He asked him the value of the counters, and again he made no reply. After Aspinall had been shown the warrant authorizing entry, he shouted: 'The bank is worth £500.'

Someone cried: 'What about the police joining in?' But no one called banco. The police posse numbered 15, including two women.

The defence was based on the fact that there was no evidence of unlawful gaming unless it was first established that the premises used were a common gaming house. One instance did not constitute 'use'. Accordingly, Mr Gilbert Beyfus, QC, submitted there was no case to answer.

Referring to the gaming laws, he said that between 1738 and 1744 six games and one class of game were made illegal: ace of hearts, faro, basset, hazard, passage and all games played with dice except backgammon. In 1744 roulette was made illegal. Lawful games could be subdivided into games which were games of mere skill and those which were not. 'The only game of mere skill that exists is Snap and as that is only played in the nursery we can disregard it for all practical purposes.'

He accepted that chemin-de-fer was 95 per cent chance and five per cent skill. It fell into precisely the same class as bridge, poker or bezique (a preposterous claim, but that was not his real point), or any of the other numerous games of cards the winning of which depended largely on chance and partly on skill. They were unlawful games only if played in a common gaming house.

'The whole secret of this case and the muddle into which the police have plunged is that it was started on a complete misconception.'

After hearing the arguments for and against, Mr Justice Cassels, the presiding chairman of the London Sessions, called in the jury and told them he had come to the conclusion that there was no case to answer. The three defendants were formally declared not guilty and discharged. They were refused costs on the ground that 'it was a case which had properly to be investigated'.

Celebrating over champagne after their acquittal, Aspinall conceded the costs of the case might be quite heavy, but said it was worth it. He was fond of giving parties. 'As for having my friends around for a friendly, casual game of poker, pontoon or chemin-de-fer, it is quite possible that in the near future I shall do the same again.'

Asked if he had started playing cards with Snap, he replied, no doubt with unconscious irony, that 'beggar my neighbour was my favourite game'.

The case was brought due to the anomalous and muddled state of British gaming law. What the police did not, apparently, notice or understand – not being too familiar with chemin-de-fer – was that although chemmy is usually a game for 9 people, Aspinall was sitting in seat number 10. He was running the game: the real point of it all was that the 'house' took five per cent of winning banks. In a game like chemmy, which is essentially a doubling-up game where the bank tries to run a succession of coups, the cut or cagnotte is huge. Players don't worry about the cut too much, in the excitement of winning: if a player holding the bank wins three times in a row, running up a £500 bank to £4,000, then the cut (each coup is 'taxed' in succession as it is played) seems relatively insignificant. In the end, though, if everyone went on playing long enough, the house would wind up with all of the money. Beggar my neighbour indeed.

The case elevated John Aspinall to fame as 'Mayfair's number one gambler'. Never a man to seek publicity, indeed assiduous in his affairs to avoid the wrong sort of publicity, 'Aspers', as he was known among his set, cut a favourite figure for gossip columnists, combining aristocratic disdain with reckless extravagance. Jane, his first wife, was dubbed by the press 'The Spirit of Park Lane'. For 30 years Aspinall has personified something a touch out of date in our times: gambling as style.

The aristocratic ethic . . . not a 'snobbish' conception so much as an expression, through gambling, of confidence, of style, of social ease, by a group of people distinguished by good manners and good taste rather than breeding, though money came into it too. For one thing, people who went to the private chemmy parties had to be able to afford to play, and that more or less excluded Aspinall's friends at that time. Most of the people he liked did not have any money, and nor did he. The mid-fifties was the heyday of the private game. Aspinall had discovered, and taken legal advice to confirm, that private games were within the law – its letter if not its spirit – if they were not habitual. He had hit upon an ingenious idea, actually a fabulously profitable idea, though he would never describe the operation in such crude terms.

He was not seeking to run a 'floating' chemmy game in the vulgar American sense, like Nathan Detroit's crap game in a backstreet garage. He was giving a private party. A party at a friend's house – what could anyone object to in that? Even two parties at the same address, if they took place over a period of a month or two, could hardly cause a raised eyebrow. Only if a succession of gaming parties were held in the same house would it lay the host open to the charge of habitual gaming. The private chemmy game exactly hit the mood of the times. The English loved to gamble. The gaming law was absurd and out of date. There was a sense of money and good times in London, as a new generation of men about town came of age, and the populace was exhorted by the Prime Minister of the day, 'You've never had it so good.' Up to then the gambling set among the upper class used to pop over to Deauville or fly down to Cannes to get its thrills at the tables. Aspinall offered a headier cocktail, shaken in Mayfair.

A lot of other people tried the same thing. I remember hoarse, mysterious voices ringing up at all hours, and inviting one over to some insalubrious dive in Earl's Court. 'C'mon, Dave, we got a

lit'le game goin' on.' There would be an assortment of young
bloods and their girls, bookies, con men from the gangster fringe,
rough drink and low laughs. And very little assurance that any
cheque passed would in fact be honoured the next morning.
Aspinall's invitations were personal, to people who knew they
would be mixing with people of their own sort, friends who could
rely on absolute discretion in such company. Aspinall understood
the social nuances of re-creating the spirit of gentlemen at cards
in an eighteenth-century salon.

Have you played chemmy? Great fun. The game has no skill
in it whatever, or none that I could detect. Each coup is decided
by whether the banker or the player gets nearer to a total of
nine, drawing two cards from the 'shoe', a long wooden box
containing six decks, with an option of drawing a third card.
The excitement of the game lies entirely in the high stakes, as
the size of the bank builds up, and the bets around the table get
higher and higher. The decision whether to stand pat on the
first two cards or draw a third card is precisely prescribed for
each case, and must be followed automatically: the only choice
for the player is on a total of five, when he may elect to draw or
not. The bank moves round and round the table, so that all the
players are gambling against one another, not the house. The
house makes its profit, as already mentioned, by cutting five per-
cent from winning banks (a net advantage of about 1 per cent).
is an elegant and stylish game, played in French – *Banco! Suivi!
Neuf à la banque!* – in which the British quality of showing a stiff
upper lip in losing, and not over-much elation in winning, is
taken for granted.

The first time Aspinall played chemmy he lost £300, but the
experience gave him the idea of running a game himself. Not so
much a 'classy' game because it would not have occurred to
him to run any other sort of game, as a game where a Greek
shipping magnate or a Persian diplomat or the wife of a British
company chairman could all come and feel secure and at ease,
and take it on trust that they were not – thanks to Aspinall's
loophole – breaking the law. Or attracting the notice of gossip
columnists.

One such person who did manage to get in was the novelist

Simon Raven. Oblivious of discretion, in the face of a juicy tale to tell, he spilled the beans in a column in the *Spectator*, much to Aspinall's annoyance. 'Lead me,' Raven's account began, 'to an enormous green baize table. Surround me with old ladies who have piggy eyes and claws for fingers. Fetch me a huge pile of counters of rare design. And let the devil himself be there as croupier.'

Raven did not name Aspinall but no one acquainted with the London social scene had the slightest doubt as to the identity of the leading character hosting the party. 'When we arrived, about twelve other people were finishing an elaborate fork supper. Some of these were girls looking apprehensive and rather bored: most of them were young men, looking far from bored and one of them at least rather drunk: and there were also two or three more mature-looking men, with soft voices, impeccable manners and very dark chins . . . Our host, who was to act as croupier, started distributing counters; his wife settled at a desk to note down the amount each player received. These amounts varied between £50 and £500.

'Play began. All the time it went on we were served with snacks of foie gras and caviare, and liberally helped, though not plied or bullied, with champagne or brandy. The play was high. Some banks started at £10 or £20, more at £50, a few, especially later in the evening, at £100 or £150 . . . So the game went on. Some got drunker, others merely poorer. Some of the girls became compulsively nervous, others began to whine and had to be sent home in taxis. People left and people arrived to take their places. When anyone left he either paid his losses direct to our host or himself received his winnings direct. The dark-chinned men showed no sign of ever leaving and never even went to the lavatory. Our host remained cool, courteous and efficient until 4 a.m., when the final coup was played and the final gains and losses calculated.'

Raven himself was a small winner. He estimated that the house, taking into account the accumulation of counters cut from winning banks, took about £2,000. Lavish as the refreshments were that their host had laid on, they were hardly that expensive.

There was the further risk of bad cheques. The host was responsible for paying the winners and dealing with losses. Did people's cheques ever bounce? Raven inquired. The host had very good backing, he was told. He could always call on enough money to pay winners and his reputation was therefore excellent. Big gambling names sometimes came to play. Greeks. Good Money. When they played the host made enough from the cagnotte in one evening to swallow any petty losses by default for the rest of the year.

A week later Paul Johnson, in those days a polemical journalist of the left, wrote a spiky little piece in the *New Statesman* contrasting the deprivations of car workers with the extravagance of the upper class, the peg for the piece being a huge party Aspinall had thrown in Belgrave Square. Johnson titled his article 'Aspers' Little Shindig'. 'I remember him as a young man at Oxford, taking a prominent part at nightly gambling sessions . . . The stakes were high and some very peculiar cheques floated around; also floating around was a young woman, who sat, as I recall, on the knee of whoever was currently winning. Even in those days Aspinall was regarded as a successful plunger. He now holds invitation-only gambling parties, in an ever-changing succession of luxury flats, to escape the rigours of the law, and makes – it is calculated – £50,000 a year, tax-free.'

The 'old nobility', according to Johnson, fell over themselves in the competition to get invitations to Aspers' little shindig. The party, for which he had flown over an 18-piece orchestra from Monte Carlo, was reputed to have cost £10,000. That very same day the Government had announced that National Assistance would be increased to 50 shillings a week, delayed to the autumn for administrative reasons. Johnson consigned the whole social scrum to perdition, but felt that the danger was more pervasive, corruption was spreading downwards. 'The day is coming,' he concluded prophetically, 'when everyone will want his invitation to Aspers' Little Shindig.'

Aspinall was furious with Raven for breaking faith but rather amused by Johnson's piece, especially his blast against the aristocracy as the last writhings of a lunatic octopus about to be swept into oblivion. Nowadays, Johnson has made a complete U-turn, and according to Aspinall would never dream of writing such stuff. He was right, though, in that most of the people in those old games have vanished, not because of the changes in the law, but – so Aspinall believes – because of the 'destitution of the English'. The 'floating' games ceased around 1960 with the new Act legalizing gaming. When he opened the Clermont Club in 1962, the clientele was still three-quarters English; today, after these changes of ownership, it's only five per cent. In the early days, the chemmy players who gambled their heads off at his parties were representative, as he saw it, of a confident ruling class, albeit the tail end of it.

'It's confidence really that makes people gamble. The old magic ruling circle had its confidence still. In my view, historically, gambling is done by a nation in a confident phase of its history. It's a popular Puritan belief that gambling is the incandescent decay of a society. The idea that the bright lights throw up a decomposing society in its death throes – that gambling is an incandescence of decay – is the exact opposite of the truth. Which is that gaming is a sign of effervescence, the bubbles of a successful society.

'So the highest gaming of the English, the Romans, was always when the nation was at its most confident. And it's the rulers of the moneyed classes who are the most confident. Namely from 1740–1840. In Rome at the time of Caesar, when the Republic was turning into an Empire. I mean Caesar was a colossal gambler. He conquered Gaul to pay his debts to Crassus – that's the only reason he went into Gaul, to pay his debts to Crassus. People forget that fact. They think of it as a great geo-political move, you know, "Let's conquer Gaul". He needed money to pay his debts. So often in history you see that.

'Look at the Arabs today. The Saudi and Gulf Arabs are very confident. They are at the apogee of their history at the moment and now they gamble like crazy all over the place, and they don't care. So confidence has got a lot to do with it really.'

Against this theory of re-writing history from the gambling point of view, Aspinall overlooks, to take one instance, the high confidence of the Victorians, who did not gamble much. In our own times, he sees the decline of the English as dating from around 1969–1972. He was out of the business for six years but when he came back in 1978, he expected a good proportion of gamblers would still be English. But no. They had all gone. There was nothing left.

So when he reopened, starting in Knightsbridge, then transferring to his present club, Aspinall's Curzon, on the site of a previous club in Curzon Street, his name was meaningless to the new swatch of gamblers. The way he describes the clientele, the establishment sounds like a mini United Nations. 'To the Arabs, the Saudis, the Gulf Arabs, the Jordanians, the Sindhis and the Punjabis (who are big gamblers), the Hong Kong Chinese, the West African Indians, who are mostly Murwaris and Sindhis, the big merchant families who gamble, the Nigerian chieftains who are another enclave of gamblers, my name meant nothing. I might have been called Parkinson or Donaldson. There was no question of being able to find any of the old business, or hardly any.'

The old English clientele had evaporated, not because they had lost their money but because they had lost their confidence. Aspinall is regretful of the passing, as he sees it, of this class, his class. 'First of all I admire the English above all other peoples, being one myself. Secondly, I've always tended to admire the leaders of the English in the 18th and early 19th centuries. If one admires those people, as I do, and I think to a large extent a lot of people are brought up to admire Pitt and Canning and Chatham and Castlereagh and so on, then you tend to admire their descendants. Because some of my clients were descendants of the great chieftains of early English history.

'Unfortunately people who inherit the name and position don't always live up in appearance and mannerisms to what one would expect of them. But I've always been very impressed with Dukes who behave like Dukes. With a Percy or a Cavendish or a Douglas or whoever it may be, who carry a great name and generations of English history. It's only a little disappointing sometimes when these people don't actually live the part too well – because of in-breeding and other factors. Disappointing. But I have in my life met some noblemen who really act the part. They are born with great aplomb and style and then I'm the first one to admire them.'

One such noble scion Aspinall admired was Sim Feversham, the Earl of Feversham. He was the epitome of an English grandee, in his confidence and his generosity. He was also a big gambler. He actually threw Aspinall a £5,000 tip across the table once. (Which indicates the size of those games.) They didn't accept tips at the private parties. Aspinall's mother took it and put it in her bag. So he had to get it out of her afterwards and give it back. Aspinall was mightily impressed by Feversham, his appearance, his manner. He would have done rather well, he thinks, in Hollywood, in the Aubrey Smith style. He also admired Lord Lucan (of whom more later), the peer whose vanishing act, after his children's nanny was found battered to death, has remained an international mystery.

He sees a cleft between the English, which can be traced back for 500 years, between the Puritans and the Cavaliers. Part of the nation has always been puritanical, he believes: the Lollards, the Levellers, the Wesleyites, the Non-Conformists, the Socialists, the Puritans. And then on the other side there are the Cavaliers. Probably they've never understood each other, but they have often acted well together, inter-locked, because Cavaliers are conquerors and adventurers, and Puritans tend to be better managers and administrators. In this sense they need each other. When they have cooperated, Aspinall avers, the nation has prospered; when they fail to understand each other, the nation droops. To take a recent example, when Labour moved too far to the Left and wanted to institute a puritanical 'Comecon' type of society, without, as Aspinall saw it, pleasure or liberty.

Aspinall admires, sympathizes and identifies with the new breed of gamblers for a particular reason. It's like musicians: instrumentalists from all over the world, even if they cannot speak each other's language, if they can play the cello well, or the xylophone, or whatever instrument you like, have something in common. Likewise there is a freemasonry among big gamblers, or gamblers of any size for that matter. It crosses the boundaries of race or language or culture. He feels happy in that company.

Because Aspinall is a gambler born and bred. It began at Oxford, where he spent his time playing the horses. Mostly the jumps. That's what kept him going in the years after Oxford, punting on the horses, poker, the occasional game of chemmy. He had no money in those days and went to private chemmy games as a small punter to try his luck. He realized at Oxford that he was not cut out for the academic world, or for a steady rise through the hierarchies in business, or a career in the Foreign Office. He probably would not even pass the exams for these sort of things, though he enjoyed the subject he was reading, English, as far as it went, which was only up to Dryden. What he did realize was that he had the temperament for gambling. He felt at ease, at home among gamblers, a rapport with them. And he realized, too, that he had an advantage through being able to accept high risks without loss of nerve. He was not a heavy drinker, either, which is another plus point in gambling.

It was at this time, soon after Oxford, that the decisive, shaping experience of Aspinall's life occurred. It's a very funny story, that begins with his step-father, Sir George Osborne, trying to find a job for him, like any other young man starting out in life. Aspinall insisted he was unemployable, because instead of taking his degree at Oxford he'd gone off to the races at Ascot. But his step-father persisted. Sir George had formed the firm view that John was a very personable young man, with his shock of fair hair and dazzling blue eyes and outgoing personality. Trustworthy and all that.

So he got him an opening with a friend of his, a tin magnate from Nigeria, who had shares in a West African trading company, headquarters in Liverpool. Aspinall, with a heavy heart, had to go up to Liverpool for an interview with the board. Still, he was consoled by the thought that he was bound to fail. There was a white-haired old gentleman, chairman of the board, and everything that Aspinall said to disparage his prospects they all thought terribly funny. 'Been to Oxford, young man?' 'Yes, sir.' 'Did you get a degree?' 'No, sir.' 'Why not?' 'Because I went to Ascot for the races.' 'You went to Ascot, by Gad! That shows enterprise, what!' Everything he said was greeted with hoots of approval and of course he got the job at once. He was to start off as a store assistant in Lagos, learning the business, then, after a year, move up country.

Aspinall was sunk, because he felt very fond of his step-father. His mother, torn between feeling he ought to get a job in a respectable firm and losing her son, reluctantly came down on the side of his taking the job. Aspinall could see no way out.

But the company made one mistake. They sent Aspinall (it's a disgraceful story, he freely admits) a tropical kit allowance of £125, to be cashed only at Austin Reed's in Regent Street. A lot of money in those days. He took the chit along to the shop and sought out the most dishonest-looking sales assistant he could find, and flashed the chit at him. 'Look, I don't really want to spend all this here. Can you do anything? I know I can't get the face value for it; work out how I can get two-thirds in cash.' So the man took the chit away, came back and told Aspinall he could get half the amount in cash, if he signed a receipt for all those clothes.

So he got £65, which was a fortune to him then. 'Obviously I realized I was cheating the wretched people who had given me the job. I was putting my foot in it, my step-father, my life. And I'd done something very bad. But nevertheless, I didn't hesitate to do it.' He took the money and backed a reverse forecast, Cock of the North and Valdesco, running at Doncaster. They came in first and second at about 18–1 and 8–1. He picked up a huge dividend of around £150. And with that he backed Flush Royal at 33–1 for the Caesarewitch, which won. So he found himself with about £1,000. At which point he was due to leave on a Union Castle liner from Southampton bound for Lagos.

The first thing he did was pay back the money. Sir George hit the roof. He probably favoured taking a horse-whip to his rascal of a step-son. Aspinall got out of the family house in Sussex in double-quick time and dashed up to London. Having nowhere to live, he decided to stay at the Ritz. But he wanted a friend to stay with him, so he sought out a chum from Oxford called Ian Maxwell-Scott (who still works for him today). Maxwell-Scott was also in difficulties, it transpired, judging from the address to which Aspinall tracked him down. He was living miles away, somewhere West, far beyond anywhere Aspinall had ever been even at his poorest; even the taxi driver baulked at driving out there because it was so slummy, doubting if Aspinall would pay the fare. Out they went, though, to find a scene like something out of Dickens, rotting cabbage stalks in the gutter, empty bottles, and finally a slum dwelling ripe for demolition.

The front door was hanging open so Aspinall picked his way through the rubbish and went in. Peering through a crack in a door he saw a figure lying on the floor underneath sheets of old newspapers. He was not even sure it was Ian; but he recognized him from their days at Balliol. He was lying on the floor because he'd hocked everything else in the room, and reading one of the papers – a five-day-old *Greyhound Express*. That's how bad it was. Aspinall relished the surprise he was about to spring.

'Ian,' he called, 'things are looking up.'

His friend let him in, then scrambled back under the newspapers, evidently feeling the cold.

'I've just booked a room,' Aspinall told him, 'number 505, a double room at the Ritz. We've got £800. We're going off to the Ritz to change our luck.'

Maxwell-Scott looked up at him from the floorboards. 'Oh no, not the Ritz.'

Aspinall never forgot that remark, from gambler to gambler. Maxwell-Scott didn't like the Ritz – 'The food's so bad. And they don't know what they're doing with the wine.' Instead of being grateful for being hauled out of the dump he was living in, he was critical of where they were going. Aspinall loved it – 'Oh no, not the Ritz' – loves that mentality. When one person is lucky and the other is busted out on his knees, you don't want gratitude. You don't want it to be 'Oh, thank you.' You just love the moment. Anyway, they did move into the Ritz and they lived there for seven months. They nearly got thrown out for not paying their bills, but in the end they just managed to pay.

How do impecunious young men manage to keep gambling in extravagant style? Aspinall and his friends had a system of 'kiting' cheques (flying 'em up like a kite) whereby you wrote out a cheque to your bookmaker, and then desperately cast around for means to cover it before it cleared – cash another cheque and go to the races in the hope of winning enough to meet the first cheque; and if that failed, borrow more money. There was always a three or four day interval after signing a cheque before it hit the bank. They didn't invent 'kiting' (it probably dates from the first cheque ever written) and it didn't always work, but they had hope. The banks were incredibly generous in those days, in the belief that they would get paid in the end. And they were paid, eventually.

Aspinall in his turn has been very accommodating about collecting debts from big losers. That is one of the reasons that his clients and friends like him even though so many of them have lost a fortune in his games. Taki, magazine columnist and jet-setter, who claims to have lost 'two or three times a six figure sum' goes even further: 'We love Aspinall because he's the man who's taken our money.' There have been bad debts. But never any real pressure, no strong-arm tactics. The assumption is that players in this closed circle will pay, though it may take a little time.

Charles Benson, former racing correspondent of the *Daily Express*, recalls an incident when Aspinall himself was put under pressure. A call came late one night from one of Benson's friends, by the name of William, saying, 'Disaster's struck, I've lost twenty-eight grand, and I'm not very happy about it.' William was a young man who in those days gambled in a very disrespectful, flippant way, which some people found distasteful, but a regular punter who won quite a lot. Benson said, 'Well, go to bed, and we'll talk about it in the morning.' William had not paid up after the game and in the morning asked Aspinall to come round to his place, where it turned out that a lady who was rather fond of William, a somewhat older woman, had marshalled a team of heavies to go round there, rough trade from the race track. When Aspinall arrived, one of the bruisers told him, 'We don't think this young man should be made to pay this debt.' Aspinall wasn't going to be remotely intimidated by these people, as Benson recalls the incident. He said: 'Don't fool about with me, I'll talk to him.' So eventually, very shamefacedly, William came down the stairs. Aspinall said: 'Look, you won a lot of money in my club. What's your problem? You know you can pay. I suggest you do.' And William agreed.

In those days credit was liberal. Benson might be having a drink with Aspers and somebody would come over and whisper that Lord so-and-so or the Duke of such-and-such or some other amazing personage wanted another £20,000 and Aspinall would say 'Fine', or 'Just make it clear to him what he's losing so he knows what the figure is', or 'Tell him it's all right with me, but is it all right with him?' The house had to pay out winners immediately, but was responsible at the same time for all the losses – because in chemin-de-fer the players are playing against each other, in a zero-sum game. The house is the banker.

Nowadays the law prohibits credit. But in the old days Aspinall went out to various Middle Eastern spots to collect his debts, or sent his brother or trusted aides. It's just something which had to be done. Sometimes they suspected that the Arabian gamblers were leading them round the desert mulberry bush, that they thought knocking their debts was rather a dare, like shoplifting on a grand scale. These were arms dealers, oil operators. By contrast, the Arab royalty, the princelings who used to play, were men of impressive dignity, generous without being flashy. The final indignity, in Aspers' code of honour, is not paying your gaming debts. But the final sanction, as all gamblers know, is being excluded from the game.

Gambling bestrides the classes, in the sense that no one cares what background a gambler is from if he's a good gambler. Aspinall with his strong sense of class has been accused of having a racialist streak in his make-up. He can on occasions hold forth, embarrassingly so for his hostess or other guests, on 'the purity of the race'. This may be a consequence of getting carried away by Nietzsche at Oxford, more likely an instinctive bias towards what he would see as the superiority of English breeding. As one dinner guest explained after enduring one of his paeans to racial purity, he can't really be taken seriously, because many of his friends, like Jimmy Goldsmith, are Jewish.

At the same time he enjoys being outrageous, like the time Benson took Mick Jagger to lunch at the club. It's like a family dining room because everybody knows everybody. Aspers called out at the top of his voice: 'Hello, Mick, good to see you, glad to see you've joined the middle classes. Because we all know you're middle class. Why do you put on that ridiculous voice when we all know you're a perfectly good middle class man like the rest of us?' And he added, 'Everybody in this room is middle class with the exception of Benson. Benson's the only upper class person and you're sitting with him. Look at those two' – and he pointed at novelist Jeffrey Archer and financier Jim Slater, who both looked a bit uncomfortable – 'they're the epitome of middle class.' Jagger just laughed, and remarked to Benson after lunch. 'I wish Aspers would come up with some new material.'

Aspinall regards himself as a very idle man, exemplifying what Tacitus called the torpor of the Saxon race. He enjoys what he does at the club. It doesn't really count as work, going up to the gaming rooms after dinner, to see what's happening; it's all exciting, especially if people are playing for high stakes. Or he'll go and play with his animals at the zoo, for hours at a time. He can't pretend it's work, in the sense that you have to do it, nine-to-five. What he hates is being at lawyers' offices all day long or waiting around at airports. It's those very boring things he regards as work.

Perhaps India gives a man that sort of attitude. He was born in India; both sides of his family had been in India for about five generations. As was the custom, he was sent back to England to a private school at the age of seven, and did not return to India until he was about sixteen. The family was thrown out of India, as he puts it, with the rest of the British in '48, and moved to places like Worthing and Littlehampton. It was astonishing how quickly all these uncles settled down to life on the south coast, giving their little houses names like 'Lucknow', changing the maidan for half an acre of garden at the back. All these men of substance who had served as colonels and commissioners. His father had been a surgeon running his own clinic in Bangalore. India was part of their life. They were all brought up to expect that they would land up in India. Aspinall goes back there quite often now. He sees (as Churchill warned) the loss of India as signalling the decline of Britain to a second or third-rate power.

He has never had any existential doubts about his identity. He learned as much about his ancestors as he could, not a particularly distinguished line, feeling a direct responsibility not to let them down, not to besmirch their name; though he himself, as the pretty Victorian term has it, was a 'love child' – not an illegitimate child, he explains, but a child born in wedlock, not of the legal father. He feels no inhibitions about it. His mother was used to little smiles about it from her old friends. Lady Osborne organized the food in the early chemmy games. Lady O's game pie was famous.

A gamesome lady, indeed, she had once been smuggled out of the Eaton Place flat in a laundry basket to avoid being photographed by the press, who had somehow got wind of the gaming going on there. If the photographers had snapped the laundry basket they would have had a scoop. The rest of the party climbed down the fire escape at the back of the house and through someone else's apartment, circumventing the *Daily Express* gossip column. The press was a killer for chemmy parties.

There was the famous story of Bill Shand-Kydd, which got exaggerated somewhat going the rounds. What happened was that Billy was having a very big win and finally left after winning about £70,000, which in today's terms would be closer to half a million. Of course when he left it meant he took virtually all the money out of the game, because the players were punting against each other, not against the house as in regular casino games. All the others, playing off their maximums, would probably be losers, and on top of that the cagnotte would have amounted to several thousand.

But just as the game was petering out, Billy reappeared. He had gone back home, had a few words, a tiff, with his wife, and decided to return to the chemmy game. At that stage racehorse trainer Bernard van Cutsem was the big loser, £80,000 down. He was a big plunger but this was the maximum he had ever lost, and it looked hopeless, certainly very unlikely he would get anything back from the other losers, at six or seven in the morning. The game was just about to break up when Billy came back in, sat down in his chair . . . and Banco! he took Bernard's bank, and suivi-ed (followed on) for what turned out to be a 7 or 8 coup winning bank. He lost his £70,000 plus another £60,000 on top of it. An incredible turn of fortune for Bernard who had been buried. Nothing came out about this, but then nine months later it got into *Time* magazine.

Aspinall himself went bust in the stock market crash of 1973. He had tried to retire from the gaming business when he sold the Clermont Club to Playboy in 1972 at the age of 45 or 46 – not give up gambling as such (even when he was living in the country he would come up to London two or three times a week to play), just the business side. One of the most elegant town houses ever built, the Clermont was designed by Thomas Kent in 1742, in Palladian style, a treasure-box of a house, whose outstanding feature is a great curving double staircase that crosses over half-way up like a figure of eight. Even after he sold it, the Club remained home from home for the young bloods about town. Unfortunately, Aspinall lost all the money he had made, speculating in shares. He went broke very, very quickly. He went zonking down in the crash, and then it took him some time to realize he had crashed that far. His second marriage to fashion model Belinda 'Min' Musker ended during this period. So to climb out, he got into the business again.

Aspinall's success, second time around, as throughout his career, stemmed from his having the social connections, the right touch, to attract the big-money players. He knew them all. They not only trusted him, they admired him: for being a player, a gambler himself, for his patrician style. The players were not all of them sprigs of the English upper class, of course. There were Greeks, then Arabs, including royal names, Americans, shipping men and oil men, race-horse owners, good-time Charlies, all lapped around in this beguiling drawly aura of English upper class style. 'Five thou' for Eddy, please,' 'Oh, better make it ten.' 'Ten thou' for Eddy, just sign the old marker will you Eddy.' *'Cinq mille à la banque!'*

Aspinall's style comes out most clearly in his attitude to parties. He loves parties, and he has thrown some memorable parties, just for the sake of giving good parties. The occasions were almost unrelated to his pecuniary interest in the guests. The parties in a mad sort of way were a form of art, he considers. They might be the most elaborate, carefully arranged, imaginative parties – but after they were over, they just disappeared. All that's left when the party's over is a memory. The ephemeral quality is part of the attraction. He gave, for example, a Babylonian party in the house of a friend in Belgrave Square. Oliver Messel did the designs for it, but as time went on they became more and more intricate. Four of the invitations are now in the Museum of Modern Art in New York: they're all that has survived. That party was modelled on the greatest party history records, when Alexander's successors divided the whole of the known world between them, over a dinner in Babylon. Another was the feast of Quatermole, inspired by a banquet given by Quatermole, nephew of Montezuma. The setting, the decoration, was sumptuous, though the historical analogy was completely lost on most of the guests, friends and punters – around 100 to 150 people would be invited to these banquets. Aspinall admits to being a bit of a showman, but his main audience is himself.

In the summer of 1986 he gave a party down at his zoo at Port Lympne which outdid in its magnificence even his own best efforts: the occasion was in honour of the Torgamba Forest Sumatran rhinoceros (a rare species which Aspinall is actively seeking to protect). Through twilit gardens, offering glimpses of wolves, Siberian tigers and snow leopards, the guests descended past cascading boxed hedges in ziggurat, to discover at the end of the long stairway, before the house, a teeming Sumatran market – dwarves stirring the air with incense, exotic natives strewing the new arrivals with rose petals, rich refreshments; thence to a tent, transformed, yet again, into a tropical rain forest, where dinner was served; followed by dancing through the night to a band from Palm Beach. According to Taki, from whose account I culled these details (not myself being of this select company) all 432 people present were known personally to the Aspinalls. (His third marriage to Lady Sarah Curzon, the widow of racing driver Piers Courage, was in 1973: by an extraordinary quirk of fate the Curzon family house in London, where she was born, was now Aspinall's club.)

Aspinall would never ask people to his parties because they were celebrities (so unlike the 'parties' of the unfortunate Hugh Hefner, one might say); on the other hand he doesn't dislike the idea of fame. It's just that journalists in his experience always get it wrong. Discretion is the soul of gaming, at this level. Nearly every big gambler in the world has some position in business or a political connection, and the last thing they want is to be in the papers. So while the parties – a celebration of the gambling milieu – attracted the gossip columnists like wasps to a jam pot (they could sting, too), Aspinall has always tried to keep them at bay.

It was the Lucan affair which brought everything out in the open. John 'Lucky' Lucan, seventh Earl, descendant of the hapless Commander of the Cavalry in the Charge of the Light Brigade (Theirs not to reason why, Theirs but to do or die) was an inner member of the Clermont Club. A peer, a gallant, a gambler, a man of unmistakable quality, golden standard-bearer of the Aspinall clique . . . a man still sought today on charges of murder. His disappearance on that night in November, 1974, after the murder of his nanny at his Belgravia home, has fascinated the media around the world. Up till now no trace of him has ever been substantiated, despite many claims and half-claims, and personally I don't think he ever will be found alive. I knew Lucan, played poker with him regularly in the early days (and I must say – whatever happened later – that I never met a man who won or lost with better grace). But that was all long before his crack-up.

What happened was . . . well, almost everyone knows what happened, in its essentials. It begins with his wife, Veronica Lucan, rushing out into the night, half-covered in blood, screaming for help. It proceeds to the discovery of the family nanny, Sandra Rivett, brutally battered to death in the basement. And it concludes with the disappearance of the noble Earl himself. The theory which was most widely scouted in the press and in subsequent police inquiries was that the intended victim was the wife, mother of Lucan's three young children, and that Sandra, in the half-dark of her room, bore some resemblance to her. The murder was a case of mistaken identity.

Lucan drove, that night, to the south coast, pausing briefly en route to make a couple of garbled phone calls to his mother before bursting in, dishevelled, at the house of Susan Maxwell-Scott (wife of the celebrated 'Oh, not the Ritz' Ian) in Uckfield. He poured out his version of events – 'I've been through the most nightmarish, awful experience' – then wrote two letters, about looking after his children, and drove off at 1.30 a.m. She was the last person to see him, before he vanished, from there to eternity.

What made the case worldwide news, of course, was Lucan's social position. But the really fascinating side of it all, in terms of English life, was the way that Lucan's friends in the Clermont closed ranks around his reputation. He was one of their own. The person whom they blamed, incredible as it might seem to those outside the charmed circle, was his hapless wife. The police, unable to trace him, claimed that they came up against a blank wall. 'Rubbish,' retort Lucan's friends; they gave the investigation maximum cooperation. Naturally, they all stood by him. 'Lucky' had had a spot of bad luck. In terms of the gambling ethic, that was it. Whatever he had done, wherever he might be, they were on his side. Certainly Aspinall admires Lucan, as a man of sterling personal qualities. All Lucan's friends give him a very high rating. The general public do not know him, so their view of him, as a man who murdered his nanny by mistake, is beside the point.

The possibility that, one day, Lucan might emerge to face the charges against him, from some hideaway in Latin America, continues to mesmerize the media. They seek him here, they seek him there. If he ever does turn up, Aspinall and his old friends will be on hand to resurrect him. The possibility, however, seems to me remote in the extreme. One theory was even so far-fetched as to suggest that Lucan's body was fed to the tigers in Aspinall's zoo. The most convincing explanation for his disappearance has been offered by the *Daily Mail*'s diarist Nigel Dempster: he suggested that Lucan consigned himself to the fate he had reserved for his wife, by disposing of his mortal remains in the waters off the south coast.

The whole case, which had a huge fall-out in terms of gossip and publicity about the life-style of the Aspinall set, took the shine off the Clermont, though the gambling among the inner group of friends continued as frenetically as ever. It was in a dimension of its own, sometimes. Charles Benson, a large, genial man and a long-standing member of the club, recalls one amazing session at backgammon, as showing the style of it. He had just got back one sunny afternoon from a trip to the South of France, having lunched extremely well in Antibes, when his friend Philip Martyn, a keen player, suggested they go off to the club to play a spot of 'gammon'.

As they walked through the door of the backgammon room a new board was just being set up. Someone shouted: 'Are you in?' and they said, 'Of course we're in.' It was £40 a point which was quite a big game in those days. They were playing chouette, which means one player is in the 'box' playing against a group of others: this sharply increases the action at backgammon, because the player taking his turn in the box wins, or loses, the stakes of all the other players. The two Sweeny brothers, Charlie and Bobby – Bobby Sweeny the great American amateur golfer and all-round sportsman – were in the box, against half a dozen others, including Aspers. Aspinall was a very big builder-up of games, and of atmosphere.

The game was doubled and redoubled fairly quickly and then the six of them doubled the two Sweenys again to £320. There was just no way, on the board, they could take it. Charlie said, 'I'm dropping,' and Bobby said, 'No, no, no, no, let's have a look.' Charlie said, 'No Bob, leave it.' Bobby stared at the board. 'I don't know, I'd like to have a look at this one.' So Aspers said, 'Go on Bobby, take it, and I'll take half your action.' So he was now playing half against himself, in fact more, because he was one of six.

The game fluctuated to the most staggering degree and eventually got to a stage where the group of six were quietly winning but had left open one combination, which would enable Bobby to hit the last remaining man they had on the board to get in. The combination is written on Benson's heart, because Bob Sweeny rolled it, 6–2. At that point the game had got up to £1,280 each for the Six. So Sweeny, with Aspinall still half in with him, immediately doubled again. What he had failed to notice, so excited was he at hitting them with his 6–2, was that they were still miles ahead, if they could get their one man back. He didn't have a full board. So – despite being pretty upset at this setback – every one of them took the double, £2,560 each.

When it came to Bobby's next throw, he rolled a double-two.

That effectively filled in the blank spaces he had on his board. So suddenly Benson, who was still metaphorically in the South of France, breathing red wine and garlic, was up against it. If Aspers hadn't changed sides, played both sides, he would have won £160, game over. But Sweeny's final throw virtually settled the match, and it cost him £2,560 on that one game – about half his annual salary in those days.

For the rest of the evening, after taking that sort of knock, Benson felt completely disoriented. The expression current in those days was 'steaming' – when you are really gambling, you 'steam'. He was steaming from the word go – you take bad doubles, play wide open, take everything, otherwise you're never going to get your money back. That evening he lost over five grand, and paid it then and there. There have been times, Benson recalls, when he couldn't pay a tenner. He once put his last sixpence on a horse, and when it lost had to walk home from Victoria station.

Lucan was good fun to play with, Benson recalls. He particularly liked to make the number one point, which is actually the worst point early on, and it became known as 'Lucky's point'. He would make it with a great flourish and say, 'The dice can only see two men!' – a ridiculous expression meaning the dice did not know which points you'd got. They used to have a lot of fun, like one night when half a dozen of them were playing blackjack in the back room, feeling in extremely good humour after dinner, and when the bank went bust Benson let out a little cheer. On the very next hand the bank went bust again and they all gave a little cheer. Then when it happened a third time in a row, they let out a fairly big cheer. The dealer looked slightly embarrassed but was enjoying it too. And then when the bank went over the top for the fourth time, a roar went up like Spurs scoring against Arsenal.

This time Aspers came out to look. There was a huge chemmy game going on next door, but he found it all highly amusing and stayed to watch. Everyone crowded around and the chemmy game ground to a halt. The blackjack dealer went bust six or seven times in a row, which is most unusual, so even the chemmy players were cheering. That sort of behaviour could never happen in an ordinary casino, but Aspers thought it great fun. One of the drawbacks of all the Arab and other foreign players who are now the lifeblood of British casinos is that they do not have any sense of fun; they just sit there and gamble.

One or two Arab gamblers might have a swing of a million in a night's play. Aspinall would cover any bet. But according to Taki, today the style of games has deteriorated, far below the point where someone like himself (if he had the money) would want to play. In the old days, it was a very elegant table ... before the English got wiped out. What constitutes vulgarity in gambling? It's akin to bravery or cowardice in battle, in Taki's estimation. It's a certain way of acting. You smile when you lose and congratulate the winner who beat you. Not playing like McEnroe plays tennis. The Arabs have money, he adds, but not courage – they bet high to impress the hookers.

Jimmy Goldsmith was the man for action, a very violent gambler. He used to like striding into the Clermont (in the days when he was not so enmeshed in business affairs) and see six or eight of them playing backgammon and say, 'Right, take you all on.' And he would, too, he would absolutely terrify them, even when there were 'real earners' in the game, professionals, like Joe Dwek. Jimmy didn't mind who he was taking on. He would give doubles that no one else would risk, what are called 'pressure doubles'. He loved pressure, inflicting pressure or having pressure put on him. He would giggle and chortle away, and laugh his head off if he lost, but very impatient for service, for getting on with it. By contrast, the financier Jim Slater (who later crashed and then recovered) liked to psych out the opposition, and talk his way through a game. He got immense satisfaction out of not losing, which is not quite the same as winning, more like chess.

An outsider's view of a night out at the Clermont, and a charming description it is, has been given by French novelist Françoise Sagan, who is, as she admits, a life-long gambler. She found herself seated at the chemin-de-fer table, in a large, comfortable, wood-panelled room, surrounded by a few 'inimitable specimens' of English society: racehorse owners who, between each banco, talked only of the turf; two outrageous old ladies with flowery hats and enormous jewels; a degenerate young heir who bore the name of one of the best English families.

The stakes were all in guineas, as Mlle Sagan recalls the scene (*With Fondest Regards*, 1986), and she had no idea of their value. Someone brought her a little pile of chips in exchange for a little piece of paper which she happily signed. To her left there was talk of horses, to her right of regattas. Meanwhile her little pile of chips disappeared, one after the other. Hardly had one pile vanished than a splendid valet would place another on a silver tray in front of her and she would sign another little piece of paper.

At length, feeling slightly alarmed, she discreetly asked the valet to write down for her the sum she now owed. 'He went over to speak to a tall, well-built man, who was very nice, and had been circling the table since play began. He was none other than the owner of the Clermont Club. He did a quick calculation, wrote a figure on a piece of paper and the trusty messenger brought it over . . . I glanced at it. I had to draw on all my moral precepts, all my strength of mind, all the good upbringing my parents had tried to give me and all the bad that I had succeeded in acquiring by myself, not to fall over backwards. My debt totalled £80,000.'

To pay off this debt, she realized, she would have to give up her flat, ask her mother to take care of her son, and spend two years working exclusively for the taxman and the Clermont. If she was going to lose two years of her life (and here Mlle Sagan showed her true, pure gambler's spirit) she might as well lose four. She called for more chips, took the bank and won it. After that she held the bank whenever she could and – by a miracle – it was all coming back. After an hour had passed she inquired of the messenger how she stood with the house. A little note came back from the proprietor, which she unfolded without betraying any haste. She now owed only £50.

She stood up and cordially took her leave of everyone at the table. She had by this time discussed the Epsom Derby with the person on her left and the attractions of Florida with the person on her right. She paid her £50 to the cashier, and the proprietor saw her out. 'It was a great pleasure to have you at my tables,' said this very friendly man, 'especially since the French are generally so lacking in sang-froid when gambling.' 'Oh,' Mlle Sagan said in a thin little voice, 'Oh, the very idea. One plays for the fun of it, don't you agree?'

It was Bobby Sweeny who introduced the wonderful word 'boff' to the group. It was just after Chappaquiddick, and Bobby said. 'I don't know what all the fuss is about. All the poor guy did was stop off for a boff.' Benson and Dominick Elwes took the word up immediately, it was such a pleasing euphemism – 'Had a great boff last night' or 'It was just a boff de politesse' (making love to a girl simply because it was expected of one) and so on. You could use it in any society. Elwes was the Clermont club wit, a brilliant mimic, a great friend of Aspinall and just about everybody there, but not really a gambler. The Lucan affaire was to cost him his life, too.

Elwes was blamed, after a detailed reconstruction of Lucan's life and times had appeared in the *Sunday Times*, for committing the cardinal sin of blabbing to the press. In punishment, he was barred from Annabel's, night club of the *jeunesse dorée* and the most stylish place in town, founded by Mark Birley underneath the Clermont, and from his ultra-exclusive luncheon club Mark's. (Aspinall himself had always been very supportive of Elwes.) It turned out later that it was a horrible mistake: according to the author of the article, Elwes was not the source of the piece, as had been supposed: the photos had come from Lady Lucan. But Elwes was judged guilty by Goldsmith and Birley of an unforgivable breach of confidence. (He did contribute a witty sketch in the style of Max Beerbohm showing some of the chaps at lunch, with one of the members, broad back bent forward, apparently relieving himself in a corner; it was nicely done and no one with any sense of humour about themselves could have taken offence.)

Deprived of the circle of friends around whom his whole life revolved, banishment was too much for such a highly-strung young man to bear. He killed himself. At his funeral, Aspers delivered a fulsome oration, 'Oh, why did you leave us, Dominick? Why did you die?' Immediately the service was over, an outraged cousin of Elwes stepped up to Aspinall and gave him a good sock on the jaw.

Veronica Lucan was completely ostracized by the group from the very moment of the tragedy of which she was the victim. How could she be to blame? How was she responsible for her husband's drinking, his debts, his fits of rage? The answer, it seems, was that she was regarded as an outsider, a usurper somehow, of Lucky's freedom. After many travails with legal and family problems, she continues to undergo treatment for severe depression.

In 1984 Aspinall, in partnership with Jimmy Goldsmith, floated their new casino, Aspinall's Curzon, on the stock market. The City went mad to buy the shares. On the plus side, the company could show an annual profit of £8m. And as its principal asset it had Aspinall's reputation and skill . . . But still . . . it was only a casino, depending for its profits on mug punters continuing to patronize it in sufficient numbers, not a 'real' business like manufacturing. The wild over-subscription for its shares showed that the investment community liked to gamble just as much as the players round the green baize. Aspinall's holding, from an original investment of £10,000, was valued at £30m. The company was sold in 1987, just before the stock market crash, for £90m.

Aspinall has never been secretive about his profits, but he is not a man who wanted to make money for its own sake. No, he has another passion. Wild animals.

His gaming clubs have financed his two private zoos, at Howletts and close by at Port Lympne, in Kent. Their upkeep costs him £750,000 a year. The zoos are not amateur little parks: Aspinall maintains some 625 wild animals, and makes a speciality of breeding Siberian tigers. When he went down in the stock market crash of '73, he sold his valuable possessions, his paintings, his furniture, his 'loot' from the years of gaming piracy, as he puts it. But he hung on to the animals, just managed to hang on.

The zoos are expensive. For one thing, they are designed to give the animals the best possible conditions in their captivity. For another, Aspinall likes to feed his animals (like his clients) only the best. Why should they be fed inferior food? They are as important to him, more important, than any human beings. Aspinall has lost three keepers over the years, two killed by a tiger, one by an elephant and has himself taken incredible risks. He likes to go into the tiger compound or the gorilla cages, and allow the animals to play with him. He has a close physical relationship with his animals. Once in the early days he was almost killed by bears: crushed and mauled, he had to be dragged out of the cage. After the ordeal he sobbed for an hour, clasping the keeper's hands. He could hardly believe it, that when it mattered most, luck had been on his side. He detests the English upper class's pursuit of hunting, seeing it as partly responsible for their terminal decline. His idea of play, as shown in this graphic account from a magazine article by Charles Maclean, is quite different.

'On the floor of the Gorillarium he sits like a Buddha in the straw and waits for one of them to make the first move. All seven around the cage have displayed distant interest; if they want to approach, they'll do it in their own time. There is no question of coercion – you can't whistle a gorilla like you can a dog. Unexpectedly a series of somersaults lands the youngest of the group in his lap. It throws a long dark arm about his neck and greets him with affectionate gutterals. Moving on to all fours he returns the compliment. At the other end of the enclosure two fully grown females confer in a corner, massive heads lowered together, small eyes evoking the pathos of intelligence imprisoned by musculature. They feign indifference but keep him under observation, casting sidelong glances, curious and jealous.

'Without warning the larger of the two suddenly breaks into a chest-thumping charge. He half turns to meet her and receives two heavy blows to the shoulder as she rushes past, deliberately not looking at him. It's a reproachful reminder, an invitation to come-and-play-with-me. Before he is fully recovered she's back, looking for action. They roll together, spar and wrestle; she sits on his back and beats her sides; he tickles her under the arms, setting off a reaction of deep reverberative laughter. Others join in the games. They come and go, always recalcitrant, sometimes aloof because of rivalries. He calls them by name, talks to them in their language, aping their vocalizations, a blond gorilla among blacks. But the true medium of their conversation is physical contact. At the end he stands alone, scratched and bruised, rugger-shirt in tatters, missing a sizeable tuft of hair and a trouser-leg, but delighted with himself, his gorillas, the whole display. Beyond the bars of the cage a manservant materializes with a change of clothes, carefully laid across his black-coated arm.'

There have been funny stories: on one occasion a keeper whom he had sacked for negligence let the pair of Himalayan bears loose; they were tempted into drinking a bucket each of green chartreuse, 60 degrees proof; when they fell asleep, they were carried back on stretchers, and slept for three days. Aspinall likes animals around the house. His first tiger cub, Tara, bought for £200 in a pet shop near the Regent's Park Zoo, was reared in his bed for her first few months. Tigers are misunderstood animals, he claims; they have a loyal and affectionate nature, and only two or three out of the 60 he has kept at Howletts have been tricky.

All right for the family, but disconcerting to visitors. Once when workmen came in to wallpaper the bedroom, and were warned by his mother-in-law, 'Whatever you do, don't wake up the gorilla,' they thought she was joking. When the gorilla peeped out from under the sheets, they fled. Or the coalman, stalked by the tiger as he carried in sacks of coal, taking a breather in the cellar; he strikes a match to light a cigarette, and sees in the flame a Siberian tiger, squatting next to him. Or Lady Diana Cooper refusing to remove her hat before a gorilla 'ramble' through the park; the gorilla snatched her hat off, to reveal . . . curlers. When Tara died, killed by a male tiger, Aspinall buried her next to his daughter who died in infancy. He also wrote a poem to Tara, the last verse of which runs:

> I swear it, I swear it, I swear it,
> To expiate man's basest crime.
> I shall increase your tribe to a thousand,
> Then join you in the jungles of time.

Aspinall believes he has 'been successful in bridging that great man-made divide that has separated us from our kindred for countless thousands of years . . . Many have feasted with kings, few with tigers . . . To those who say how dull must be the company of creatures that have no language or learning, I would answer that the most profound communications are often mute.'

Other zoologists have saluted Aspinall's dedication and originality. But in this field, as in gambling, his idiosyncratic approach has aroused jealousy. The very success of his zoos – in encouraging breeding (which animals will only do if they feel content), in the upkeep and display of his animals, in the atmosphere of family freedom – is taken, so he feels, by some other zoos as implicit criticism of their own activities. He, after all, is only an amateur, a dilettante. He felt particularly upset when the *Smithsonian* magazine was prevailed upon to reject an article about his zoos, simply because the writer, an expert in the field, turned in a rather flattering report. In general, though, his work is more respected abroad than in England.

His knack of handling people, he has said, especially rich and powerful people, has been transferred to handling wild animals. It is dangerous, getting close to wild animals. He thrives on all kinds of risk. But he does not make a direct connection between his love of gambling and his love of wild animals, except for the obvious fact that the former has enabled him to afford the latter.

Ultimately, Aspinall believes in some cloudy apocalyptic way in a vast reduction of the human species in the British Isles, and in the world, so as to make room for the animals, and atone for man's sin of 'speciocide'. 'Some of us are now driven to believe,' he declared in a final credo in his book about his zoos, *The Best of Friends* (1976), 'that a demo-catastrophe will be an eco-bonanza. In other words, a population readjustment on a planetary scale from 4,000 million to something in the nature of 200 million would be the only possible solution for the survival of our own species and of the eco-system or systems that nurtured us. The reduced figure would represent a human population approximately equivalent to that of Julius Caesar's time, and may be too large for the earth to sustain in perpetuity.'

In his despair over the survival of the animal species, Aspinall has been driven to the horrible analogy of comparing wildlife workers with the *Sondergruppen* of Auschwitz, who knew the day they and their ward were to be executed and yet went on with their tasks . . . (He seems actually to approve of genocide if staged over a period of a few hundred years, his only regret being that a nuclear holocaust would annihilate merely some 200–300 million.)

'The grand design of all wildlife workers must be to protect the threatened through this difficult time . . . No longer can it be said that peace, plenty and plurality are worthy ends . . . Homo sapiens is an uncontrolled, cancerous growth . . . Unfortunately its efforts (medical research) to neutralize our time-honoured, natural beneficial predators like bubonic bacillus, the anopheles mosquito and the typhoid bacterium have proved only too successful . . . The choice before us is a qualitative life for 200,000,000 humans in perpetuity in a partially restored paradise, or a quantitative countdown to Armageddon on a raped planet gutted of most of its resources.'

Will there ever be a shift in human opinion large enough to save the animal species? Aspinall thinks not. 'I think the odds are stacked against success; but I know of no other wager worth a bet.' In late 1985 Aspinall suffered a minor stroke, which has not, he says, served to reduce his physical involvement with animals. He faces death 'in the jungles of time' with equanimity, hoping – but very much doubting – that one of his three children may, perhaps, want to continue his self-appointed task.

Aspinall's success as gamester-extraordinary to the English aristocracy and the international set may be compared with the achievement of the celebrated 'Greek Syndicate' in the years between the two world wars. The Greek syndicate ran the baccarat games in Deauville, Cannes and Monte Carlo. Its motto *'Tout va'* – the sky's the limit. This famous challenge murmured politely by dealer Nico Zographos, at the start of the big week at Deauville in 1923, created a sensation in that golden arc of high society which frequented the continental spas. *'Tout va'* was an invitation, a 'come-on', as the organizing spirits behind the syndicate, notably François André who managed the Deauville and Ostend casinos, well knew, which no big player could resist – to try to break the bank at baccarat. The game itself is exactly like chemin-de-fer, except that instead of the players all gambling against each other, the two halves of the table, six players on each side, bet against the house as banker.

A throng of rich old men, kings and captains and sportsmen of a Europe forever gone, fastened on the challenge. Over the years they tilted at the Greek syndicate, and sometimes they won huge sums. Zographos, described as small and dark, rather like Charlie Chaplin with deep pouches under his eyes, was an unemotional player. His worst moment came at Cannes in 1928. Running the bank on a float of 30 million francs, he was down to his last million. Baccarat is a game in which a sudden swing of luck for the players, ten or a dozen coups in a row on each side of the table, can wipe out the banker, despite his theoretical 0.8 per cent advantage.

The Greek's last million was riding on a single coup, as Charles Graves describes the moment in *None But The Rich* (1963). Zographos dealt the cards – both opponents said *'Non'*, meaning they held likely winning hands. He turned over his own cards – a king and a queen – *'bouche, bouche'* – nothing! Word had gone round that Zographos' credit was exhausted. This was it. As the players and onlookers around the table craned forward, he drew the third card and quietly turned it over – it was a nine, the perfect card. To celebrate the coup, which broke the losing sequence against the syndicate, Zographos bought a nine of diamonds tie-pin with cuff links to match; the nine of diamonds became the pennant on his yacht.

And what about the customers' yachts? Very, very few of those baccarat players rose from the table as rich as when they sat down. Of course they won, but they came back, and came back again. For four decades the syndicate held the gamblers of Europe in thrall. When Zographos died in 1953 he left over £5m, despite large sums disbursed to family and friends before his death. No gambler before or after has left such a vast fortune amassed entirely from card playing, and that from only one form of it, claims Charles Graves.

Zographos' record, and his achievement in sustaining it so long, must be judged greater than Aspinall's own success, because baccarat is a game in which the banker relies on his skill to win. On every hand, he has the option of whether to stand or draw, depending on his assessment of the players' hands against his own, compared with the money being wagered on either side of the table. By contrast at chemin-de-fer, the game which launched Aspinall, the cagnotte or five per cent cut on winning banks will automatically destroy the players, and progressively enrich the house, the longer the game goes on.

Baccarat is seldom played nowadays in the old way, except at Monte Carlo and one or two French casinos, having been superseded by the mechanical and uninteresting modern version of the game known as Punto Banco in England and Nevada Baccarat in America. According to Zographos, there is as big a difference between a good baccarat player and a poor one as there is between a scratch golfer and a man with an eighteen handicap.

'There is no such thing as luck,' he once observed. 'It is all mathematics. There are three kinds of cards – good cards, bad cards and indifferent cards. You must play them according to what they are. That is not a contradiction. You may have luck for an hour or two, even a day or two, even a week ... What people call luck is merely an established fact seen through the spectacles of after events ... the main difference is that the punters usually double up when they are losing and hedge when they are winning. I will put it another way: the bank plays baccarat as though it were contract bridge; the punters play baccarat as though it were poker.'

Despite the syndicate's motto of *tout va*, Zographos showed excellent judgement when things did occasionally get out of hand, like the night Sidney Beer the racehorse owner and orchestral conductor kept turning up 8s and 9s and simply obliterated the bank. Beer had the kind of streak which happens to a few lucky people once in a lifetime: he won 12 coups consecutively in a series in which his side of the table won 26 out of 29 times.

He had bet this phenomenal run with great courage or great recklessness according, as he said, to how you like to look at it, and retired to the bar for a celebratory drink.

Summoned to the table when it was his turn to play the hand again, he won another five coups in a row, doubling up. Zographos showed no emotion, but suddenly rose from the table, bowed to the assembled company and said politely: *'C'est assez pour ce soir.'* Within two years Sidney Beer had lost all of it back and was a heavy loser to boot.

Zographos gave up the game at the onset of war in Europe, retiring to Switzerland, where he concentrated on his golf and his skiing. He resisted all blandishments to resume dealing for the syndicate in the years after the war. He was waiting, he said, for the good days to come·back. He meant when people had money again – the English in those days were limited to an annual travel allowance of £25. On Zographos' death in 1953, the syndicate required new partners. They were forthcoming, but the risks were underlined when the new syndicate, which had started out with 300m. francs (worth then about £320,000) got wiped out in ten days at Cannes in August 1957, despite being over 120m. francs ahead one night.

The bank hit a run of 14 losing coups which, so dealer Sammy Denoune told Charles Graves, should not happen more than once in a decade. On the final coup, tableau one asked for a card and the bank dealt out a 2, tableau two asked for a card and the bank dealt a 3. Denoune himself had a 5. With the odds so heavily in his favour, he stood pat – the chances were that both tableaux were less than 5 and quite possibly baccarat, 1, 2 or 3, so it was about two to one his winning on both sides of the table and about three to one his winning one side and being *égalité* with the other. In the event tableau one was drawing on a 4 and tableau 2 on a 5, so he lost to both.

That night Jack Warner won £50,000 and Darryl Zanuck £15,000. It was no consolation that the pair of them, having busted that game, went over to Monte Carlo and lost it all back at the baccarat table there. In any case, the syndicate was coming to an end, in the new social milieu of the swinging sixties. Aspinall's private parties had already set the new style.

The final survivor of the old gang was François André, who had run the Deauville casino where Zographos first announced 'tout va', and had been the *éminence grise* of the syndicate ever since. Reflecting on his long career as his life neared its end, in his private suite at the Majestic Hotel in Cannes, he confided that he was dying with a clear conscience. He believed it was a grievous mistake to make too much money. (Among other good works, he had built a hospital in his native Ardèche.)

The gambler who had impresssed him most, in the 40 years of the syndicate, was Zographos. 'He always had the absolute conviction when dealing the cards that he could not possibly lose. He gambled for fantastic sums. By contrast, he would never have risked five francs if he had been punting against the bank.'

André's last English visitor was golfer Henry Cotton. Lying back weakly on his bed, André waved his gnarled hands round the bedroom: 'Et voilà! Mon Empire.'

When the stakes are so high that it really hurts, gambling may be called 'deep'. The concept of 'deep play' was well expressed by Jeremy Bentham in his treatise *The Theory of Legislation*, published in 1790. By it he meant play in which the stakes are so high that it was (from his utilitarian standpoint) irrational to engage in it at all. As he put it:

Though the chances, so far as relates to money, are equal, in regard to pleasure, they are always unfavourable. I have a thousand pounds. The stake is five hundred. If I lose, my fortune is diminished one-half; if I gain it is increased only by a third. Suppose the stake to be a thousand pounds. If I gain, my happiness is not doubled with my fortune; if I lose, my happiness is destroyed; I am reduced to indigence.

There were many aristocratic young sprigs frittering away their fortunes in Aspinall's games, who would have done well to heed this early statement by Bentham of what is now known as the theory of marginal utility. Young men who played (as we all have done in our time) over their heads but, in this rakish ambiance, lost more than just money – heirlooms, inheritances, even houses slipped away across the baize. Deep play is sustainable, perhaps, if you are the Duke of A or the Earl of B, owning houses stuffed with family treasures: such a man can always sell off a Goya or a piece of Georgian silver and hardly notice its absence: for the lesser men among the gamesters, it went harder.

What induces people to engage in deep play? The Clermont might seem to have been in its heyday a peculiarly English sort of club, harking back in its style and exclusiveness to the gamesters of some candle-lit salon of the eighteenth century; but I am inclined to think, human nature being what it is, that deep play, in its own social context, exists in many other cultures around the world. As an illuminating sidelight on the derring-do at the Clermont, one may cite an experience of gambling quite strange to our own society, the Balinese cockfight.

Cockfighting to Bali is like horse-racing in our own society, not just a sport, but part of the fabric of social life, in which the top owners, by their wealth and standing, set the standards for the sport as a whole. Actually, cockfighting in Bali is more akin to illegal gambling here, because it is forbidden fruit, banned by the authorities, and forbidden fruit is always far spicier than the ordinary variety.

Gambling, intense and continuous and extraordinary, according to anthropologist Clifford Geertz (*The Interpretation of Cultures*, 1975), is what characterizes cockfighting in Bali. In the period under review, fights were held three times a week, and fortunes wagered on them. Stakes were many times in excess of a man's monthly earnings, whole villages and kinships were swept up in the fever to back their own cock, such was the enthusiasm for gambling on the contest. The betting was usually close to even money, because the cocks were closely matched, a further inducement to high stakes.

'As much of America surfaces in a ball park, on a golf links, at a race track, or around a poker table, much of Bali surfaces in a cock ring. For it is only apparently cocks that are fighting there,' Geertz says. 'Actually it is men.' Why do they, village people, people living off the ricefields, close to their temples, with a rich and elaborate culture, why do they gamble so wildly, go so far over their heads in their betting?

For people who think like Bentham (nowadays mainly law-yers, economists and a few psychiatrists, says Geertz) the ex-planation is that such men are irrational – addicts, fetishists, children, fools, savages, who need only to be protected against themselves. For the Balinese, the explanation lies in the fact that in deep play – where men bet so high above their normal standards of economic value – money is less a measure of utility, to be won or lost, than it is a symbol of moral import.

In deep games, more is at stake than material gain: namely, esteem, honour, dignity, respect – in a word, status. Yet it is at stake symbolically. No one's status (leaving aside a few ruined gamblers) is actually altered, it turns out, by the outcome of a Balinese cockfight; it is only momentarily affirmed or diminished. This is not to say that the money does not matter: it is because it does matter that the more money a cock's owner and his backers risk, the more of other things, such as their pride, their poise, their dispassion, their masculinity, are also risked. It is because the 'marginal disutility' of loss is so great at the higher levels of betting that in this kind of deep play a man lays his public self, through the medium of his fighting cock, on the line, says Geertz.

To a Benthamite, this might seem merely to increase the irrationality of the enterprise that much further; but to the Balinese what it mainly increases is the meaningfulness of it all. By contrast, the smaller 'shallow' cockfights, where the money is important to the players, are regarded as of no social signifi-cance. This graduation of status gambling with deeper fights and, inversely, money gambling with shallower fights, is exactly like the graduation of horse-racing in our own society: to win the Derby is a public triumph, whereas the outcome of a selling plate on some provincial track is of no account – likewise with the betting involved.

What makes Balinese cockfighting deep is thus not money in itself, but what money causes to happen ... a psychological release of emotion, in a representation of the interactions of everyday life ... 'a migration of the Balinese status hierarchy into the body of the cockfight'.

Or, to translate the jargon of social psychology into everyday terms, the cockfight is a kind of replica of real life, in which the tensions of living, social and psychological and violent, are displayed in a deliberate way in a 'game'. In this process, the Balinese are put in touch with themselves, or an essential part of their being, as we are in our society, so Geertz concludes, by seeing a performance of *King Lear* or *Macbeth* or reading *Crime and Punishment*. The cockfight is like a text which takes up the themes of death, masculinity, rage, pride, loss, beneficence, chance, and orders them into a comprehensible structure. It expresses the thrill of risk, the despair of loss, the pleasure of triumph ... but not merely these things, which in themselves are obvious, but these emotions as a paradigm of the way society itself is constructed. The cockfight focuses in a small space governed by strict rules a people's experience of their life: but without the intensity given by the betting, the effect could not be achieved.

Well! I am not seeking to imply that the scions of English nobility who frequented Aspinall's chemmy games were duplicating the experience of going to the theatre at Stratford-on-Avon, still less that they were somehow re-living in the play of the cards the tensions of the British body politic. But there is a parallel with the cockpits of Bali. It is certainly true that 'deep play' has a social dimension, of conferring and reducing status, without necessarily altering the players' material position. In these games the players are rivals but act as gentlemen; to lose gracefully is the highest attribute, to win well hardly less so. Those who do both have popularity and standing among their peers; those who fail are regarded as 'bad sports', uncompanionable. To bet for such high stakes, losing as one young man was reputed to have done 'the most beautiful house in England', is madness. Yet without the high stakes none of the ritual or the manners of the game carry any weight or feeling: that is really what it's all about: a way of feeling things more intensely.

If one asks such players why they engage in gambling for absurdly high stakes they do not offer very articulate answers. It is 'exciting' yes; but it comes down, very often, to the reverse side of that, to being 'bored' by not playing, a feeling that to stand aside from the group would be to lose out, to miss the whole point of being a member of such fast company. Deep play is not utilitarian, unless like Aspinall you are running the game as well as gambling in it; whether viewed as a pastime or a social rite, or if you like, a 'text', those who engage in it feel, probably not at the conscious level, involved in something which goes beyond mere gambling. Does the Balinese instance seem too remote from our own experience? If so, there are examples closer to home. The aficionados at a bullfight are not just watching a man kill a bull, are they? Style is everything. Aspinall always had it. In any case, Aspinall couldn't stay away for long. In 1992, in a blaze of publicity, he opened a new casino in Curzon Street. With his usual candour, he explained: "I need the money."

3

A VIEW FROM THE DOWNSIDE

> True, out of a hundred persons,
> only one can win; yet what busi-
> ness is that of yours or of mine?
> Dostoyevsky, *The Gambler*

Gordon Moody has that fresh-air, alert, well-scrubbed look of a bookish boy scout. In his early seventies, his step has the same spring, his eye the same gleam of humour and interest, as in those far-off days when he started out as a Methodist minister, on circuit around the English shires. He inherited a strong and simple faith from his parents, particularly his mother who took him to church on Sunday mornings; but in the week there was no contact with the church at all, none of his close friends were from church-going families. Belief became a part of him, mixed with a good streak of old-English common sense.

At the age of 11 at his London high school, the biology teacher asked the class how different languages had come about. Gordon upped his hand: 'The tower of Babel!' He was dismissed as an idiot, and from that moment came to accept that religious belief must be accompanied by a scientific approach to the understanding of life. The early chapters of Genesis, he realized, were a myth, albeit with a colossal message wrapped up in it.

He grew up to feel there were two parts of his life: he lived in the world, and the beliefs he accepted from the church lived in him. He learned, as he put it, not to turn the world inside out but to accept it, as it is. A quality of mind summed up in the young Gordon's estimation that 'People are people' – regardless of who they are or what they may believe.

Or whether they are in trouble from gambling. Over the years no individual has had more influence on or a closer knowledge of the social issues involved in gambling in Britain than the

Rev. Gordon Moody. Yet his own involvement with gambling was the purest chance.

When he left school, where he had been regarded as a no-hoper, he managed to find a job with an import firm in the City of London. At the age of 19 it suddenly struck him, as he describes it, that he ought to be ordained. He was accepted into the Methodist ministry, and this time went to college with a will; next came probationary service, travelling around country parishes, leading to his ordination in 1942, the year he got married. The young couple were as poor as church mice. Moody got on fine with his congregation, but still felt claustrophobic. The church did not seem to realize that it cost more to have a minister with a wife than a man on his own – it seemed in those days to be acting stingily. His wife Jess felt depressed. Moreover, the Rev. Moody with his motto of 'People are people' was not used to confining his activities to churchy folk. He was a mixer. Volunteering as a chaplain to the forces, he was accepted by the Royal Air Force. Mixing with all ranks, being treated as an equal by all ranks, was a great release. The question was what to do in 1958, after his term of six years was up. Out of the blue a friend suggested he should become Secretary to the Churches' Council on Gambling.

Moody had never heard of it. He guessed it must follow some kind of temperance approach and felt a bit insulted. He wrote back and asked what qualifications were required. His friend told him he could get on all right with the Anglicans. And secondly, as regards the job itself, Moody knew how to talk to 'lewd fellows of the baser sort' as the New Testament expression has it, people like bookmakers; for he too was a man who did not speak the language of Zion. In short the job was like a frontier post from which he could go out and meet his fellow men on their own ground. His motivation for accepting, he recalls, was of the lowest, but he rather esteems low motivations. 'They get you through, they go on. High motivations burn you out. They really only operate at key points.' He took the job on.

Street bookmaking, illegal bookmaking, was the dominant characteristic of gambling in Britain in 1958. The well-heeled punters, the owners and trainers at the upper end of the racing fraternity, had telephone credit accounts with bookmakers, who were themselves, in their brown trilbys and tweed suits, treated almost as gentlemen. 'Five 'undred pounds the favourite, m'Lord? Very good, m'Lord. Five 'undred invested.' (They always used that word.) 'Thanks ver' much, Billy.' As so often in England, class distinction set the rule. The ordinary working bloke without a bank account or references could never open a telephone credit account for off-course betting. But damn nearly everybody in the country wanted to bet, especially on Derby day. The result was the proliferation of street bookies with their runners watching out for the police. Only in the north and in Scotland were there any betting shops, under arrangement with the local police. There were no casinos. Instead the smart set had private gaming parties, whose 'scandalous' goings-on from time to time fizzed into the popular papers (see chapter 2).

In Britain when the Government of the day wants to review policy about something but does not quite know how to go about it – typically on big social issues – it appoints a Royal Commission on the subject. This committee of the great and the good, experts and lay people, then deliberates for a year or so, publishes its report, sometimes with dissenting opinions, and sets the stage for a grand debate which rolls gently on, allowing the Government, if it so chooses, to take no further action at all. That is how British public life works. The Royal Commission on Gambling of 1949–51, however, annoyed the Churches' Council on Gambling very much. Its report was adjudged to be light-hearted and shallow compared with the Royal Commission on Gambling of 1932–33. The latter said that there were serious social consequences from gambling. The new report said not so.

Gordon Moody in his new job was inclined to side with the new report. He put it to himself that with high unemployment, half a crown a week (this coin, long since withdrawn, was a handsome silver piece, then the price of a good dinner) wagered on a horse made serious inroads on a man's wages back in the thirties, but in the 1950s it had no effect at all. He felt as un-enlightened on the subject of gambling as everyone else. Reading through the Churches' Council evidence and submissions to the Royal Commission, some of it seemed unreal. For instance the churchmen claimed that starting quietly with football pools, the public were led on in a fever of desire to all types of gambling. Moody felt that was not right – so far as the pools were concerned it was obvious that what attracted people was the lure of a big prize; most people would go on with their lives as they always had done. When the church looked at these things, it did not seem to have the human race in view.

His position brought him on to various Methodist committees where he had the same experience, for instance the fear expressed that if divorce were made easier, everyone would go wild. Likewise with abortion: the official line seemed to base itself on the need for new law, taking no account of the strong natural pull of motherhood; if that ever changed, something would have changed in human nature itself. Some people, Moody felt, seemed to believe in the power of evil more than the power of good. The same principle applied to the Royal Commission report. When it came down to doing something, like opening betting shops, the Churches' Council resisted it. It was also part of human nature to seize on any argument, good or bad, to bolster a moral view, and the churchmen were no exception. Moody concluded early on that the Council was playing charades. What they were saying about gambling had got nothing to do with what people were doing when they were out gambling.

The first thing to do was to discover what gambling was all about. He did not pursue the ethical discussion of gambling – the high church view was that gambling was not wrong unless taken to excess, as opposed to the low church view that it was wrong in itself – which he had been drawn into many times. No one ever changed their minds in such discussions. (When he had worked in the City, and people had offered him sweepstake tickets in the office lottery for the Derby or the Oaks he had sometimes bought them, and sometimes refused, feeling bad either way for judging people he could see were doing no harm.) What was it which attracted people to gambling? Why did people bet? He began to look around for ways of finding out.

Moody got talking to the porter at the Churches' Council building, whom he thought might know a thing or two. The man tried to introduce him to a bookie but couldn't find one who would talk to him, but he did know a chap who would take him to the dogs. So off they went. In each race of the night, the bets that this fellow made went down. Mindful of his reputation as a good mixer, Moody suggested he pick a dog in the next race, number three. It was the only winner they had all night. It did not take long after he started going to the greyhounds on his own to realize that serious social consequences did stem from gambling. Gathered together in the cheap enclosure at the tracks, he saw people not adequately dressed or fed, who looked very pinched and hard pressed. They looked like the miners seen on a hunger march at Durham.

In 1959 the Betting and Gaming Bill was coming in and Moody led for the Churches' Council. He still hadn't got much real knowledge. The one advantage he had, so he felt, was his dog collar. At one of the hearings a man came up to him and asked if he took a special interest in the proposed legislation. He was a street bookie. Moody asked if he would take him down to his pitch, which was in Bermondsey in the East End. It was quite a revelation. The bookie had a man standing on his pitch, taking in betting slips and stakes, and a look-out man round the corner, while he himself kept right out of sight. If any client had a dispute, he was directed to the bookie to sort it out.

The visit confirmed for Moody the idea that betting shops should be opened. It wouldn't change the ethos of people having a bet every day, but it would be a far better way of doing it. The mistake in his view was to have the shops open throughout racing hours, which encouraged gambling by continuous betting. Gradually Moody became acquainted with a wider circle of people engaged in the business of gambling. A greyhound stadium manager spoke up to support the need for legal controls at the Council's annual meeting and press conference: 'If you don't prune the trees, you don't get the apples.' He went to gaming clubs. His experience of mixing with so many different people in the Royal Air Force was paying off. He saw that if the Council was going to have any value, he had to get close to gambling.

He went to the Derby and had a wonderful day. He did not watch the races, he watched the people. He ate sweetmeats he hadn't tasted since he was a child, went to the fair and saw the boxing, joined in the shouts of protest when the all-in wrestler kicked the amateur. The Derby was more than betting and racing, he realized, it was about life; people left their problems behind them. It was another stage in his enlightenment. It helped persuade him, in writing reports for the Council, to get the relevant facts checked out by people who knew gambling from the inside.

The darker side of gambling had impressed itself on him quite early on, during his visits to the dogs. One day he saw a cutting in the *Daily Express*, only a couple of inches long, about Gamblers' Anonymous being set up in the United States. Was this a bona fide organization? He wondered if something similar might be started in England. On May 27, 1964 (he remembers the date) Moody went to address a meeting about gambling in Croydon and was asked some questions about addiction. Afterwards a fellow came up to him and said he knew about GA because, as a compulsive gambler, he was a member of it. He was an American called Henry. 'Right, let's get cracking!' said Moody. He invited him to attend a meeting of the executive committee of the Churches' Council.

Henry had ruined himself through petty crookery to get money for gambling. The committee gave permission to hold a press conference to launch him. Moody gave out the Council's telephone number for anyone who might want help. They got enormous press coverage. No one had ever heard a story like Henry's before, and Moody's phone didn't stop ringing for three days. It was like taking the lid off a sewer. The stories came pouring out. A meeting was arranged one evening for these desperate people and about a dozen turned up. Henry told his story. Then he asked if anyone else would like to recount his own experience. Everyone did. The effect was sensational. The last person to speak was a taxi driver. He said how he couldn't go on any more, how he had gambled the money put by for his wife's birthday present, how he'd become sick and tired of gambling. 'Is there anything you can do to stop gambling?' the taxi driver demanded rhetorically. 'Yes! You've just got to stop.' On that ring of truth, the meeting closed itself.

A side-effect of being listed in the telephone book as

headquarters of GA was that any homeless person who came to Moody's office was fixed up in a hostel or helped to get back on his feet. The idea was to get them off the street. Thus occurred one of the finest experiences of his life. One morning a chap appeared outside his door looking terrible. It turned out he had been sleeping rough for three weeks. Without more ado, Moody took him to a barber's shop and had him cleaned up, then gave him a good breakfast in a café, whereupon the man fell asleep in his chair. He was a businessman from Liverpool. Moody rang his wife and told her he was all right. It so happened that this was the day of the Methodists' luncheon club. Moody didn't want to leave the man on his own, so he took him along. As there was no extra space, he squeezed him in at the top table. The President came over and said how honoured they were he could join them.

When lunch was over, but before the speaker was called, the extra guest felt sufficiently restored to tell his companions at the top table a funny story. 'The Bishop of Chester,' he said, 'looks like the pop singer Frankie Vaughan. One day the Bishop was returning to his hotel and was waylaid by a lady in the lobby. "Oh, Frankie!" she called. "I am the Bishop of Chester," he replied, "I have been to a conference, I am very tired and I am going straight to bed." At the foot of the stairs a second lady greeted him in the same way and was given the same response. As the Bishop proceeded to his room, a door was opened across the way, and yet another pretty young woman appeared, this time in a negligee. "Oh, Frankie!" she cried. The Bishop of Chester flung his arms wide. "Give me the mo-o-onlight!" he sang.'

Moody watched the expressionless faces of his Methodist brethren at the top table. He longed to tell them that according to the best Methodist doctrines, here was one newly raised from the spiritually dead.

Of course the failure level at GA was very high. People slipped back again in their own environment, because it was too long to wait a whole week until the next meeting of GA. Moody would have liked a special hostel for gamblers but there was never enough money.

Around this time Moody met a welfare officer at Pentonville prison named Michael Sorensen. He did not see gambling as a problem on its own; what puzzled him was that the same bunch of petty thieves kept turning up at Pentonville, time after time. Why? One day Sorensen discovered that they were all hooked on gambling. Gambling had made them broke, being broke had got them into debt, getting into debt had led to borrowing more, being unable to repay had led to thieving and petty crime. When at Sorensen's request Moody took a psychologist along to the prison, he learned that there was more to this than just a Rake's Progress.

Moody was struck by their spontaneous answer to the question: what is your experience nearest to gambling? 'Being on the job,' they cried; breaking and entering was just like gambling – the same excitement of getting away with it, the same nervous thrill – will you be caught or not? – as in winning or losing; a story of twin excitements, not just simple villainy.

Generally, probation officers or social workers were quite used to dealing with alcoholics and drug addicts, but few of them were aware of compulsive gambling or could recognize its symptoms. And no one knew its causes. Often it seemed to start from 'beginner's luck', which rapidly engendered a habit and liking for gambling, which accelerated, as the luck ran out, into more intensive gambling. It is certainly a common experience of Gamblers Anonymous that people are driven to stealing from their friends and families – even from their children, so desperate are they to get money – and are thus drawn on into all kinds of larceny. They are not really 'criminals'. Moody's aim was to get wider discussion and understanding of the problem in prisons, and help such men when they came out.

Many magistrates and probation officers had never heard of Gamblers Anonymous. At the ad hoc meetings Moody organized in those early days, questions were raised as to whether there was such a thing as expert treatment. Magistrates saw it as their duty to interpret and apply the law. In spite of being sympathetic 'nothing could be done', as a chilling phrase from one discussion put it, 'in an official capacity'. The fact which had to be faced, Moody continued to argue, was that many people spent years of their lives inside, contributing nothing to society. They needed help. GA groups were started in Pentonville, with some success.

The link between gambling and crime is not a simple one, obviously: it is hard to distinguish between criminals who gamble and gamblers who are led into crime. (The partial survey done at Pentonville showed an incidence of heavy or excessive gambling amongst at least ten per cent of the prison population; but no individual who was in prison solely as a consequence of excessive gambling.) One of the strangest things about gambling is how it is bracketed at either end of the social scale by the criminal element. At the lower end, gamblers in trouble slip into crime like fish into water. At the upper end, organized crime has its dirty hands on the operation. There are many honourable men in between (we are all, all honourable men) but there is no doubt that there is something inherent in gambling which attracts criminality, and that something is ready money. In reality, as Moody pointed out, gambling is expensive: people's debts always seem vast relative to their income.

When social workers and others telephoned GA for advice about clients who gambled, Moody used their experience to build up a backlog of case histories and information about gambling. This in turn encouraged him to arrange the first conference on compulsive gambling, held in London in 1967. The conference continued on an occasional basis in London, Manchester and Glasgow. Moody served as chairman, secretary and treasurer, but he saw that to be effective the group had to get away from the churches and be seen as independent.

Among the experts drawn into the GA circle was a psychiatrist, Dr Emanuel Moran. He had discovered a different link with gambling through his experience with attempted suicides. A quiet, dumpy, self-effacing man, swamped by the papers and letters brimming over his in-tray, Moran runs a busy department at a North London hospital. As a young doctor, he was puzzled when in the space of a fortnight two patients were admitted to hospital after taking an overdose, yet there seemed to be no obvious explanation of why they had done it. He went into their cases and found they were both gamblers. In his early training, experience with alcoholism had given him an insight into the problems of excess; gambling was something new. Yet there is always a 'gamble', a degree of uncertainty, as to whether a suicide attempt will result in death or not. Chance factors in the environment, such as the arrival of another person on the scene, may be all-important in determining the outcome.

He looked up the subject and found there was very little published on it back in 1964. Nosing about, he discovered the newly formed Gamblers' Anonymous, and that was how he made contact with Gordon Moody. Together they would sit in at meetings of GA, in a dingy hall in Victoria, and listen to the lurid stories recounted by the hapless victims of excessive gambling. Moran's role was not to participate but to listen and learn. Gradually he acquired a wider knowledge of gamblers' problems.

The tone was a bit emotional and evangelistic for Moran's taste – 'therapy' transferred from medicine to a personal 'confession' – but the help given was clearly worthwhile. At the time there were only two such meetings in the whole country. Sometimes when invited to make a comment his advice might be criticized; but there was always a halo around Gordon Moody's head, he recalls, as there has tended to be all his life.

So far as psychiatry in general was concerned, treatment of gamblers stemmed from the single case of Freud on Dostoyevsky. This famous essay, 'Dostoyevsky and Parricide' (completed around 1928), was more of an occasional piece stemming from Freud's admiration of the novelist than a deep psychoanalytic study. But like all Freud's work, it is a good read. It falls into two parts: first, a discussion of Dostoyevsky's character and second, his passion for gambling, with special reference to a short story by Stefan Zweig.

For those who may not be familiar with the piece, Freud focuses on the period when Dostoyevsky was in Germany, consumed by a mania for gambling. Although he had the pretext that he was trying to win at the tables so as to return to Russia and pay off his debts, Freud notes that he was acute enough to recognize that this was only a pretext, and honest enough to admit it. 'He knew that the chief thing was gambling for its own sake – *le jeu pour le jeu.*'

All the details of his impulsively irrational conduct show this,

Freud says, and something more besides. He never stopped until he had lost everything. For him gambling was a method of self-punishment as well. Time after time he gave his young wife his word of honour not to play any more or not to play any more on that particular day, and he almost invariably broke it.

What part of a gambler's long-buried childhood is it that forces its way to repetition in his obsession for play, Freud asks. He elicits the answer from a story by Stefan Zweig: *Twenty-four Hours in a Woman's Life.* On a visit to the gaming salons of Monte Carlo a lady, widowed young, has a strange experience: she finds herself fascinated by the sight of a pair of hands, hands which seem to betray all the feelings of the unlucky gambler with terrifying sincerity and intensity. The hands belong to a handsome young man, who after losing everything leaves the salon in despair, with the evident intention of ending his life in the casino gardens. The lady, inexplicably drawn to him – the difference in their ages makes him young enough to be her son – follows him outside, and manages to dissuade him, eventually accompanying him back to his apartment, and his bed. She exacts a solemn vow from the young man that he will never play again and provides him with money to return home.

Next day she decides to join him at the station, to go away with him, but misses the train. Revisiting, sadly, the gaming rooms she sees, to her horror, the same pair of hands which had first excited her sympathy. Obsessed by his passion to gamble, her protégé cruelly rejects all her entreaties. She hurries away, to learn, soon after, that she had failed to save him from suicide.

While paying high tribute to the story as art, Freud maintains that its invention is based on a wishful fantasy deriving from puberty. 'The fantasy embodies a boy's wish that his mother should herself initiate him into sexual life in order to save him from the dreaded injuries caused by masturbation . . . The "vice" of masturbation is replaced by the addiction to gambling; and the emphasis laid upon the passionate activity of the hands betrays this derivation.' Freud adds, in what has become a classic formulation: 'The irresistible nature of the temptation, the solemn resolutions, which are nevertheless invariably broken, never to do it again, the stupefying pleasure and the bad conscience which tells the subject he is ruining himself (committing suicide) – all these elements remain unaltered in the process of substitution.'

Powerful stuff: it seems to have come as quite a surprise to the author, Stefan Zweig, when Freud, who was a personal friend, put this interpretation to him! The essay has had a seminal influence – Freud concluded that this analysis in large measure explained Dostoyevsky's addiction to gambling. It is certainly very suggestive; but it can hardly be taken as the last word on the psychological motivation of gamblers – certainly not when it comes to dealing with gamblers in trouble in our own social milieu.

Moran set out to look at the field in a broader way. It was the heyday of casinos in Britain, following the new Gaming Act. He collected a lot of data. As his interest became known, numbers of gamblers in need of help were referred to him for treatment. A majority of them he sent on to GA which seemed to provide valuable support. And from study of these 50 or 60 cases he was able to propose a new classification of the problem.

(1) Subcultural gambling, arising from the individual's background, which is one of heavy gambling. (2) Impulsive gambling, associated with loss of control and ambivalence – while longed for, it is also dreaded. (3) Neurotic gambling, which is a response to a stressful situation or emotional problem. (4) Psychopathic gambling as part of the overall disturbance in a psychopathic condition. (5) Symptomatic gambling, in the context of mental illness, most usually due to depression. (Proceedings of the Royal Society of Medicine, December 1970.)

The real point of such a classification – its categories overlap and its precise validity is, of course, open to question – was that it got away from the idea of gambling as a mental illness. The popular term 'compulsive' as applied to gamblers in trouble was, in Moran's view, quite mistaken. In practice, gamblers turned out to be a homogeneous group of people whose common feature was that excessive gambling had resulted in economic, social or psychological disturbance. Since none of these conditions had the characteristics of a true compulsive disorder, he argued, the syndrome was more accurately referred to as 'pathological'. In popular usage, 'compulsive' and 'addictive' still tend to be used interchangeably.

He suggested that the syndrome of pathological gambling could be recognized by any of the following:

1. Concern on the part of the gambler and/or the family about the amount of gambling which is considered to be excessive.

2. The presence of an overwhelming urge to gamble so that the individual may be intermittently or continuously preoccupied with thoughts of gambling; this is usually associated with the subjective experience of tension which is found to be relieved only by further gambling.

3. The subjective experience of an inability to control the amount once gambling has started, in spite of the realization that damage is resulting from this.

4. Disturbances of economic, social and/or psychological functioning of the gambler and/or the family as a result of persistent gambling.

(a) Economic disturbances: debt, shortage.
(b) Social disturbances: loss of employment and friends, absconding from home, eviction, criminality, imprisonment, marital problems, divorce, problem family.
(c) Psychological disturbances: depression, attempted suicide, behaviour disorders in children.

Nowadays Moran would prefer the neutral term 'problem' gambling. He describes people's gambling behaviour as on a sliding scale, ranging from nil, to light gambling, to moderate, through to heavy, up to very heavy or problem gambling. In other words it is one of those forms of behaviour in which people are liable to go to excess: not, as GA likes to see it, an 'illness', over which the unfortunate sufferer has no more control than a man with pneumonia is in control of his cough. In the majority of problem gamblers, the disturbance was socially determined, as distinct from an illness arising from some individual abnormality. Accordingly (like crime) it admits a wide variety of explanations. Despite his own more analytical approach, Moran still felt that the fellowship GA offered to gamblers was very useful. Over the years, he has put patients with gambling problems in touch with GA as a matter of course.

There was also a public dimension to Gordon Moody's work, in press conferences and so on. *The Times*, in particular, was very supportive. Moran had written a letter to the paper protesting against a crude suggestion that compulsive gamblers should undergo lobotomy; when he was contradicted a few days later by an irate sociologist, Moody fired off a heated reply in Moran's defence. After that little exchange *The Times* took a continuing interest in Moody's views on gambling, regularly reviewing the Churches' Council's reports and statements in leading articles. Given the importance of the letters column in *The Times* – which serves as a kind of establishment notice-board – this was very valuable back-up, even when points of disagreement arose.

In effect Moody had emerged as spokesman for the one group of people none of the official authorities ever bothered to talk to – the gamblers themselves. Indeed, so great was his success in persuading MPs and others to take account of the gamblers' interests that he began to feel, light-headedly, that he was the world's greatest political lobbyist. When gambling was such a live issue, especially in that peak year of 1968 when the House of Commons was thrashing out the new Gaming Act, everything he said was heard and heeded: he certainly enjoyed special (and perhaps disproportionate) influence in the public debate on the kind of reforms needed to clear up the anomalies of the unworkable legislation of 1960. (In recognition of his contribution he got an MBE in the 1969 Birthday Honours list.)

Moody also set about organizing a series of conferences on gambling: his idea was to bring together academics and experts, including people in the casino industry itself. Their efforts were complementary: the churchman trying to knock some sense into people, the psychiatrists pursuing a scientific approach, the operators representing the business interest. The purpose of such meetings was, in a word, enlightenment. The people who attended accepted gambling as part of life; Moody himself was neither for it nor against it. His experience was that, whenever he met someone for the first time, he always had to fight to show he was not a stereotyped do-gooder. (One of the reasons gambling legislation goes wrong is that the people in favour of gaming have got the most money – look at New Jersey.)

The first meeting happened to be on the day of the Grand National. Moran's wife Jane, whom he fondly describes as an unpredictable person, put 25 pence on a 100 to one shot. It romped home an easy winner. A writer of children's books on social education, Jane Moran's particular speciality is to devise little playlets for children to perform, the themes of which can then be understood and discussed by the class in terms of the drama, rather than simply as abstract ideas. (Her cautionary tale on drugs attracted the enthusiastic notice of Mrs Reagan.) Moran suggested that it might be useful in schools if she wrote a playlet on gambling. The result was *A Mug's Game* (included in *Mind Out*, published by Edward Arnold, 1979).

The story opens with the children talking about buying birthday presents for their mother. But Tom is off to the dogs, where his friend has a hot tip:

Tom: I lost so much at the last meeting. I daren't lose tonight.

Sindy: You can't lose if you use Pat's tips!

Tom: So long as I leave enough to buy my Mum a birthday present, that's all.

Pat: Listen, Tom, you follow my advice and you'll double your money.

Meanwhile, back at home, his mother has come in from work:

Mrs Moore: Tom not in yet? . . . If he's gone down to the dog track again, I'll give him what for!

Jill: He'll only be watching, Mum. He's too young to bet.

Mrs Moore: Who are you kidding, Jill? Tom just watching, don't be daft!

Ben: He's hardly got any money to use, Mum. He's almost broke.

Mrs Moore: I'm not surprised! He lost enough the week before last. He must know he's playing a mug's game. I would have thought he'd have learnt enough from your Dad.

Jill: But Dad doesn't bet any more now, does he?

Mrs Moore: No, that's the whole point. At last he's managed to stop . . .

Ben: It was Gamblers Anonymous that helped him, wasn't it, Mum?

Mrs Moore: Helped him? They saved us all from the gutter if you ask me. I just hope Tom won't go and start everything up again!

Cut to the track where, as may be imagined, disaster has struck and Tom has lost everything. On the morning of their mother's birthday, the other children give her their presents. Then, enter, very quietly:

Tom: I'm sorry I haven't been able to . . .

Mrs Moore: To buy me a present! Tom, if you think I want presents, you're wrong. What I want is a happy family. And you're not happy.

Tom: You know what happened the other night?

Mrs Moore: I can guess. I've seen it all so many times before!

Tom: I've learnt my lesson this time, I promise . . .

Mrs Moore: . . . If that's true, Tom, then you've given me the best birthday present you could have done.

After the play comes follow-up work, e.g. What do you think of Mrs Moore's attitude towards Tom's gambling? Pat was a great believer in 'hot tips'. Why was this rather foolish? There is then a discussion of gambling, what it is and how it works and people's motivation. The section concludes with a list of the Don'ts of Gambling, which is a useful model for schoolchildren or grown-ups. The first one would certainly have saved all of us a lot of money if we had been taught it properly at school: Always decide upon a set limit to your total stakes. Then DON'T exceed this amount under any circumstances. Moran's view as a clinician is that if youngsters could be given a true idea of the ins and outs of gambling as part of their schooling, it might save a lot of blood, sweat and tears in later life.

As I mentioned in the foreword to this book, I have gambled from time to time, occasionally quite heavily, but without ever getting over my head: so I had only a very amateurish idea about what compulsive or problem gamblers were like, and how they felt, before it struck me that it might be a good idea to attend a meeting of Gamblers Anonymous. It was a shock. Or if not exactly a shock, because I was expecting to hear a fair catalogue of misery, a revelation into what had moved a man like Gordon Moody to devote his life's work to such people. Actually the atmosphere was cheerful – resolutely so, on a snowy night, with little self-help notices around the walls of the bare room declaring 'Keep It Simple', 'First Things First' and 'Easy Does It'.

About a dozen people turned up, aged between 20 and 50, all men on this occasion, and it was at once apparent that, though they sat apart and looked a bit forlorn, they knew each other and were all – in a slightly edgy way, as if not showing their feelings – backing each other up. One of the group, as chairman, then invited everyone to read a few lines from the GA leaflet, known as their 'Bible', which sets out the Recovery Program. GA is not a religious movement but it is based on spiritual values. Thus:

'What is the First Thing a Compulsive Gambler ought to do in Order to Stop Gambling?'

'He must accept the fact that he is in the grip of a progressive illness and have the desire to get well. Our experience has shown that the GA program will always work for anyone who wants to stop gambling. It will seldom work for the man who cannot, or will not, squarely face the facts about his illness.

'Only you can make that decision.'

The Recovery Program sets out 12 steps: 1. We admitted we were powerless over gambling – that our lives had become unmanageable. 2. Came to believe that a Power greater than ourselves could restore us to a normal way of thinking and living. 3. Made a decision to turn our will and our lives over to the care of this Power and of our own understanding. 4. Made a searching and fearless moral and financial inventory of ourselves. And so on. (It is notable that although GA portrays compulsive gambling as an illness – which in a sense absolves those who apply for help from blaming themselves for what they've done – the program itself implies that it is not an illness.)

The men then came out one by one, some eagerly, some reluctantly, to 'give a therapy' i.e. report on their symptoms and state of progress. 'My name is Jack and I am a compulsive gambler. I haven't had a bet for 42 days . . .' Or alternatively, 'My name is

Terry, I'm a compulsive gambler. I'm ashamed of myself, I got my wages and I thought I would have just one go on the fruit machine in the pub, and then I had another go, and then I had another go, and then I got into a card game, and then . . .'

These stories were sad and funny and moving and terrible, and could be duplicated, no doubt word for word, in any town anywhere in the world where gambling is rife. They combined at one and the same time a dread of going back to betting, of the endless suffering that came from uncontrolled gambling, and a vivid, barely suppressed sense of the awful elation such activity gives its devotees. GA is neither for nor against abolishing gambling as such – it simply concentrates on immediate help for those who want it. Another sign on the wall proclaimed: 'Live and Let Live.'

As an outsider one is bound to feel humbled – 'There but for the Grace of God go I' – and to ponder what pushes a man or a woman over the line, that fine line which everyone who has ever made a bet has walked along. Meeting over a drink after the GA session, members of the group looked and sounded as 'normal' as any other people in a neighbourhood pub. To gamble, after all, is human. I'm afraid the conclusion I drew wasn't very profound: Those who defy the laws of probability the gods of chance destroy.

Alongside the sessions of GA, but in another room, spouses or friends of the gamblers in the supporting group known as Gam-Anon, meet to compare notes. 'My name is Connie, and I am the wife of a compulsive gambler . . .' Their role is to provide the right kind of family back-up. As more than one woman told me, an addiction to gambling is quite different from an addiction to alcohol or drugs, because it doesn't show in the person concerned. He doesn't topple over like a drunk. Above all, gamblers can conceal their activities for a long time, quite easily, by lying and stealing and other deceptions. That is why it is so hard to live with.

So Gam-Anon offers helpful advice. e.g. 'To question or interrogate the gambler will serve no purpose. You are powerless over this situation. If he has something he wishes to hide, the truth cannot be forced from him. Why try?' It also advises against paying the gambler's debts for him. 'The gambler, not his wife, should be responsible for calling his creditors to make restitution. Don't take this responsibility from him.'

With the aim of fostering spiritual strength, Gam-Anon also recommends 12 steps, similar to the GA program. Self-help is the key. 'There are two days in every week about which we should not worry . . . One of these is yesterday with its mistakes and cares . . . All the money in the world cannot bring back yesterday . . . The other day we should not worry about is tomorrow with its possible adversities . . . This leaves only one day – TODAY . . . Let us, therefore, live one day at a time.' At the end of the session the women held hands and recited a prayer together: 'God grant me the Serenity to accept the things I cannot change . . . Courage to change the things I can . . . and Wisdom to know the difference.'

Moody's reports for the Churches' Council in the early years had a centrality and clarity which were impressive. Successive titles told the story: A Nation's Responsibility . . . Time to Think Again . . . A Bad Risk for Britain. Thus in 1965 he set out a particular problem. Parliament had legalized certain forms of gambling in 1960, hoping this would not lead to an increase or excess of gambling, but the results had been quite the opposite. Public opinion had become anaemic, he wrote, because many people who wished to resist the spread of gambling hesitated to take action, feeling they would be adopting a 'moral' position, and be thought 'puritan'. This was unfortunate, because it involved a misconception.

'It has come to be accepted that the moral question can be expressed in terms of one man and his money. This is a proper question for individuals to resolve, but the discussion is inadequate for the practical task of containing gambling as an element in society. The argument that gambling is all right in moderation leads to a laissez-faire attitude towards gambling and its results in society generally. The attitude that gambling is essentially wrong on every occasion leads to a rigorist approach which is equally ineffective.'

The 1960 Act, which legalized betting offices for horse racing, also had a section on casino games. To combat illegal back-street gaming, the Home Office experts who framed the Act had hit upon the theoretically ingenious but in practice hopeless idea that the odds in games of chance should be the same for the player as for the house – instead, a cover charge (as in restaurants) would be made on the players. This was all right for 'soft' gaming like bingo, the British equivalent of the American Keno, where players buy a card and try to match a series of numbers – 'Clickety-click, all the sixes!' – called at random, but hopeless for action games like roulette. Apart from customer resistance, the house wouldn't make any money, or even risk losing quite a lot – and that would never do, would it? So clubs got round the law by a variety of devices such as keeping the zero on the wheel but allowing players a turn to hold the bank. Far from equalizing the chances, that put the players (if they understood anything about probability in the short run) at considerably greater risk! Instead of casino gaming being brought under official control, over 1,000 casinos and dubious 'clubs' had opened up across the country, exploiting loopholes in the law, and the unwary public was being taken for a ride – wheels with three zeros for example, which one might describe as the casino operator's dream of Heaven.

Moody nailed parliamentary responsibility: 'No one knows how many gaming clubs there are, nor how many people are involved. The intention of the law is ignored. As gaming is conducted in some clubs, it is quite illegal even as the law now stands. Its legality in many others is doubtful.'

His point was that before the 1960 Act most people in Britain had never gone in for casino gaming. It was in the main an upper class foible, indulged on summer holidays in the French resorts of Nice, Cannes or, nearer to home, Deauville, plus a few private parties in Mayfair. At the other end of the social scale there had always been shady dice and card clubs in London's East End. Yet now, like a pincer movement from these opposite ends of the social scale, gaming was tightening its grip on the whole population, for the benefit of commercial interests. 'It is reasonable to argue that people should be free to take part in gaming if they wish to do so,' Moody concluded. 'It is unreasonable not to consider deeply the probable consequences of frankly encouraging people to gamble.'

Later, Moody hit upon an old-fashioned simile which he became rather fond of. It happened that his daughter was leaving for Spain on a package holiday, while he was due to preach at Windsor on the theme of the good shepherd. At the same time he noticed an advertisement in *The Times* offering guided tours for top people. The thought struck him that, just as his daughter needed to be shepherded on her trip and 'top people' on theirs, so everyone in daily life needed shepherding – the customers in the shops, as much as the manufacturers providing the goods. At different times we are all shepherds and we are all sheep.

It was corny, he knew, but he risked it in a valedictory comment to the Home Secretary on the Royal Commission Report on Gambling of 1978. The Commission wished to avoid paternalism which it thought of as 'protecting members of the public against their own gambling instincts or idiosyncrasies'. The Churches' Council approached the matter another way: that gambling facilities should be provided so as to enable those who use them to guard themselves against excess.

'That may be shepherding,' Moody wrote, '... but it is nevertheless a common feature of life ... there is always the need of the law, a kind of chief shepherd, to make sure that the sheep are not fleeced. The same considerations apply to gambling, to those who promote it and to the gambling law.' He added: 'Gambling promoters may smile, and perhaps be pleased, when a churchman compares them with shepherds and not with wolves.'

A true moral approach, Moody had argued back in his very first report, should take into account, among other things, that some people are prone to become addicted to gambling. Conditions which afford opportunities to gamble for some involved enormous temptations for others. 'It is morally indefensible to ignore either this fact or its consequences. At the present time both the law and public opinion incline to assume that everyone is equally able to look after himself. Because it is thoughtless, it is immoral to dismiss anyone who gambles to excess as necessarily either a fool or a knave, when he may be only more vulnerable than the rest.'

In this context, one may note a crucial difference between regulation of casino gambling in Britain and America. In the U.S. the characteristic motive has been production of revenue, suggests Jerome Skolnick in his comprehensive account of the Nevada casino industry *House of Cards* (1978), whereas in Britain gambling, especially casino gambling, is viewed as a social problem to be 'controlled'. It is therefore the responsibility of the Home Office – 'deploring gambling while at the same time accepting it' – rather than the Treasury.

'The attitudes of the British Government towards the gambler in general, but particularly the working-class "punter", are rather like those displayed in the past by benign colonial administrations: a combination of paternalism, benevolence and sharp autocracy,' Skolnick says. Probably he over-states the class divisions in British gaming (he believes that official policy is to 'suppress casino gambling, particularly for the working class', which is manifestly not the case); though as an outsider perhaps he sees these things more clearly than the British themselves. As he concedes, the trouble with taking economic success as the criterion for policy, as in Las Vegas and Atlantic City, is to foreclose social and philosophical discussion of the issue.

The Gaming Act of 1968, which Moody had followed so closely in its various stages through the Commons, established the format for casino gaming in Britain. It has been widely admired in other countries, but it is so idiosyncratically English – for example, the chairman of the Gaming Board need have no qualifications whatever in terms of gaming experience (the man appointed in 1985 told me that he had up to then never even visited a casino!) – that it could hardly be applied elsewhere.

It is a two-tier system: licensing of clubs is run locally, supervision nationally. This had interesting consequences when, in later years, several big clubs stepped out of line. Multi-million-dollar enterprises, like the Playboy Club in Mayfair (which at the time was bankrolling the Hefner empire virtually on its own) found themselves answerable to neighbourhood justices who might hardly know how to run a whelk stall.

The role of the Gaming Board is to examine would-be operators to ensure they have the right sort of management and funding. If so, they are granted a certificate of consent to apply for a licence in the area where they propose to operate. This procedure had the inestimable advantage of keeping out Mafia and kindred undesirables who were finagling to get into London. (A prominent casualty was movie star George Raft, noted for his gangster roles on the screen; engaged to 'host' a big Mayfair club, he was informed that his continued presence in the country was not welcome.) The test at the local level is what is termed 'unstimulated demand' – an estimate that sufficient numbers of people want to gamble to justify provision of gaming facilities. This is another very English concept: for the fact that facilities for gaming are known to exist will itself stimulate more gambling. The law as such is enforced by the police.

Moody felt gratified that, while they did not achieve everything they wanted in detail, the principal concerns of the Churches' Council had been met. First, the number of clubs had been restricted; and secondly, gaming was to be kept separate from entertainment. (Compare the scene in Las Vegas, where the only exit for the audience after the floor show is through the gaming tables.) Bingo, the housewives' little flutter, was also set apart. In sum, the Act set reasonable limitations on the promoters' opportunities to induce people to gamble. A typical instance (which many foreign visitors find a very annoying restriction) is that you cannot just walk off the street into a casino: a player has to become a club 'member', which means waiting a period of 48 hours after formally 'joining'. Likewise, the ban on entertainment – cabaret or otherwise – in casinos, means that there is no showbiz razzamatazz to 'induce' people to gamble. Moody's other main concern was that the new Act should be capable of being strictly enforced. This it was – as future events were to show (see chapter 9) with surprising results.

In the next year or two after the Act came into force in 1970 the number of casinos in Britain fell sharply, from over 1,000 to some 120, which is around the present total. In London, where 70 per cent of the action takes place, the total hovers around 19 to 21, according to who's been closed down or taken over. Moody was enthusiastic at the enlightened attitude shown by the new Gaming Board. It had, he wrote in 1974, 'made energetic and imaginative use of its powers' and was 'interpreting its social function effectively'. (He argued strongly for a similar Betting Board to cover horse racing, but in vain.)

A Royal Commission on Gambling was set up in 1976 under the chairmanship of Lord Rothschild. I can't resist quoting a few lines from the Royal Warrant to show how these things are done in Britain:

ELIZABETH THE SECOND, by the Grace of God of the United Kingdom of Great Britain and Northern Ireland and of Our other Realms and Territories QUEEN, Head of the Commonwealth, Defender of the Faith, to

Our Right Trusty and Well-Beloved Nathaniel Mayer Victor, Baron Rothschild, Knight Grand Cross of Our Most Excellent Order of the British Empire, upon whom has been conferred the George Medal . . .

WHEREAS we have deemed it expedient that a Commission should forthwith issue to inquire into the existing law, and practice there-under, relating to betting, gaming, lotteries and prize competitions . . .

. . . Our further will and pleasure is that . . . you do, with as little delay as possible, report to Us your opinion . . .

The resulting report, running to nearly 600 pages in two volumes, was both comprehensive and highly readable. The members of the Commission not only reviewed and analysed all aspects of gaming in Britain, and made numerous recommendations for future policy, they also set out some practical advice for would-be gamblers. Moody was one of many people who gave evidence to the Commission; he was listened to seriously, even if his advice, this time, was not followed.

It so happened that the report was published in July, 1978, just two weeks before the day came for Moody to retire. He was the only full-time employee in gambling who was not working either for the promoters or for the controllers of gambling.

He was, in a word, irreplaceable. There was also a problem of money which the Churches' Council had to face. For several years Moody had economized by using a room in his home as an office, and handling such matters as post and filing himself. His wife Jess dealt with the phone in his absence. This sort of thing could not really go on. Given the plain choice of finding the money to appoint a successor on his retirement in 1978 or closing down its office, the Council reluctantly opted for the latter. Its hope was that some kind of National Council on Gambling would emerge to take over its role as adviser, protector and spokesman of the public's interest.

For some time this looked to be only a pious hope – though the Royal Commission's very first recommendation was that the Government should establish a Gambling Research Unit 'to monitor and study the incidence, sociology and psychology of gambling'. This was, in effect, what Moody had tried to do, as a one-man band, by turning his occasional conferences into a Society for the Study of Gambling. Until its launch in 1977 no such group existed – which goes to show how study of the impact of gambling on society in Britain has been neglected. Even now there is no money behind it. Fortunately, colleagues who appreciated the value of the Council as a research and lobbying body, like Dr Moran, persisted in the attempt to set up a national council, which they succeeded in doing in 1980.

Moody's true memorial came in another form altogether. A hostel was set up in Beckenham, South London, for looking after single, homeless, compulsive gamblers. It was essential, if such people were to have a chance of pulling through, to get them off the streets; otherwise they went straight back into trouble. The hostel, which could take care of up to eight people, now receives an annual grant from the Home Office. It was named Gordon House.

Looking back, Moody believes that the record of the Churches' Council, its successes and failures, were due not so much to skill as to luck – a surprisingly 'gambling' view of life! He means that when they were successful they were ridiculously successful, because they were riding the wave of political opinion, like a winning streak. Where they failed, for instance on the Horse Totalisator and Betting Levy Board Act (when no one was thinking at all about the poor old punter at the bottom of the crock of gold) or on the legislation for lotteries (where the local authorities were siphoning off all the profits for their own ends) it was not through bad work, but bad luck. The political tide was running the other way.

Always active on behalf of gamblers, Moody's thoughts in retirement had been much troubled by a new social problem, or an old problem in new guise: teenage gambling: kids who became hooked on slot machines – whirring, flashing little slots which paid out a derisory maximum pot of £1.50 in cash, or tokens for free plays. Such kids, apart from being the despair of their mothers, were a category of compulsive gambler for whom there was no remedy to hand. They were not hard cases fleeing to GA; their parents could not relate to Gam-Anon – they would arrive at a meeting saying, 'How long before Johnnie is cured? Can we do it this afternoon or will it be next week?' Such parents couldn't believe it was a long-term addiction, that their kids did not want to give up. Yet such children displayed all the destructive traits of adult compulsive gamblers.

Youngsters who got addicted to these slot machines might have started at the age of 9 or 10. They ran through their pocket money, school dinner money, and loose change around the house. A year or two on and boys began stealing things. Everything would be sold from the child's own room, bats, books, even treasures like record players: other children would find their own toys gone too. Nothing in the house was safe. Moody heard of desperate mothers piling up their possessions in one room so as to sit guard over them, or having to hide their handbags under the bedclothes when they went to sleep. Frantic, such mothers could no more comprehend what was happening to their offspring than nesting birds robbed by a cuckoo. The kids still managed to steal from somewhere. By the age of 16, the police would be knocking on the door.

Moody, stuck down in Devon, couldn't see any way he could crack the issue. Then he got a letter from a young mother living not far away in Newton Abbot. What this mother had to say about her errant son was so clear and intelligent that Moody got in touch. They talked things over and decided to act. So, with the help of a charity in Taunton called Spectrum Children's Trust, they launched a telephone service for parents. Thus was started the Society for the Problems of Young Gamblers.

The missing ingredient was to do something directly for the children. Parents had to learn not to shout and lose control, but to reorganize their own reactions, so as to bring the situation under control. This, in turn, would have some beneficial effect on the children: but the problem itself remained. There is nothing that can be done for a juvenile gambler, Moody has to explain, unless the child positively wants to change his ways. In that sense it's exactly the opposite of GA, where all those who join do so because they have been driven to it, as a last resort.

One sunny day at the end of 1986 a newly decorated and expanded Gordon House – rooms for 15 residents – was opened in south-east London. Moody, spruce and pink and jolly as ever, held a pair of golden scissors for the tape across the front door to be ceremonially cut. A little crowd of well-wishers and residents gathered round him in the forecourt.

'We're going to open a door in a minute,' Moody began, 'and it reminded me (I don't often worry people when I'm not in the pulpit about what it says in the Bible) of Jesus telling Peter that he is giving him the keys of the Kingdom of Heaven: what he sets free will be free and what he binds will be bound. Tremendous responsibility!' When he was young and interested mainly in theology, Moody explained, there was a great argument over who held these keys, whether it was the Pope or the Archbishop of Canterbury or the President of the Methodist Church, or just the priesthood in general.

But since he had got mixed up with Gamblers Anonymous and Gordon House and its residents and staff, he had come down to earth and realized that what this was all about was that in life some people – either by their situation of birth or their circumstances or by their own actions – had got themselves outside the door, and wanted to get through the door, back into life.

'And I've realized, too, that all of us as members of the human race very often hold for others the keys of life, and if we open a door then those who wish to go through can go through. Now often when that's thought about by people I know in ordinary life they think it's a matter of the staff at Gordon House saying, "Oh yes, come in," and in comes an outcast, who is then put under instruction and very great discipline, and who may eventually become some kind of a human being, but will live for ever afterwards under a shadow, because of the past. But what goes on here, and has done from the beginning, I'd like you to know, is that when the door opens, it's opened as much by the residents as by the staff, and there is a welcoming hand to a fellow human being, coming back into life, with no reservation. And for that I'm jolly glad about Gordon House.'

4
THE GAMBLERS' HOSPITAL

> Getting married can cause trouble
> for a gambler.
> Henry Lesieur, *The Chase*

In 1972 the American Psychiatric Association formally classified compulsive gambling as a disease. This was an unusual step to take. We all know when we catch measles that it is a disease, or regard a common cold as an annoying minor illness. But compulsive gambling? This was something new.

The decision by the A P A was the result of pioneering work in the field by Dr Robert Custer, and his wife Lilian. Custer, a big, gentle man now in his sixties (no relation to the hero of Little Big Horn), has devoted a lifetime to treating gamblers; in particular, he was the moving spirit behind the so-called 'hospital for compulsive gamblers', set up in Brecksville, Ohio. This out-of-the-way unit is located within the big, clean-swept neuro-psychiatric hospital south of Cleveland, part of the Veterans' administration network of medical care for ex-servicemen; there are 30 million veterans in the United States and the V A, far the biggest medical institution in the country, disposes of an annual budget running into hundreds of millions.

When Custer went to Brecksville as consultant psychiatrist back in 1969 he found, as might be expected, that drinking problems were quite common among veterans. He set up a 50-bed unit for alcoholics. Then one morning he received a curious call: three men who were already members of Alcoholics Anonymous had come back to the hospital to tell him they couldn't stop gambling; they had been diagnosed as suicidal, and Custer decided they would benefit from a short stay in the hospital. He did not know anything about gambling, so he started going to Gamblers Anonymous meetings, and his wife Lilian to Gam-Anon, the family members group which supports G A. His growing interest in the subject led him to get eight beds set aside for treating gambling cases. The old guard at the hospital was mistrustful, but the staff recruited from the alcoholics program was enthusiastic, and from its inception in April, 1972 the unit took off. About a third of the patients were active GA members, the others had been admitted for various psychological disorders.

It was the only such program in the world and Custer got calls from far and wide about it. What really put Brecksville on the map was the media, which latched on to what looked like a hot news story. After all, everyone has gambled at some time in their life, but to go to hospital for it! Half the referrals to the unit came via press reports.

Perhaps the media imagined hardened gamblers, trying to kick the habit, lying back on fresh laundered sheets being fed sweet California grapes by soft-eyed nurses. The reality was somewhat harsher. 'We insisted on total abstinence, as we do with alcoholics,' Custer recalls. Patients were allowed to play competitive games – checkers, pool and cards – but without betting; they were discouraged from watching sports on television, and told to take exercise themselves. This did little to relieve the agitation and tension they felt, in their desperate urge to gamble – but there they were. 'The hospital,' as one report by the medical team frankly conceded, 'is not a pleasant place to be.'

The first weeks were pure trial and error, Custer recalled in his book *When Luck Runs Out* (written with Harry Milt, 1985). 'We just worked and waited to see what would happen. We only had a vague idea about what we were dealing with and how it ought to be handled.' The program was designed by Custer and his associate Dr Alida Glen on the pattern of their treatment of alcoholics. 'But when we got together in our staff conferences – the counsellors, psychologists, psychiatrists, social workers and nurses – we found ourselves zeroing in on something. As these patients began to tell us in detail about what they had done in the course of their compulsive gambling, we realized that they all had in common several negative traits of personality and behaviour.'

To appreciate what Custer and his team meant by 'negative

traits' and what they were up against – the abysmal depth of the human problem – you need to have some idea of the degradation and despair which many of the men had sunk to. Some of the gamblers' case histories recounted in *When Luck Runs Out* could provide material for *cinema-verité* almost too painful to contemplate – though such experiences in this milieu of habitual losers are quite common. I quote a couple of brief scenes to convey the awfulness of it all.

First, black comedy. Here's Rachel, a serviceman's loyal wife, who for many months had been unable to grasp the extent of her husband's secret gambling, facing the final moment of disillusion:

It was our wedding anniversary and he said he would take me to some elegant place for the weekend . . . When we got there, and I saw the hotel, I was thrilled. It was just as beautiful as the pictures in the brochure . . . It was one of those heavenly southern nights, with a soft, warm breeze coming off the ocean, the scent of night-blooming flowers floating to us from below . . . In the magic of the night and the wine all my concerns about his gambling melted away, all my anger was gone . . . We sat on the balcony for a while, and then, with the unspoken understanding of lovers, I got undressed and changed into my flimsiest negligee. While I was still in the bathroom, he shouted to me that he had just remembered and had to go down to the desk and straighten out something about our reservations. He suggested I get into bed and wait for him . . .

The next thing I knew I was being awakened out of a deep sleep by the loud barking of some dogs . . . The lights in the room were still on . . .

By seven o'clock I had my bags packed and called a taxi to take me to the airport. He walked in just as the bellhop was coming to get my bag . . . dishevelled, grimy, unshaven . . . I didn't even bother to listen to the rest of it.

This might be taken as black comedy but for the fact that Rachel later miscarried. Here's another story which is simply black tragedy:

Ralph had cashed a lot of little cheques around town and got away with it, but one night the police came out and took him off to jail; with no funds in the house, he told his wife to get some money from his mother to bail him out, which she did.

We were out there standing in front of the police station, and I asked her where the rest of the money was. She asked me, 'What rest of the money?' 'The money to bet with . . .' I screamed at her . . . I figured I could still make the late afternoon races . . .

As his wife had only got him bail money, with nothing over, the infuriated Ralph left her standing there and drove over to his mother's.

My mother was 80 years old. She was all bent over from having worked at a sewing machine in the factory most of her life. I had already gotten $35,000 from her. That was what she had left from her savings and what she got out of my father's insurance when he died. I had cleaned out all that . . . She started to cry and pleaded with me, 'Ralphie, what do you want from me? I gave you everything. Now you want to take the food out of my mouth . . .'
I didn't even hear what she was saying. I had to have the money. So I got on my knees and began to cry and I promised her by all the saints that this was the last time, that I would just pay off that check and my gambling would be finished. I would go straight and my wife and kids would get all my salary. And she believed me. She went down to the bank with me and cashed her Social Security check and gave me $200. An hour later I was at the track.

But just to emphasize that the problem is not confined to small-time gamblers, here's Louis, a big player, who had run through his multi-million-dollar clothing business in less than a year, on his return home one night after dropping another $150,000 in Las Vegas:

When I came upstairs, there was Lisa on the bedroom floor, half-conscious, the kids were in there crying. The housekeeper had gone home, and the kids didn't know what to do. Do you know what I was thinking? I was wishing Lisa would die so I could collect the $500,000 insurance.

You get the picture? As Custer recalled, these people were not just gamblers, they were dishonest. They had lied, cheated and deceived in order to get money to gamble. 'They were abysmally insensitive to other people's needs and feelings, borrowing without any intention to repay, stripping their nearest and dearest of their money and possessions. We did not know, at that point, whether these traits were there before the gambling problem began or whether they developed as a result of the addiction. We subsequently learned that it was the latter, that these had been honest, responsible, considerate people before they had become addicted.'

The immediate challenge was to the tolerance and stamina of doctors and nurses. For the patients, inevitably, turned their talents for manipulation on the staff – not to get money, but to ease the strictness of their regime in hospital. They were, by turns, evasive, abusive, obstinate in having their own way, refusing to see themselves as sick, yet insisting on a quick cure, intolerant of anyone not like themselves, negative to all advice. 'At this stage, the compulsive gambler is very hard to take, to like or even to sympathize with.'

The staff met in one strategy session after another, trying to identify the basic mode of treatment. Out of this came a clear decision: to deal with the behavioural problems which underlay the gambling. 'We decided that the most effective way to take on this rather formidable task . . . would be to concentrate on group therapy. Group therapy permitted open confrontation . . . by the patients themselves.' (A technique which had the further advantage, presumably, of placing the long-suffering analyst or doctor at one remove from the somewhat hard-to-take personalities of the patients.) In group therapy, people relate to each other the way they have been relating to other people in real life, but in real life people can run away and evade the consequences of their behaviour; in group therapy, they cannot. It's all up-front. The others, the victims, will hit right back, even though they themselves may be guilty of the same offence.

'Each person is compelled to sit there and face the group's reaction, which may be a very tough one, the kind he never had to contend with before. This forces the individual to see himself the way others see him, to come face to face with his faults and maladaptive behaviour, and to correct them. Why correct them? Because few people – least of all compulsive gamblers – can stand disapproval and rejection by the group.'

Thus Custer – but can one suppose that people who had acted out the kind of monstrous experiences described above, in one variation or another, could be 'cured' by a few sessions of group therapy? Well ... Custer believes so. Changes can take place very quickly in group therapy, he says. 'Lifelong ways of feeling, thinking and behaving can be changed in just a few sessions, and this is what we counted on in our daily group-therapy encounters.'

In support of this view one may say that everyone who chose to go to Brecksville wanted to be cured. These were people who had hit rock bottom. They had been driven to the hospital in desperation, there was no other escape route (bar suicide) out of it. That motivation was the pre-condition for any change. But it only works, of course, while the gambler sticks at it. In other words, the four brief weeks of group therapy and individual counselling had to be seen as a prelude to a whole lifetime of self-enforced abstinence through attending Gamblers Anonymous.

Custer devised an acrostic on the word GAMBLING: G – Gambling; A – Alienation; M – marital problems; B – behaviour problems; L – legal problems; I – indebtedness; N – needs, mainly money with which to support the family; G – goallessness, so as to break down the problems for each patient as an individual. Restitution was one of the most important elements. The process of repaying debts, monetary and moral, was seen as binding the gambler to a realistic and tough programme of action that would instil in him new self-respect. Such restitution, which might not be more than $25 or $50 a week and take years to complete, was regarded as a fundamental part of a man's rehabilitation. All this stemmed directly from GA's 12 steps to recovery (e.g. make a list of all persons who have been harmed and make direct amends wherever possible) which the Brecksville programme took as its model. The practical arrangements indeed were turned over to GA.

Next, Custer tried to bring the wives in. Long-suffering women, they had had it up to here. So when he arranged for the spouse of each gambler to attend a therapy session with her husband, it turned out to be a complete disaster. 'The wives were so full of rage and hostility, they could not do anything but vent their violent emotions on the gambler husband. This was something they had been aching to do, and here was their chance. This was the last thing Custer wanted, so another approach was tried, assigning a therapist to talk to the wife on her own, during her husband's four weeks of treatment. These sessions went on weekly for three months, enabling the wife to work out her hostility and to view the husband, so Custer hoped, as a sick person who had taken a positive step to get rid of his addiction.

The men also continued with individual therapy after their discharge from the hospital. Only when the staff felt a husband and wife were sufficiently on the way to recovery to meet together without an explosion would they attend a joint session. One problem that always came up was who was going to handle the family's money. Generally it was agreed that the husband would relinquish control, at least for a period. After some months of this joint therapy, the sessions would be spaced out to fortnightly or monthly intervals, gradually tailing off as the couple made it back to 'normal' life. Such was the Brecksville program, which has served as the model for treatment of gamblers in other veterans' hospitals as well as programs outside the V A.

Almost all of the veterans treated at Brecksville were men. Very few women who served Uncle Sam came forward as patients. This is not to say that female compulsive gamblers do not have their own problems. Custer believes that society applies a double standard: a man who gambles may be disapproved of but he's still tolerated. Not so a woman gambler: 'There is a quality of dissoluteness, immorality and indecency that people read into it, exceeding even that attributed to women alcoholics.'

Sensing this, women compulsive gamblers do everything they can to hide their problem, from their husbands and everybody else. According to Custer they see themselves the way they think other people regard them – with loathing and contempt; they are ashamed even to come in for treatment (which may explain why there are so few women in GA). This sort of attitude prevailed despite the advances in women's status and self-confidence brought about by the women's movement.

The difference in male and female attitudes was evident 'in a second', in Custer's experience. 'No matter how badly depressed the male compulsive gambler may be, no matter how much havoc he has wrought on himself and his family and with creditors and the law, he still, somehow, manages to retain a "hang-tough", combative, challenging attitude, almost a cockiness, as if he feels he is justified in what he has done, that there really is nothing wrong with him, that the problem is everybody else's fault.' By contrast, the woman who comes in for treatment is 'subdued, withdrawn, frightened, abject and almost cringing in her demeanour'. She finds it difficult to admit she's got an illness because she's ashamed, whereas the male compulsive gambler refuses to admit it because he's egotistic and 'proud'.

Women's feelings of self-contempt are often induced by the punishing attitude of the husbands: 'They would almost rather the wife be an alcoholic or even a prostitute. They see the wife ... as dissolute and immoral ... of betraying the trust that he and the children have put in her as wife and mother.' Wives of male compulsive gamblers may hate their husbands for the harm they have done, but they do not reject them as sinners; they still find it possible, ultimately, to forgive them, and build a new life. Husbands of gambling wives seem unable to do this, Custer says; they are likely to head straight for divorce. Only a few are prepared to go to Gam-Anon, or do anything to help their wives recover.

Custer takes a basic psychoanalytical approach in explaining compulsive gambling, but draws a sharp distinction between the sexes in the causes and development of addiction. For males:

In childhood, this person is subjected to indifference, rejection, or outright abuse, as a result of which he grows up feeling inadequate, insecure, unliked, worthless and helpless. In order to compensate for these unbearable feelings, he does things through which he tries to prove to others that he is superior and for which he should be liked and admired.

For women, he believes the causes go deeper:

In every instance that has come to our attention, the woman's childhood was marked not only by rejection or indifference, but by trauma. Several were illegitimate and grew up without a father. Others were abandoned by fathers when they were still children. Others were humiliated, punished and abused by a mother, father or stepfather. In a few cases, there was sexual abuse.

Feeling unloved, unwanted, disliked and worthless is equally painful to boys or girls, Custer goes on, but whereas boys are conditioned by their upbringing to masculine solutions – to overcome, 'be a man', 'fight back', 'show them', to win acceptance and approval from the crowd – girls are given a different role to model – to be liked, accepted, wanted, loved, protected. 'That is what these mistreated, rejected girls most desperately want, and they try, but their self-esteem has been so badly battered that they find it difficult.' When in adult life they are unable to achieve this state – when in consequence they land up with unsuitable men, reliving the drama of their childhood, or fail to achieve love and acceptance as women – they turn to a life of illusion, in drinking, drugs or gambling.

In short, the classic Freudian explanation of neurosis. Though neither for men nor for women, one must say, does this explain the attraction of gambling itself, over other forms of 'illusion'.

It is generally those who win early and consistently in their gambling career who become compulsive gamblers. 'Having caught the "fever" and experienced the excitement and magic of money, they come back to gamble some more,' Custer says, describing the onset of the urge in vulnerable teenage boys who have suffered rejection at home. 'The longer the winning edge is sustained, the more confident he becomes and the larger are his bets . . . Then, somewhere along the line – earlier for some, later for others – something happens that changes the course of the gambling career and of the gambler's entire life. He makes his first big win.' This emphasis on 'beginner's luck' accords well with Moran's findings, in his prior classification of gambling types in England (see pages 91–2).

There were, so it appears, contradictions in Custer's position. Were the negative traits in the men who went to Brecksville a result of gambling, or did they precede it? Were these men, as Custer says, honest, responsible, considerate people before they became addicted, or were they, as his theoretical approach would imply, reacting against unhappy experiences in childhood? Gordon Moody never heard anything about his psychoanalytic theories when he talked to Custer: they discussed gamblers like any other people they knew, as people with good points and bad points. Gordon and his wife Jess became lifelong friends of Bob and Lilian. Sometimes they went to the races together; but there was one slightly secretive thing about Bob; he would never let anyone else see him placing his bets or reveal afterwards how much he had won or lost.

In April, 1974, Custer was sent by the VA to Washington as director of treatment services and his role changed, so far as the gambler's unit was concerned, to one of well-wisher at a distance. His successor, Dr Glen, had a hard time keeping the program going; a new hospital director turned out to be less than sympathetic to the project; but she weathered the storm. Meanwhile people back at headquarters had begun to question whether veterans who gambled really needed in-patient treatment.

Red tape finally snarled Brecksville up. Soon after Dr Julian Taber took over in 1978, he found himself in the unfortunate position of being deprived of his patients altogether. The gamblers' beds were abruptly closed down pending 'clarification' of the program being funded out of the alcoholism budget. There was an immediate public outcry, encouraging recognition, as Taber saw it, of the unit's standing, and after ten weeks it re-opened with the VA's formal seal of approval. No one could now accuse the gambling unit, Taber quipped, of being a 'bootlegged' program.

In any case it was clear that the problems of compulsive gambling went far beyond the VA. It was on the basis of research by Custer and his wife Lilian that the American Psychiatric Association recognized pathological gambling in its *Diagnostic and Statistical Manual* as a 'Disorder of Impulse Control' (see following page).

AMERICAN PSYCHIATRIC ASSOCIATION DIAGNOSTIC CRITERIA FOR PATHOLOGICAL GAMBLING

A. The individual is chronically and progressively unable to resist impulses to gamble.

B. Gambling compromises, disrupts, or damages family, personal and vocational pursuits, as indicated by at least three of the following:

   (1) arrest for forgery, fraud, embezzlement, or income tax evasion due to attempts to obtain money for gambling

   (2) default on debts or other financial responsibilities

   (3) disrupted family or spouse relationship due to gambling

   (4) borrowing of money from illegal sources (loan sharks)

   (5) inability to account for loss of money or to produce evidence of winning money, if this is claimed

   (6) loss of work due to absenteeism in order to pursue gambling activity

   (7) necessity for another person to provide money to relieve a desperate financial situation

C. The gambling is not due to Antisocial Personality Disorder.

One consequence of classifying compulsive gambling as an illness, instead of wilful misconduct, was that it enabled evidence on behalf of gamblers to be given to the courts. In some cases, for instance where mental health workers could support gambler's plea of diminished responsibility, judges were prepared to allow offenders the benefit of treatment, rather than send them to prison, which would be worse than useless in terms of curing them of their addiction. Gamblers, too, were quick to take advantage of the new ruling, in counter-suing casinos for enticement (see Chapter 10).

The question whether disorders of impulse control like compulsive gambling may have a physical basis – though there are no visible signs of illness – is well worth pursuing, Custer believes. How is it that gamblers get the physical sensations they do from gambling? – the stimulus and excitement that enables them to keep going for five days without sleep; the depression when they can't gamble, manifested in chills, headaches, aches and pains, which vanish when the gambling starts again. The chemistry of the brain may provide an answer. Recent research on the chemicals (known as monoamines) found in the cerebrospinal fluid of neurologically and psychiatrically ill patients suggests that some of these chemicals play an important role in the control of impulsive behaviour. New studies are now going on to compare the brain chemistry of compulsive gamblers with other groups of people. If an abnormal concentration of monoamines and other chemicals were to be found among compulsive gamblers, it might imply an underlying biological malfunction.

The APA set of criteria has been criticized, notably for having 'a middle class bias' in emphasizing white collar offences like income tax evasion. Henry Lesieur, in his entertaining study of the career of the compulsive gambler, *The Chase* (1984), notes that the arrest criterion overlooks bookmaking, fencing stolen goods, burglary, robbery and other crimes. Moreover, not everyone who commits a crime will be arrested. He suggests that a better definition would be 'committed a crime to support the gambling habit'. He also notes that the last criterion 'C' – that gambling is not due to Antisocial Personality Disorder – was added to the list partly to make it easier for psychiatrists to go on the stand in the courtroom. The idea was to persuade public opinion, in particular a jury, that pathological gambling was really a disease, not a criminal act: i.e. when such gamblers are in the money, they don't go in for crime.

It has also been pointed out that many 'compulsive' gamblers, in the course of treatment, promise themselves 'slips' or 'falls' from abstinence, such relapses often being planned long in advance and then carried out very precisely. A rather strange manifestation, surely, of what is supposed to be a disorder of impulse control?

Custer did a lot of lobbying on the National Council on Compulsive Gambling, set up in 1972 with the express purpose of convincing public opinion that compulsive gambling was a treatable illness. This, in turn, helped in persuading several states with lottery or other gambling interests to allocate funds for treating gamblers who had fallen victim, as it were, of the state's exploitation of their weakness – half of one per cent of the profits was the target figure, a not inconsiderable sum. Even in a small state like Iowa, for instance, it yielded between $500,000 and $700,000 a year. The campaign had its slip-ups, too. In Washington a national Bill to establish a Commission to study problems of gambling fell through when, as luck would have it, the Senator who was sponsoring it was convicted of bribery and sent to gaol.

Maryland was the first state to legislate for treatment of compulsive gamblers, in May, 1978. The Bill was quite concise, declaring simply that Maryland with its extensive legalized gambling had an obligation to provide a program of treatment for people who became addicted to gambling. A centre was set up as a pilot project in Johns Hopkins University, which continued until 1983; now replaced by a program at Taylor Manor Hospital in Endicott, Maryland.

When Julian Taber took over at Brecksville, he formed a quite different view from the psychoanalytic diagnosis proselytized by Custer: compulsive gambling, so he came to believe, wasn't deeply psychological – it was a character defect. A roly-poly, genial man with round spectacles, Taber has a down-to-earth, slightly mocking air about him – not at all an evangelist. He ran the program for eight years. By the time he left Brecksville in 1985, he had become thoroughly disillusioned. 'I don't want to have anything to do with gamblers ever again,' he told me.

His work with alcoholics, gamblers, overeaters and sexual deviates led him to formulate for his own use a notion of limited character disorder. 'The impulsive disorders or, as I like to call them, the "Disorders of Desire", seem to represent severe but limited developmental or character flaws,' as he told the American Psychiatric Association (1979). 'The afflicted individuals demonstrate mature and sophisticated self-discipline in most critical life areas such as work, family obligations, schooling and community.' For example, gamblers when they are using money in everyday life, as a medium of exchange, often display prudence and frugality to high degree, in order to gamble. 'Similarly those who impulsively eat, drink, smoke, steal and so forth are usually well able to run their lives in other areas, although the quality of life in all areas is eventually eroded by their specific out of control behaviour.'

Hamlet's comment on the King's ostentatious relish for drinking, one might say, hit the mark exactly:

> So, oft it chances in particular men,
> That for some vicious mole of nature in them,
> As, in their birth – wherein they are not guilty . . .
> Or by some habit that too much o'er-leavens
> The form of plausive manners; that these men . . .
> Shall in the general censure take corruption
> From that particular fault   (1.iv. 23)

Anyway, Taber formed the view that total or general loss of impulse control was much rarer than a severe but specific loss. Reviewing the life histories of alcoholics, gamblers and over-eaters, he concluded that the root of the trouble lay in 'parental failure to impose conditioning discipline in selected areas of gratification'. And if this was so, therapy must provide op-portunities to practise and to learn the rewards of responsibility: acceptance, patience, self-discipline and sensitivity. These are the qualities which the process of group therapy is designed to bring out and foster – as it were, a training ground for tolerance.

Gamblers are easy to work with (less passive than alcoholics), being direct, talkative and challenging. Each new group member would prepare an account of his own experience to present to the others. In daily sessions discussion focused on the feelings and problems which result from individuals' behaviour as compulsive gamblers: social stigma, personal failure, alienation and distrust, inability to express love, 'magic' thinking, and so on. The therapist must try to avoid being assertive. 'The worst an inexperienced therapist can do, in my opinion,' Taber added, 'is to treat the addicted person as some kind of neurotic and set out to probe the past for psychic distortions.'

'No one knows,' he declared, 'which features of our program contribute materially to long-term abstinence . . . One suspects that the drastic step of surrender to hospitalization is itself the first major curative step in the required life-style change and that it really may not make too much difference exactly what we do by way of a program so long as we encourage the practice of a mature and controlled existence.'

In the absence of factual data, it was likely that treatment would continue to be based on 'theory', so it was important, Taber suggested, to look carefully at the credentials of the theorists themselves. Thus he is somewhat sceptical of claims by Custer and others that about 50 per cent of gamblers going through a treatment program achieved an appreciable period of abstinence. 'I can accept political and economic needs (he meant the need to convince the people back at HQ) for simple outcome statistics such as recovery rate, but I see neither a professional nor scientific purpose for this information. Slips occur and may serve a therapeutic role in the long-term turn-around of a life style.'

After patients left Brecksville things like length of abstinence, dollar value of gambling losses and the duration and frequency of slips could be measured, but only imperfectly. As a behaviourist, following Skinner rather than Freud, Taber dislikes such statistical analysis in making what are essentially value judgements. 'We must measure something, but how do we measure the quality of life? . . . Gamblers, their habits, and their personalities,' he concluded in this report, 'display a variance that will confound every effort at normative analysis . . . I feel we must learn to listen to recovering gamblers when they tell us what they think helped them the most . . . What successful abstainers tell us probably deserves greater credence than our theories, personality tests, and professional opinions . . . There is so much to ask him other than, "Have you gambled lately?" If this is all we can ask we shall deserve the answers we get.'

This scepticism about the value of the professionals' contribution seems to have deepened in Taber. By the time he left Brecksville he had become disenchanted, to put it mildly, with gamblers. 'They're awful, they're fakers, they went there, to Brecksville, to get out of their legal obligations and their debts, to gain a breathing space.' What, all of them? 'Well . . . yeah . . . that was the obvious temptation, to escape. I don't want to have anything to do with gamblers ever again.' In response, I suggested that he was like one of Graham Greene's lapsed believers, a burnt-out case: he still believed in the program, but he had been too closely involved with compulsive gamblers for too long.

Certainly he remains committed to treating patients suffering from 'disorders of desire', gambling excepted, as can be seen from his new job, which is even more demanding: running a special clinic for drug addicts, this time in Reno (where many of the cases are inevitably gambling-related). But Taber has pushed his theory still further, that the patients as a group know better than the professionals how to deal with their problems.

'I let the group decide what to do, how to handle each case.' What if the patient doesn't accept, doesn't agree? 'He can leave. I ask each man who comes in, "Do you want to be cured?" If he wants to be cured, he joins the group. He accepts what the group says. Most of these guys, what they need is to find some simple job, like working at a filling station. Then they can start to learn how to become a decent human being again.' Yes indeed, but what happens if a patient who is told by the group to get a new job and start a new life has other commitments, has been living far away from Reno, say in Oklahoma, leaving a family behind? Taber gives a shrug. 'Does the man want to be cured or not? If he does, he stays. If not he can quit.'

Taber's model, one might sum up, is valid for him; Custer's approach for others. In gambling, as in treatment of other addictive disorders, no single approach has the imprimatur of a proven 'cure'. Theories have their uses, certainly, but they also have their limitations. And just as there are different models of alcoholism, so there is a variety of medical as well as social models to explain compulsive gambling.

Reviewing the field, Iain Brown (whose experiment to test gambler's heartbeats is reported at the end of Chapter 5) notes that if a social learning theory of gambling was patterned on theories of drinking and drug abuse, it would probably suggest that gambling begins with imitation learning, perhaps copying a hero figure in adolescence, but more commonly that gamblers pick up the habit from their social group. Once it takes hold, major losses occur, 'chasing' begins; the gambler then devises new ways of raising money, leading in turn to a life crisis.

The disease and social learning models each have their drawbacks, Brown adds. One danger of the medical model is its concentration on extreme cases, leading to treatment suitable only for the seriously sick. A weakness of the social learning model is that it underestimates the importance of internal responses (such as arousal). On the other hand the disease analogy is easily understandable, whereas behaviourist explanations offer no familiar analogy in everyday life, which makes it harder for the gambler and his family to adapt to change.

The conclusion offered is that exclusive reliance on any one model leads to impoverishment of both research and methods of help. Even if a social learning theory of gambling were to become dominant, 'the medical, moral and other perspectives on gambling and problem gambling will always remain ... important ... and sometimes useful.' (Paper on Gambling and Gambling Addictions).

So far as Brecksville is concerned, a key point is to keep in touch with people who have been through treatment. Custer encouraged 'graduates' of the hospital to maintain contact by phone; some return on a monthly basis; nearly all keep going to GA. Experience has shown that the further away a man lived, the more likely he was to slip back into gambling. If a man did not make contact the case was assumed to have been a failure. Holding down a job – vocational training was included at Brecksville – offered the best chance of a return to normal life. Custer believes they were 50 per cent successful in the Cleveland area; the GA rate of success across the country is usually put at around 5 to 20 per cent.

Given the variety of 'substance abuse' as the problem is known, it would be gratifying to have a general theory of addictions, comparing similarities and differences between alcoholics, heavy smokers, drug takers, over-eaters and pathological gamblers (who are not involved with a 'substance' as such). Fortunately, such a theory is to hand, conceived by one of the founding psychologists at Brecksville, Durand Jacobs, now chief of the Psychology Service at a veterans' hospital in Loma

Linda, California. Whereas the usual practice is to study each type of addiction as a separate entity, Jacobs and his colleagues set about cross-checking the behaviour and background of different types of addicts. What they found is that all addicts share the same objective – a common aim – what Jacobs and his colleagues term 'a dissociated state', meaning a state of altered identity.

From the very start, they say, the addict's pattern of use provides relief from distressingly high or subnormal levels of physiological tension. 'In addition the manner and circumstances under which the chosen substance is used, or how the chosen activity is pursued, concurrently serves to release the would-be addict from longstanding psychological maladjustments and permits fantasies of being wanted, successful, recognized and admired.' This doubly gratifying physiological and psychological end-state powerfully reinforces the behaviour that produced it.

Of course many casual users experience the same sort of physiological release or high. Only the addict, according to this theory, finds the additional psychological reward of entering a dissociative end-state, where it is possible to live out his fantasies. 'It is this double-barrelled end-state that constitutes the common denominator which binds different kinds of addicts into a community of fellow travellers.'

The addictive pattern of behaviour is maintained by a series of positive (i.e. reward) and negative (i.e. escape from pain) reinforcements:

> What is the nature of this end point gratifying experience? Does the drug addict experience it all that differently than the alcoholic, or the compulsive gambler, or the overeater, or the addicted runner or sky-diver, or the addicted commodity trader, or the helplessly infatuated lover? We believe that, while there may be wide differences in the means (i.e. the substances or activities chosen for pursuing an addictive form of behaviour), certain aspects of the end state may be much the same for all addicts. That is: the attainment of a dissociated state. (Jacobs, Marston, Singer, 1984)

As Jacobs explained his theory to me, an element of chance – in the form of the first opportunity to indulge – has also to be present, for a user to turn into an abuser and thence into an addict. Adolescents, naturally, are particularly vulnerable to such chance encounters.

'It's like fire. You need a substance, which is the physical arousal level. You need kindling, which is the psychological flashpoint. And for a fire to burn you must have oxygen, which is analogous to a conducive situation. If these three elements do not co-exist, you don't get a flame.' In other words, a person who might be, by his physical and psychological make-up, a potential compulsive gambler, runs no risk of addiction if the opportunity to gamble isn't there. If he lives, shall we say, in the middle of Alaska rather than a couple of blocks off Las Vegas Boulevard South.

Fire is an attractive analogy. If one or other of these three elements is lowered, the flame of an addictive form of behaviour can be extinguished, at least temporarily. Treatment, therefore, must take account of psychological and physical stresses and the environment too. The practical aim of all this theoretical work, which Jacobs and others are continuing, is to develop an early warning system – a way of screening high-risk adolescents before they get caught in an addictive pattern of behaviour.

'Everybody has got his own theory,' Custer summed it up, 'It's up to them to prove it.'

Edward O. Thorp

John Aspinall

Compulsive Gamblin

Occasional gambling

WINNING

Frequent winning

Excitement prior to and while gambling

More frequent gambling

Increase betting amounts

Fantansies about winning

Big win

Unreasonable optimism

Gambling alone

Bragging about winning

Thinking only about gambling

Prolonged losing episodes

Can't stop gambling

Covering up, lying

LOSING

Careless about family

Losing time from work

Delay paying debts

Personality changes
Irritable, restless, withdrawn

Homelife unhappy

Heavy legal
and illegal borrowing

Unable to pay debts

Reputation affected

Bailouts

Alienation from
family and frien

Marked increase in amount
and time spent gambling

DESPERATION

Blaming othe

Remorse

Panic

Illegal a

- Hopelessnes
- Suicidal
  thoughts
- Arrests
- Divorce

nd Recovery Chart

GROWTH

New Way of Life

Sacraficing for others

Understanding self and others

Giving affection to others

Facing problems promptly

Insight into self

Preoccupation with gambling decreases

More relaxed

More family time

Less irritating behavior

Less impatience

Family and friends begin to trust

Resolve legal problems

Self-respect returning

Develop goals

Accept self-weaknesses
and strengths

New interests

REBUILDING

Restitution plans

Improved family relationships

Return to work

Paying bills, budgeting

Decision making

Problem solving

Spiritual needs
examined

Thinking clearer

Responsible
thinking

Personal stock

CRITICAL

Realistic, stops gambling

Hopeful

Honest desire for help

- Alcoholism
- Emotional
  breakdown
- Withdrawl
  symptoms

Rev. Gordon Moody

Dr. Robert Custer

II
MOTIVATION

5

IN THE CASINO

To be on the wire is life; the rest
is waiting.

Karl Wallenda,
high wire artist

We all take risks every day of our lives. Driving to work, catching
an aeroplane, even crossing the road. These sorts of risk are
quantified by actuaries and covered by insurance policies. The
insurance company, working on the past record of many hundreds of thousands of instances, calculates the probability of a
particular accident befalling the individual seeking cover and sets
its premium for the policy accordingly, plus a healthy margin to
take care of its operating costs and profits. Exactly as the casinos
do. But whereas most prudent people would take out an
insurance policy, as a basic part of their game-plan for living,
gamblers choose to take a wholly unnecessary and avoidable
risk. Seeking risk for its own sake, as a diversion.

In this book I concentrate on casino gambling, because it is so
intense and so fast. If you buy a ticket in a lottery it may be
weeks or months before the draw is made. If you go horse-racing,
you may find six or eight events in an afternoon to bet on, with
long intervals in between. If you have a bet on a football match,
you have 90 minutes play in which the outcome is in suspense.
But if you play roulette or blackjack or dice . . . you can expect a
rate of betting of over 60 coups an hour! On a slot machine,
which may pay out anything from a few bucks to a million
dollars on the jackpot, you get maybe five coups a minute!

Part of this attraction, I feel sure, is the physical sensations
offered. Consider simply the case of someone like you or me,
planning to spend a night out at the casino. First comes the
pleasure of anticipation, thinking through the day about going
out to gamble; then perhaps comes the agreeable social pleasure

of making arrangements to meet friends, other gamblers; not forgetting the important point of ensuring you have the money to gamble . . . That may well be a nervous-making element, especially if you can't really afford it, or can't afford to lose (which is always the case as a young man); then comes the physical sensation, the pitter-patter of excitement as you walk through the doors of the casino, the sight and sound of action in the gambling rooms . . . twitches of nervous tension . . . finally the see-saw sensations of each coup, one after the other in rapid succession, as the wheel spins or the dice roll or the cards fall; the exhilaration of winning and the depression of losing.

The same sequence of sensations applies to any other kind of bet, or, for that matter, an investment in the stock market. Currency speculation, which I have tried, is much the best for round-the-clock action: as soon as the market in London closes, the dealing starts up in New York, then moves to the Far East, and so back to London again. All bets are essentially the same, it is the time scale that's different. However this amalgam of sensations, of anticipation, excitement and resolution, may be described, the impact is in the body, physical.

Such feelings are not limited to gamblers. The same sort of sensations, I suppose, are felt by glider pilots, racing drivers, deep-sea divers, to name but three (operating as it were above, on and below the level of everyday living). The difference is in the pay-off: the thrill of trusting to the wind, speed around the track, piercing the darkness of deep water. When you come to think about it, almost all human activities carry an emotional charge, in varying degrees – the actor going on stage, the politician at a public meeting, the salesman trying to close a deal. In this sense gamblers are not so different. The emotional charge is a common experience, known colloquially as 'getting the adrenalin going'.

The classic expression of this highly complex bodily reaction was given in Walter B. Cannon's *The Wisdom of the Body* in 1932, long a standard text for medical students. 'Our bodies,' he wrote in his introduction, 'are made of extraordinarily unstable material. Pulses of energy, so minute that very delicate methods are required to measure them, course along our nerves. On reaching muscles they find there a substance so delicately

sensitive to slight disturbance that, like an explosive touched off
by a fuse, it may discharge in a powerful movement. Our sense
organs are responsive to almost incredibly minute stimulations.'

'Fight and flight' is the formulation – the body had to react to
give primitive man the capacity to get out of trouble, to run, to
survive. As Cannon put it:

In the long history of the race bacteria have not been the only living
foes of man, and in wild life, perhaps, they have not been the most
important. There have been savage creatures, human and subhuman,
watching with stealth and ready to attack without a moment's warning.
And there has been, also, the necessity of fighting, for revenge, for
safety and for prey. In that harsh school fear and anger have served as
a preparation for action. Fear has become associated with the instinct
to run, to escape; and anger or aggressive feeling, with the instinct to
attack. These are fundamental emotions and instincts which have
resulted from the experience of multitudes of generations in the fierce
struggle for existence and which have their values in that struggle.

It is remarkable that most of the reactions thus noted occur as
the accompaniment to rage and fear. 'Respiration deepens, the
heart beats more rapidly, the arterial pressure rises, the blood is
shifted away from the stomach and intestines to the heart and
central nervous system and the muscles, the processes in the
alimentary canal cease, sugar is freed from the reserves in the
liver, the spleen contracts and discharges its content of concentrated corpuscles, and adrenalin is secreted from the adrenalin
medulla.' These transformations in the body stem from fear and
rage – running away in order to escape from danger, and
attacking in order to be dominant. Either way, a life-or-death
struggle.

Easy to see that many of these bodily changes occur when one
is engaged in gambling. One may be only subconsciously aware
of a heightened sense of physical tension, but it's there all right.
Rapid breathing and a faster heart beat are well attested reactions to excitement. There are many others, whose force one
doesn't need a medical explanation to appreciate – dryness in
the throat, sweaty palms, tautness in the pit of the stomach as
the cards come off the deck, and – excuse the crudity – the

favourite threat of a former airforce captain with whom I used to play poker in Washington, as he put in a heavy raise, 'Boy, this'll make your asshole pucker!' This pepping up of the body is what is meant by 'getting the adrenalin going'. In gambling it is not a life-or-death struggle (leaving aside Russian roulette); nor is it, in modern terms, enhancing the capacity for flight or fight exactly.

It is, rather, the accentuation of alertness, as it were doing battle over the green baize, which is what the gambler feels. And – this is the point – it is a highly pleasurable sensation. It's good to get pepped up, to feel the adrenalin going. The 'arousal' takes place in the brain when one is faced with uncertainty or probability decisions. It is a way of alerting one to signals, to be more aware, like picking up blips on a radar screen. This is its purpose. But it also has a secondary effect of being pleasurable in itself. Asleep, the pattern of cells in this part of the brain are like waves, in unison; in arousal, millions of cells are agitated, dancing about so to speak. It feels good because one is on top of things, in expectation of performing well. This is part of the pay-off for gambling, just as it is for gliding, motor racing and diving. People do these things for a variety of motives and one of them is feeling the experience of being alive more intensely.

The same idea was expressed for different reasons by Thorstein Veblen in his classic critique *The Theory of the Leisure Class*, which first appeared in 1899. He saw sports, or the sport of the upper class and nouveaux riches, as a modern manifestation of an ancient, predatory instinct for fighting and displaying prowess. 'Sports of all kinds are of the same general character, including prize-fights, bull-fights, athletics, shooting, angling, yachting and games of skill, even where the element of destructive physical efficiency is not an obtrusive feature. Sports shade off from the basis of hostile combat, through skill to cunning and chicanery, without its being possible to draw a line at any point.' (He might have mentioned poker, above all.)

The propensity to gambling, he goes on, is another aspect of the predatory temperament, of almost universal prevalence among sporting men. Belief in luck – stemming from the remote past when man apprehended the natural world through spirits which could be moved and propitiated – is the basis of the gambling habit. But betting on the outcome of contests of strength and skill has a further motive, without which the belief in luck would hardly figure so prominently in sporting life. 'This further motive is the desire of the anticipated winner, or the partisan of the anticipated winning side, to heighten his side's ascendancy at the cost of the loser. Not only does the stronger side score a more signal victory, and the losing side suffer a more painful and humiliating defeat, in proportion as the pecuniary gain and loss in the wager is large . . . But the wager is commonly laid also with a view . . . to enhancing the chances of success for the contestant on which it is laid.' Such bets, Veblen adds, serve to encourage a victorious outcome.

I stress the physical sensations aroused in gambling because I think in the extensive investigations of psychological motives that have been conducted by psychoanalysts and psychologists over the years, this aspect of the matter has been undervalued. It's what we laymen call fun. Gambling awakens and stimulates deep animal instincts in the bodily reactions it sets in motion. This is not to suggest that study of the psychology of gambling has been overvalued: it is obviously crucial to any understanding of gambling. But psychological drives cannot exist without a physical base. A gambler is not two beings, one acting and the other feeling.

The term 'emotion' should not really be used in psychology, it has been argued, because it is only a convenient label for behaviour which cannot be explained in physical terms. A man's actions, his thoughts and his emotions are different aspects of the single complex of processes in the interacting organs which comprise the individual, and which interact in turn with the environment. 'One is justified, therefore, in seeking the changing patterns of material substrata that must, in all reason, be part and parcel of those phenomena that we call emotions,' (*Emotions and Emotional Disorders*, Ernst Gellhorn & G. N. Loufbourrow, 1963). Because everyone has experienced states of elation, indifference and depression, fear and anger, anticipation and dread, it tends to be forgotten that such feelings are the result of changes in activity of the central nervous system. They are heightened in gambling because there is no exercise involved to 'burn off' adrenalin.

There is one key difference, though, which distinguishes the activity of gambling from gliding, racing, diving and all the other things that people do when they are enjoying themselves. In all these activities, the pilot, driver, swimmer, or whoever, has trained or practised or worked out the right and the wrong way of doing it, has been taught and tested at some length how to perform and has, in sum, established that he or she is in a position to carry through the action successfully. There may be accidents – freak winds, oil on the track, oxygen failure – but the chances are very strongly in their favour. In gambling it is exactly the opposite! The odds are against the player, and everyone knows it. The risk is worse than fifty-fifty. Gamblers who manage to get a 50-50 break, as with the odds bets at craps, count themselves lucky!

After all, you cannot win at gambling in the long run, and that is the basic truth and the basic point about it. The very point that makes the motive for gambling such a mystery. Put it this way: suppose you're walking down the street and you meet some fellow who offers to toss a coin with you, heads or tails: the only snag is, when you lose you pay a dollar, when you win, you get paid only 99 cents. You wouldn't do it, would you? You'd be out of your mind to do it. But that is what happens, exactly what happens, when you bet in a casino. I do it, you do it, and everybody does it. That is how the casinos make their huge profits.

Note that the casinos' advantage, their profit, comes from players' winning bets, by paying out less than the true odds. In the coin-tossing encounter you would on average win half the flips and lose half the flips, so that for every two coups you would win back 99 cents for the other dollar you lost. All right, one cent in two tosses may not seem too serious. But in fact it is one-half of one per cent of the two bucks wagered, which is 0.5 per cent. The odds are in the other fellow's favour – the casinos' favour – and that is an unalterable law of probability. (See my calculations on pages 149–151.)

No 'system' can overturn that law, not varying the stakes, or waiting for a run one way and betting the other, least of all doubling up your stakes. You get to an impossibly high figure too quickly: 1, 2, 4, 8, 16, 32 . . . ten bets from the start of such a sequence you are up to 1,024, and if you still went on doubling up at, say, roulette you would reach, after another ten losses, a figure of over a million, 1,048,576 to be precise – far beyond the table limit even if you had the money. The chances of the next spin coming up red or black, as everyone knows but so often prefers to ignore, are the same as they were on each separate spin, namely evens. (And this is to leave out of account the unfortunate little matter of zero, or in American casinos the doubly unfortunate zero and double zero, which makes the true chance of winning significantly less than evens.)

So why gamble? The reasons are as many and various as the stars in the sky. I prefer to take the question the other way round. Why do some people not gamble? It's such a widespread trait of human conduct that it might be considered abnormal not to do it. The thought is not new. Gaming in all its various forms – casinos, horse-racing, lotteries, card games – is simply too large an industry to be based on services catering for a deviant sub-group of the population. As the great gambler and early student of probability, Girolamo Cardano (c. 1530) observed, 'Even if gambling were altogether an evil, still on account of the very large number of people who play, it would seem to be a natural evil . . . Thus it is not absurd for me to discuss gambling, not in order to praise it, but in order to point out the advantages in it, and, of course, also its disadvantages, so they may be reduced to a minimum.'

One of the very few proponents of this point of view in modern times is Dr Felicia Campbell, who teaches literature at the University of Nevada at Las Vegas. Perhaps you didn't suppose Las Vegas and Reno went in for academic life? Well, these two campuses, oases in the desert, offer degree courses to some 20,000 students, studying everything from hotel management to desert biology. Dr Campbell, a bit of a gambler in her own life, (her marriage, made on impulse, was over in about five minutes, as she cheerfully admits) has noted that the professional literature, at least that in English, largely ignores gambling as a normal part of human behaviour, treating it as the Victorians treated sex. Most of the behaviour studies are flawed, she maintains, either because the investigators have known too few gamblers, are too little familiar with gambling, or because of cultural and emotional bias of which they are largely unaware.

She is particularly severe on Dr Edmund Bergler, whose findings in *The Psychology of Gambling* (first published in 1958) that people gamble in order to lose, to punish themselves, has had a seminal influence on psychological studies of gambling. His work was based on a group of sixty neurotic patients, most of whom did not consider their gambling a harmful activity, she says, until Bergler had convinced them of it through long analysis. He saw any consistent gambling as psychomasochistic, and termed the gambler a rebel against his own self. (An approach which echoes Veblen's censure of gambling as 'a hindrance to the highest industrial efficiency of the aggregate in any community where it prevails.')

By contrast, Dr Campbell's own research among gamblers in Las Vegas led her to the opposite conclusion, that 'by and large gambling is beneficial to the gambler and increases rather than decreases his efficiency and productivity.' In one study she interviewed elderly people in the downtown casinos, local or retired people, eking out a living on small means; most of them elderly women, they were all utterly absorbed in their play at the slot machines. That absorption, she felt, was the clue: they were once more engaged in life. (A point which superior people, so dismissive of the little old ladies with their plastic cups of nickels and dimes, usually ignore.) Thus one woman, who had turned down the offer of living with her daughter in Kansas: 'Here I can wear what I want and play the machines. I never lose much and I like to play. Whenever the money drops, I feel real good. I won something, and I ain't won a lot of things in my life.'

Stakes are not important, in the sense that such people get as much thrill from playing penny slots as do high rollers ten feet across the floor betting thousands at the craps table. It's all relative to a player's resources. The winnings go back into the machines, of course, but that doesn't matter. What counts, Dr

Campbell maintains, is not how much is taken home but how many jackpots are won and the amount of play that people were able to sustain on the little money they had. Many old men frequent the downtown casinos. Far from being shells of human beings who have destroyed themselves gambling, as tourists usually assume, many are retired blue collar workers such as railroad men and factory hands. Quite a bit of socializing goes on, especially at bingo. 'Momentarily they feel alive, involved, possibilities exist, victories are possible, and tomorrow the game exists to be played again.' Dr Campbell thinks that old peoples' homes might do well to include some form of gambling in their routine, to add spice to fading lives.

The value of social life among gamblers can be similarly seen in the day-by-day routine of a group of horse-race punters, as reported by John Rosecrance under the ironic title *The Degenerates of Lake Tahoe* (1985). The relationship between these mostly down-and-out players was less than friendship, but more than acquaintance, a kind of comradeship without entanglements. The relationship was defined by the shared preoccupation of playing the horses and (as in a poker school) did not go beyond that. The advantages are listed as 'empathy without deep emotional involvement, interaction on demand, ease of exit and entry (to the group), and absence of the "strain towards totality" ' (i.e. not trying to get to know the whole person). The key to all such special interest groups, whether in gambling or the wider world, is involvement, or at least understanding of the common activity.

In the neighbouring town of Henderson just outside Las Vegas – an industrial area half-smothered by chemical fumes – many workers, Dr Campbell found, managed to relieve the soulless blight of their existence through gambling. As in downtown Vegas, the casinos in Henderson offer a spit-and-sawdust style with low stakes. Just what people on low incomes with no hope of bettering themselves or of getting away from Henderson need. 'It buys me some time for myself. It's the only way I can get anything for me.' For people who feel they have no influence over the forces which rule their lives, such gambling is not rebelling against the self, but the system. 'All day long, you do what them dumb supervisors tell you. Don't make no difference if it makes sense or not.' Dr Campbell goes further in adducing the therapeutic benefits of small-time gambling by suggesting that, if factory workers were given 'gambling breaks' like coffee breaks, it is possible that absenteeism would be reduced and the accident rate cut.

Likewise in prisons: picking up another point from Cardano that 'play may be beneficial in times of grief and that the law permits it to the sick and those in prison and those condemned to death,' she observes that it is a pity that Nevada prisons have given up the practice of recent years of allowing some gambling. As one prisoner told Dr Campbell, being allowed to gamble was all that saved his sanity during years of incarceration in ver-minous, brutalizing conditions. In such play, prisoners could lose themselves; in making decisions, feel human again. Why shouldn't gambling, along with re-training, have positive use as a recreation for prisoners?

Well it has, at least once. This episode, which must be one of the most extraordinary in the whole history of gambling, deserves celebration in a movie one day, like *Birdman of Alcatraz*. It centres on the imaginative approach to running a modern prison by a former warden of Carson City prison, Jack Fogliani. During his six years as superintendent and eight years as warden (1953–67), social conditions were unusually good, thanks in large measure, so it appears, to the use of a casino in the prison itself, to reduce tension. Thus, there were no riots at Carson City during Mr Fogliani's time. When he left, trouble started.

Metallic chips made of brass, called brass money, were used; there was a cashier in the prison to take charge of the money won or lost in the card and dice games; the playing tables were made by the prisoners, on the model of real casinos. 'It may be against all precepts of prison administration elsewhere,' a report ran in *The Sacramento Bee* in 1962, 'but here behind the old limestone walls of the institution two miles east of Carson City, gambling – legal, above board, sanctioned, aided and abetted by prison officials – is high on the list of approved recreation.'

The precise beginning of the Carson City prison casino is not clear, but officially it dates from the legalization of gambling in

Nevada in 1931. Interviewed at the age of 82, Fogliani assured Tomas Martinez, Professor of Criminology at California State University, Fresno, that there had been gambling at the prison for 100 years. 'Mr Fogliani seems to have been a very sensitive and sensible warden in his use of the casino to control the prison population,' Martinez says (*The Gambling Scene*, 1983). But then, the day after Fogliani retired, the new warden shut the casino down. 'Warder Hocker did not study the function of the casino because he did not have an interest in doing so.' But he did provide some activities to replace the gambling. The main one was . . . knitting!

Defending this change of policy by the new warden, a public information sheet from the prison stated: 'When the brass money . . . was retrieved . . . it was found that one inmate had virtually all the cash in the institution . . . at one time the Bullpen (as the locale was called) was out of bounds to institution staff. Many beatings and other nefarious activities took place under these conditions. This was the most degrading, non-productive activity that Warden Hocker had seen in thirty years of prison work.' What the official hand-out failed to add was that tension among the prisoners began building up as soon as the new warden arrived and shut the 'casino' down. Tension has remained high through the years since then, with periodic outbursts never seen in Fogliani's days.

The trouble is, as Dr Campbell says, that the gambler has acquired a bad press. He is frequently viewed as an erratic, unstable and irresponsible sort, driven by unknown forces to take foolish and unnecessary chances. The consequences of this risk-taking, so the public feels, may be financially and psychologically dangerous to the player, as well as to those whose lives interact with his. (I am not, it goes without saying, recommending people risking more than they can afford; as with alcohol, excess is dangerous and destructive.)

The reason why society disapproves of gambling is that the very process of taking risks, 'bucking the odds', goes against the socially accepted norm of realistic and attainable goals achieved through conformity and hard work – 'a spouse, a home in the suburbs and 2.2 children'. People who do not fit into this pattern tend to be seen as either not trying hard enough or misfits, maladjusted; those who find the adjustment too difficult to make are given pills to speed them up or slow them down, so as to match the pace required for 'success'. It is as if the human being was being re-designed to fit the model of a citizen, without knowing what makes up a fully-functioning individual.

The gambling impulse, Campbell affirms, is part of what has been called 'the adventurer within us' – that part of human nature which desires change, the unknown, chance, danger, all that is new. It is the impulse which draws people to the gaming tables – and also up to the moon. 'Contrary to the popular belief, I have found gambling to be largely beneficial to the gambler . . . Gambling stimulates, offers hope, and allows decision-making. In many cases it provides the gambler with a "peak experience", that godlike feeling that occurs when all of one's physical and emotional senses are "go".'

Campbell managed to achieve this state of heightened consciousness for herself recently, not at the tables in Las Vegas, but in the Himalayas. She had won a long-running lawsuit against the University over equal pay for women and decided to blow the money on a climbing expedition. She did not take a medical before the trip in case the doctor told her at the age of 50 not to go. She flew to Islamabad and took a bush plane out to the wilds of northern Pakistan. Her idea was that if she got too tired making the ascent of some glacial peak, she could simply call a halt, because she was the one paying the porters; she had not foreseen there would be no place flat enough to pitch a tent and that you have to go on or give up. 'My Madam can do it,' her porters told her each time they came to the next unclimbable obstacle, and then, beaming, 'My Madam is strong.' She was struck down by illness at one stage and had to camp on her own for several days while the others went higher. But that too turned into a peak experience of inner reflection.

The most intense moment of the trip came crossing a very cold, very swift, waist-deep river. 'I've always been afraid of water. Yet it was the most exhilarating thing I have ever done. The swiftness of the water, and the realization we could really die, seemed to contribute to it. I was doing it and laughing at the same time.' Another kind of peak came when she realized, at the end, that she was no longer lagging behind; she could make the pace. As a result of the expedition, Campbell felt she could take on any challenge, including starting writing about gambling again. She is not proposing that people's problems can be solved by turning the world into a giant casino; simply that it is wrong to suppress an aspect of human nature which may be a key to more creative living, or at least release from daily tension.

Another academic who believes that we have come a long way since Bergler's original interpretation of gambling as psychic masochism is Igor Kusyszyn. He sees gambling as 'adult play'. For the vast majority of people who gamble it is, without doubt, psychic pleasure. In addition to teaching psychology at York University, Toronto, Dr Kusyszyn has the distinction of having written a technical manual on how to beat blackjack, under the name of 'Lance Humble', humbly titled *The World's Greatest Blackjack Book.* (He has also written on how to beat the horses, unfortunately getting busted in the process for illegal book-making.)

Kusyszyn observes that for every pathological gambler there are at least 100 social gamblers. 'These nonpathological gamblers have been taken for granted by both the media and social scientists, and little attention has been paid to them. Yet, if we include lottery, bingo, and numbers players, the nonpathological gamblers are seen to comprise approximately 60 per cent of the adult North American population.'

When it came to research on real-life gambling behaviour, Kusyszyn complains, he could find very little material. One such study showed that housewives who were habitual players in the poker clubs of Gardena, near Los Angeles, were significantly better adjusted, on the average, than female adults of the general population, so far as emotional, home and social life were concerned. He tends to believe from his own research that gamblers have healthier personalities than non-gamblers: for instance, in a questionnaire comparing risk-taking and other characteristics between race-track gamblers and psychology graduate students, the former group was found to be lower on hostility, familial discord, anxiety, and the internalizing of emotion. In Kusyszyn's view, gamblers confirm their existence and affirm their worth through their play (*The Psychology of Gambling*, 1984).

In defining gambling in terms of its physical surroundings as well as the state of mind of its participants, he has some good points to make. Thus he notes that gambling is self-contained; there is almost always a special place for it, with physical boundaries, such as a racetrack, casino, card room or bingo hall. It is completely apart from the routine activities of everyday life. In addition, gambling occurs during leisure time. People do it of their own volition. 'Gambling is complex and cyclical. It is composed of continuous chains of events that include decision making, wagering, an outcome, emotional reaction to the outcome, cognitive appraisal of one's actions in relation to the outcome, further decision-making, further wagering, and so on. Each chain is unique; although succeeding chains are almost always variations of previous chains, no chain is identical to any other. The novelty of each chain and the gambler's freedom to participate in it as a creative agent allow gambling to be an absorbing activity.'

The hardest thing for non-gamblers to understand, it seems to me, is that money loses its economic value in gambling, a process powerfully reinforced by the use of plastic chips instead of banknotes. In the casinos, the transformation of money into coloured counters, children's playthings, into a part of the game itself, serves to weaken the players' natural instinct, instilled in us all every day of our lives since we first had pocket money, to hold on to our cash. The only time you notice money, as world poker champion Doyle Brunson has said, is when you put your hand in your pocket and find it empty. That is when the chips do take on a terrible significance by their absence. Imaginary or mental bets do not work. The gambler's involvement in such wagers – for example players who have gone broke still hanging around the table – is token, and as such carries only a vicarious emotional charge. The real importance of money is that it is the indispensable condition for being able to continue gambling.

The uncertainty of the gambling event, Kusyszyn concludes, and the risk that is an integral part of it provide for the cognitive, emotional and physical arousal of the individual. 'It can be spoken of as a mood state, a peak, a trance, a high, or even a mystic state. It is not, however, uniform. It is a general state that is altered many times – or more precisely, different mini-states pass through the generally pervasive state – during a session of gambling by the individual's actions . . . This self-regulated playing within the pleasantly safe, fantasy mood state is probably the most important feature of gambling.'

The trouble comes, one may add, when the peak experience costs more than the outlay in achieving it – like the pigeon in B. F. Skinner's experiments which exerts more energy to gain a pellet than is contained in the pellet, and thus literally works itself to death. Or, if you like, slot machine players who go on pulling the one-armed bandits until they are in a state of collapse.

A number of laboratory experiments have been carried out to determine how people feel when they are gambling; but the trouble with a laboratory test is that it is nothing like a casino. A basic flaw is that in an artificial test, the players are not risking anything; they may be rewarded for winning, but in terms of excitement, playing without the possibility of loss is like drinking a dry martini without gin.

In a novel attempt to get around this problem, an experiment was devised by two researchers in Glasgow which compared reactions of gamblers in a laboratory test with their reactions in a casino. This last was achieved by wiring up a number of players to monitor their heartbeats, while playing blackjack, via a re-corder switch attached to the tail of the player's jacket, operated by an experimenter standing behind him. 'This does not look out of place in a casino setting where it is common for people to crowd round a table. Recording of subjects' stakes, cards and outcome was done by speaking a running commentary into an audio mini cassette recorder in the experimenter's breast pocket.' (Real and laboratory gambling, sensation-seeking and arousal, G. Anderson and R. I. F. Brown, *British Journal of Psychology*, 1984). The laboratory test, which also compared the reactions of a group of students who were not gamblers, sought to replicate casino conditions with dim lighting, a croupier with a real blackjack shoe and chips (maximum prize £10) and soft music in the background; the students were not tested in a casino 'for ethical reasons', but had two sessions in the mock casino. Twelve gamblers and twelve students were tested.

Since excitement in real gambling was being measured for the first time, the study also sought to discover what aspects of blackjack were most stimulating. The test was divided into three periods, corresponding to the sequence of events at blackjack, described as a two-decision game divided by a 'hopeful' period in between: 1. placing the stake; 2. being dealt two cards; 3. resolution of the hand. Heart-rate signals were later passed from tape to a polygraph where they were recorded for visual analysis by counting the beats between the events marking the beginning and end of the periods of the game, and expressing the rate in beats per minute.

And what did they show? That there was no significant difference between the students and gamblers in the artificial casino, but a highly significant difference in heart rate increase between gamblers in the artificial and real casinos. Surprise, surprise! you may say; but the figures are revealing. 'A round of the game in a simulated casino only produced a tiny increase in heart rates but in the real casino, they shot up,' noted Iain Brown, a psychology lecturer at Glasgow University. 'One subject began with a pulse rate of 72 but when he started gambling it raced up to 130 – a rise of 58 beats a minute. The average rise was 25.' These increases seem to be on a par with strong physical exercise.

'The constant repetition of major changes in autonomic or other kinds of arousal associated in time and place with various forms of gambling activity is likely to have a powerful classical or Pavlovian conditioning effect on gambling behaviour,' the study concludes, 'and may contribute significantly to the development of gambling addiction. . . . If, as appears likely, arousal and excitement are major mediators of reinforcement and internal cues for gambling behaviour, especially for regular gamblers, pathological gamblers may become addicted to their own arousal and its physical and psychological effects.' In some individuals such high and in-

Increases in heart-rate (beats per minute) at different stages of play

| | Students | | Gamblers | | | |
| | | | Artificial | | Real | |
	X̄	SD	X̄	SD	X̄	SD
Increase period 1	2.4	1.9	6.1	1.8	23.2	3.5
2	6.3	3.3	8.1	2.5	25.1	4.9
3	4.0	2.6	9.0	3.1	22.5	4.0
Increase overall	4.1	3.7	6.8	3.4	23.1	6.8

creasing arousal in the course of a gambling session could produce a narrowing of attention and hence a secondary reward in an escape from disturbing factors in their normal life, the authors suggest; and, with further increases, changes in short-term memory and accuracy, and even a state of confusion and disordered thinking.

All this seems to me very persuasive. One gets a strong sense in gambling, as in an addictive time-consuming game like chess, that the activity is not pursued to win as such. It is far more an activity which 'takes you out of yourself', actually turns you in on yourself, so that the increased focus on doing it – making the right moves – is both highly gratifying in itself, and at the same time blocks out any thoughts about the real world beyond the table. (Like President Truman, on being interrupted in the course of a poker game by his daughter to give him the results of mid-term elections: 'Thank you, my dear – thank you – Okay, deal!' An experience which any card player can instantly identify with.)

On a sensation-seeking scale, which combined a variety of personality tests, no significant difference was found between the students and the gamblers. But the results did show a positive correlation with heart-rate increase for gamblers in the real casino. In other words, gamblers most inclined to seek sensation make larger bets than those who are less inclined to do so in real casinos, but in artificial ones they bet the same amount. (The gamblers' responses as to why they gambled regularly were: 50 per cent for enjoyment or excitement; 33 per cent to be sociable; 8.5 per cent to pass the time; and 8.5 per cent to win money.) Whether sensation-seekers place higher bets as a way of obtaining higher arousal, or whether high arousal makes for higher bets, or how they reinforce each other, is an open question. Brown believes that the constant 'jolts to the system' provided by gambling can produce a powerful Pavlovian conditioning effect. As the study concludes, 'excitement or arousal . . . not sexual, but probably autonomic, might be seen as being sought repeatedly by the regular gambler for its own sake.'

Next, a word about odds.

6

PERCENTAGES AND CHANCES

Figures can't lie but liars sure can
figure.

Bob Beckman

"Ain't only three things to gamblin',' former world poker
champion Pug Pearson remarked to me one fine morning.
'Knowin' the 60-40 end of a proposition, money management,
and knowin' yourself.' Puggy, dressed in his 'work' attire of red
satin shorts and open-necked shirt, cigars sticking up out of his
breast pocket like a battery of missiles, gave me a shrewd look:
'Any donkey knows that.'

Sitting at an empty poker table in the card room of the Golden
Nugget in Las Vegas, Puggy was waiting for new players to
arrive to start up a game. 'Siddown,' he invited me. One of the
poker players already waiting at the table looked up, 'Ya gotta
be playin' to siddown.' 'Aw right,' Puggy commanded, tossing
me a huge roll of hundred-dollar bills trussed together with elastic
bands, 'Siddown here. You can play this game, can't ya?' I had
just vacated my seat at the $3–$6 limit game to talk to him. 'Er
– sure can, Pug.'

On the instant, the table filled up with four or five hungry-
looking guys, eyes agleam. Pug made a rapid reassessment of
the situation. 'Yeah, well, okay – gimme the money back.' He
had evidently concluded that staking me in a high rollers' game
meant that he himself would be taking the 40-60 end of the
proposition. I tossed the roll back again – it has a comfortable
heft to it, ten thousand bucks – and stood up, to resume my seat
in the tourists' game.

We had both of us demonstrated his definition of the winning
gambling formula cited above.

As a matter of fact most people do know the 60-40 end of a
proposition when they see it. The trouble is the attraction of the

gamble is so strong that the bet overrides their judgement. This is especially true of bets on sporting events, where enthusiasm, not to say blind fervour, for backing one's fancy, or local team, or favourite player, frequently warps any prudent estimation of true odds or value. Money management simply means making your bets in sensible proportion to your funds. The commonest mistake people make in casinos is over-betting their bankroll. They get in too far.

So the real contest is not between the player and the house, whether it is a sports bet or a casino game, but between the player and himself. And despite what Puggy says, the injunction to 'know yourself' is rather difficult to fulfil, as moral philosophers down the ages have pointed out. Do you want to win or do you want the sensation of action for its own sake?

If you are an occasional player, buying say ten or twenty pounds – or dollars – worth of chips after enjoying a good dinner in the casino, what are your chances of winning or losing? And how much?

At blackjack, playing basic strategy, the house edge against you is reduced to around a mere 0.5 per cent – which all in all seems pretty insignificant. Or perhaps your fancy turns towards the faster action of craps, when the house edge rises a notch but is still only 1.4 per cent against you – provided, that is, you stick to the basic line bets and don't go in for proposition bets, like throwing double sixes, where the house edge rises in American casinos to 16.6 per cent (in Britain it is a mere 5.5 per cent).

At roulette, of course, it all depends if you play the European game with one zero, or the American game with zero and double zero. In the single zero game the odds against you, playing red or black or other even money chances, are only 1.35 per cent (when zero comes up you lose only half your stake), which is virtually the same as at dice; betting the numbers, the odds against you rise to 2.7 per cent. At American roulette, with two zeros, the house edge rises to a whopping 5.26 per cent, whether you choose to play 'even money chances' like red and black or numbers.

Regardless of which of these games you choose, if you make ten straight bets at the same stake, the chances of breaking dead

The first diagram shows what percentage of players will win, lose or break even at the three main casino games, blackjack, craps and roulette, after 100 bets, 1,000 bets and 10,000 bets, at level stakes.

At blackjack, the calculation is based on the assumption that the player is following basic strategy (see chapter 1) which is an edge of 0.5 per cent in the house's favour. (As can be seen from the left-hand column of chips, after 100 coups, 51 per cent of players will be behind, 47 per cent will be ahead and 2 per cent will be even.) The middle section on craps also stands for European roulette, because the edge against the player is virtually the same – 1.4 per cent at craps, playing line bets, and 1.35 per cent at roulette, on the 'even money' chances (not numbers). At American roulette, when the edge against the player rises to 5.26 per cent on 'colour' bets, there will in the long run be no winners.

In practice, of course, good gamblers never stick to level stakes. They increase their bets as the dice or the cards get hot, or they feel lucky. The corollary of winning at a faster rate, however, is risking losing at a faster rate: varying the stakes, therefore, will not alter the basic findings set out here – provided that the gambler goes on playing.

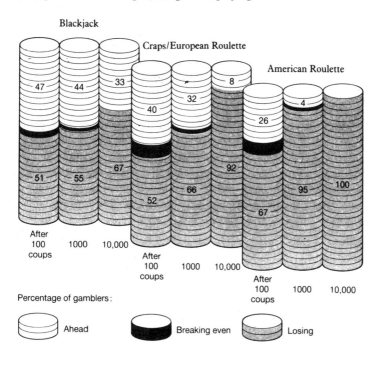

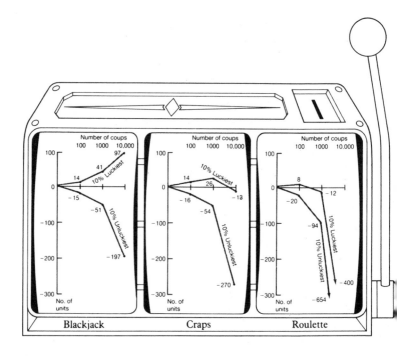

The second diagram shows in graphic form how many units – that is how much money – the luckiest and unluckiest 10 per cent of players will win or lose in the course of making 100, 1,000 or 10,000 bets at level stakes.

Figures on the plus line mean more than that amount ahead; minuses signify that amount or more behind (e.g. at blackjack, the luckiest 10 per cent of players will be more than 97 units ahead after 10,000 coups, while the unluckiest 10 per cent will be 197 units or more behind). When even the luckiest players still lose, as occurs at craps and roulette, the minus figures signify no more than that amount behind.

At the extremes (not shown in the graphs) the luckiest 1 per cent of players will win 218 or more at blackjack after 10,000 coups and the unluckiest lose 318 or more; at craps, the luckiest 1 per cent win 92 or more and the unluckiest lose 374 or more; and at roulette the luckiest 1 per cent will be no more than 294 behind and the unluckiest, with the profound blessing of the casino, be 750 or more behind. The house wins what the players lose.

even are about 25 per cent. The luckiest 1 per cent of players will be eight or more units ahead and the unluckiest 1 per cent of players will be 8 or more units behind. In any case, making ten bets is not too serious, whatever happens.

The outcome looks very, very different if you play for long periods of time and make, say, 100, 1,000, or 10,000 bets.

You'll never see the kind of figures which I present in these previous pages displayed in a casino. They have been calculated for me by Professor Peter Griffin of California State University, Sacramento (the blackjack expert, see chapter 1). My thanks are also due to Edward Rothman in London, who wrote a computer program for me to show how any particular edge against the player, after any given number of coups, works out.

So, suppose you spend a couple of hours in a casino and make 100 bets at the same stake, what is the result likely to be? Or suppose you are on a four-day vacation or business convention with time and money to burn, and indulge yourself by spending four or five hours a night at the tables, making a total of 1,000 bets. (A rate of 50 coups an hour is quite normal.) How does that change things?

Or suppose, finally, that you are a 'serious' gambler. You take off every weekend for Atlantic City or Lake Tahoe, or trawl around Mayfair: over a few months of regular punting you can easily rack up 10,000, bets – and over a lifetime's play 100,000. It's not so much as it seems, if you play several hours a night. My figures show what to expect.

7

ACTION MAN

> Uncertainty is the normal state.
> You're nobody special.
> Tom Stoppard, *Rosencrantz and*
> *Guildenstern Are Dead*

One of the most intriguing aspects of gambling is how people make up their minds when they are taking chances. At its most basic, how do you decide whether to back red or black? Why do you choose one number over another? How do you assess the various factors in more complicated decisions in taking chances? How good is people's judgement in uncertainty?

According to academic studies on these matters, many decisions are based on beliefs concerning the likelihood of uncertain events such as the outcome of an election, the guilt of a defendant, or the future value of the dollar: beliefs usually expressed in statements such as: 'I think that . . .', 'Chances are . . .', 'It is unlikely that . . .', and so forth. Occasionally beliefs concerning uncertain events are expressed in numerical form as odds or subjective probabilities.

People rely on a limited number of heuristic (problem solving) principles, which reduce the complex task of assessing probabilities and predicting values to simpler operations of judgement. In general these methods are quite useful, but sometimes they lead to severe and systematic errors. ('Judgement under Uncertainty: Heuristics and Biases', Amos Tversky and Daniel Kahneman, *Science*, 1974.)

One of the most common mistakes is known as the 'gambler's fallacy': the belief that the law of large numbers applies also to small numbers. People expect that a sequence of events in a random process – say the tossing of a coin – will represent the essential characteristics of the process even when the sequence is short. In tossing a coin heads or tails people regard the sequence H–T–H–T–T–H as more likely than the sequence H–H–H–T–T–T, because the latter does not appear to be random, and more likely than the sequence H–H–H–H–T–H which does not seem to reflect the 'fairness' of the coin. Thus people expect the essential characteristics of the process of a very long series of tosses to be shown in each of its parts. Look at the roulette players in any casino in the world! (I am ashamed to confess that the first time I went to Las Vegas, when I was old enough to know better, I had a system based on waiting for a sequence of eight reds before backing black; it took less than two hours for the system to be shredded.) In other words, people view chance as a self-correcting process in which a deviation in one direction induces a deviation in the opposite direction to restore the balance. In fact deviations are not 'corrected' as a chance process goes on, they are merely diluted.

All right, but this habit of mind is for simple folk, not one which sophisticated people adopt. Not so, according to Tversky and Kahneman, who found that experienced research psychologists had a lingering belief in the 'law of small numbers' too. In this particular heuristic or method of judgement, known as 'representativeness', an event is judged probable to the extent that it represents the essential features of the structure from which it originates. Probability is judged by similarity.

Very many questions of probability belong to the type: What is the probability that event A belongs to class B? Or what is the probability that process B will generate event A? In answering such questions people typically estimate the probability by the degree to which A is representative of B.

For instance, suppose you are trying to predict the future value of a stock or a commodity. Given a description of a company which is very favourable, a very high profit will appear most representative of that description; if the description is mediocre, a mediocre performance will appear most representative. What people overlook is the degree to which the description itself is reliable, and the degree to which it permits accurate prediction. So if people make investments, or bets, solely on the basis of the favourableness of the description, their decision will not take into account the reliability of the evidence and the expected accuracy of the prediction. This mode of judgement violates statistical theory: if the descriptions of companies provide no information relevant to profit, then average profit should be predicted.

In another heuristic known as 'availability', probability is judged by association, or what comes easily to mind. For example, the divorce rate in a given community may be assessed by recalling divorces among one's acquaintances. The sight of a car overturned on the side of the road certainly gives one a heightened sense of the risks of driving. In other words the estimate of probability is influenced by the way in which instances or associations seem to run in parallel. A doctor who has heard a patient complain that he is tired of life and wonders whether that patient is likely to commit suicide may recall similar patients he has known. What the doctor ought to think about is patients who resemble the present case and attempt suicide: the relevant statistic is the frequency of attempted suicides in this class. The example doesn't have to be a doctor. 'We know of no reason to believe that the intuitive predictions of stockbrokers, sportscasters, political analysts or research psychologists are less susceptible to biases,' say the authors.

Essentially, what is in question is the gap between subjective thinking and cognitive thinking. Subjective thinking resembles assessment of physical phenomena like distance or size. For instance, the apparent distance of an object is determined by its clarity: the more sharply it is seen, the closer it appears to be. However, reliance on this rule leads to systematic errors. Distances are often over-estimated when visibility is poor because the contours of objects are blurred; on the other hand distances are often under-estimated when visibility is good, because objects are seen sharply. Such biases are also found in the intuitive judgement of probability.

Here's an example which you can test for yourself. In many situations people make estimates by starting from an initial value that is adjusted to yield the final answer, a method of judgement termed 'adjustment' or 'anchoring'. Typically, adjustments are insufficient at both ends of the scale. And different starting points yield different estimates, which are biased towards the initial value. Take five seconds to estimate the total product of this line of numbers going from left to right:

$$8 \times 7 \times 6 \times 5 \times 4 \times 3 \times 2 \times 1$$

then five seconds to estimate

$$1 \times 2 \times 3 \times 4 \times 5 \times 6 \times 7 \times 8$$

or try it on any two acquaintances with ten seconds to spare.

To answer such questions rapidly, people perform a few steps of computation and estimate the final total by extrapolation or adjustment. Because the results of the first few steps of multiplication are higher in the descending sequence than in the ascending one, the former is judged higher than the latter. When the test was given to high school students, the median answer for the ascending sequence was 512, while the median answer for the descending sequence was 2,250. What did you get? The correct answer is 40,320.

It is also worth noting, so far as gambling is concerned, that different people have different feelings about the same bet. In other words that there is a subjective estimate of value. Two quarters risked on a pinball machine by a pair of teenage boys may be every bit as significant to them as twenty-five dollars doubled down on a blackjack hand to their parents on a night out at a casino, while the same twenty-five chip might be flipped to the cocktail waitress by a gambler betting in units of five hundred. It's all according. A still further distinction exists between this subjective value of the bet itself and the subjective value or 'pleasure' afforded by the actual process of playing the machine or playing the blackjack hand – positive or negative – in the excitement and anxiety it arouses. As has been pointed out, we all have different base-lines from which to measure risk and opportunity. So, quite apart from the odds, there are three elements in a bet: its real value, its subjective worth and its excitement quotient.

To take a personal illustration: I am a member of a group of friends who play five-minute chess for 50 pence a game. The monetary result is insignificant, the price of a cup of coffee; but the subjective value of winning those games goes beyond mere price, and I have witnessed more rows at the chessboard over these trivial sums than I ever have at the poker table playing for hundreds.

When the big money players in Las Vegas play a game of golf, for instance, the amounts wagered are by any ordinary standards, hysterical. A $10,000 Nassau – ten grand on the first nine holes, ten on the second, and ten on the overall result – is merely for starters. With side bets, a round can easily get up to six figures. The players simply wouldn't 'feel' it playing for hundreds.

I have been particularly struck by the colossal bets which the top poker players like to wager on football and other sports, because, properly speaking, these men are not 'gamblers' in their chosen calling. They play a game of skill and depend on their talent at it to survive, like chess masters. Anyone among them can reel off percentages down to three places of decimals, on the probabilities of a particular hand of cards. Yet in sports bets they go wild. They wager $50,000 or $100,000 on events which are not only inherently unpredictable, and on which the odds are against them, but on which their own evidence (going back to the 'representative' heuristic) is hopelessly subjective. What happens is that one team 'looks good', while the rival quarterback couldn't throw a tea-towel. Or the full-back had a problem with his girlfriend last week, but now they're back together. 'I tell ya, I wouldn't give a wooden nickel for that bunch of no-hopers from the East Coast,' and so on. Evidence? Schmevidence.

Betting on horses and football is a huge business in Las Vegas. While off-track betting is illegal in the rest of the United States, a good deal of money finds its way to Nevada. I must admit that the set-up in the Nevada sports books, as betting shops are called, is the nearest thing to gambling Heaven yet devised.

Imagine a lecture hall, with long rows of seats, each with its own table top, banked up around a wide semi-circle. Down below, across the front of the room, is a line of six or eight television monitors showing, thanks to satellite, every race meeting, every football game, every important sporting event, taking place in the United States. To the side of the TV screens are the betting windows.

Imagine, further, that while you sit there, studying the form and racing sheets and all the other paraphernalia available, that you can order up any drinks you like, on the house. What a deal! It's like being a student all over again but without any grades. Only one tiny snag . . . you gotta pick the winner.

You want a line on a football match, a baseball game, college basketball or any other event coast to coast, the sports book has got it. As one of the leading oddsmakers in town, Michael Roxborough, known everywhere as Roxy, explained it to me, the line is calculated on the basis that each bettor wages 11 to win 10, which gives the bookmakers a theoretical edge of $4\frac{1}{2}$ per cent. (The bookmaker takes in 22 dollars and pays out 21, leaving a profit of $\frac{1}{22} = 4.55$ per cent.)

The line reflects the oddsmaker's assessment of the teams, but is also cunningly designed to look attractive to supporters of both sides, to encourage betting on each. The sports books work to a fine margin, but they do have an ace in the hole: the set-up in the casinos is located close to the gaming tables. Anyone clever or lucky enough to call it right and walk away with a fistful of dollars has got to navigate his way past the tables on the way out.

Sports bettors are not the only ones given to self-delusion. Another aspect of anchoring is that people tend to over-estimate the probability of events which are joined together (conjunctive events) and under-estimate events which seem to be separate (disjunctive events). This kind of bias is especially prevalent in political life. It leads to over-optimism in assessing the likelihood that a plan with many steps in it (like managing the economy) will succeed or a long-range project be completed on time. Conversely it leads to under-estimation of the risk that, say, a nuclear reactor, dependent on many separate components, will malfunction (look at Chernobyl or the U S space program); or for that matter, that a complex system like one's own body will continue in good working order.

Conjunctive events make good sucker bets. One of the most familiar, which I repeat here in case you don't know it, concerns how many people need to be in the same room before it is better than an even money bet that at least two of them share the same birthday. The answer, which confounds most people's intuitive reaction, based on the fact that there are 365 days in the year, is surprising: 23.

The probability of a second person in the room having the same birthday as the first person is $1/365$, so the probability of having a different birthday is $364/365$. The probability for the third person having a different birthday from each of the other two is $363/365$, for the fourth person $362/365$, and so on. The probability that they will all have different birthdays is the product of all these individual probabilities, i.e. $364/365 \times 363/365 \times 362/365 \times \ldots\ldots$, and by the time there are 23 people in the room, this sum works out at just under 0.5. So, with 23 people in the room it is slightly more than 50 per cent likely that at least two of them will have the same birthday.

The essential point which intuitive judgement misses in assessing conjunctive events is that when a lot of probabilities are multiplied together, even if they are all very near to 1 (i.e. the likelihood of each individual case is close to 100 per cent), their product gets smaller very quickly. By contrast, in disjunctive events intuition tends to underestimate probabilities: if every single component in an aeroplane is 99.9999 per cent reliable, and there are half a million components in the plane, the probability of at least one component breaking down is approximately $500,000 \times 0.0001$ per cent, which is 50 per cent.

The argument put forward by psychologists like Tversky and Kahneman (whose findings I have considerably over-simplified) is that an analysis of the heuristics that a person uses in judging the probability of an event may reveal whether his judgement is likely to be too high or too low. Subjective probabilities play an important role in everyone's life.

The decisions we make, the conclusions we reach, and the explanations we offer are usually based on the judgements of the likelihood of uncertain events such as success in a new job, the outcome of an election, or the state of the market . . . Although no systematic theory about the psychology of uncertainty has emerged . . . perhaps the most general conclusion obtained from numerous investigations is that people do not follow the principles of probability theory in judging the likelihood of uncertain events.

Biases that people have are inherent in their way of judging things, not a product of differences in motivation, such as wishful thinking or monetary reward. Experienced people, trained in statistics, may avoid elementary errors such as the gambler's fallacy, but they also go wrong when they think intuitively about more complex problems.

The reason why we do not learn what our personal biases are from everyday experience is that the relevant information isn't in a form that can be easily checked out. If one kept a record of events that actually occurred, measured against the probability that one assigned to them in advance, that would help. But that is not the way people think. If it were one might discover, for example, that only 50 per cent of the predictions to which one gave a very high probability, say 0.9, came true. (In my own work, as a journalist commenting on foreign affairs, I have found that one tends to savour the times that one calls it right – like making a winning bet – but tends even more to have total amnesia over the many other times one gets it wrong. The prudent newspaper reader or TV viewer makes, instinctively, an estimate of the reliability, that is the probability, of the journalist's or broadcaster's accuracy. When it comes to official Government statements, people frequently assume the opposite of what is claimed is the truth!)

Yes, to err is human, and to err in assessment of probability is all too human. That is what the human mind is like, an uncertain instrument. Of course one may say that, given a little practice, given a few lessons in probability theory, one wouldn't make these mistakes. Not so: experts make mistakes too. Besides, gamblers do not normally think in this way. Quite the reverse: they operate on a hunch, feel, lucky numbers, a sense of the dice being hot, intuitive feelings, omens, random happenings about them, flying high on a wing and a prayer. 'Although a rational mind (as playwright Jack Richardson has put it) must insist that the grimace of a stranger or a moment of intestinal agony has no causal link to the way cards will fall, it is nevertheless true that a gambler's instinct comprehends relations between events that are perhaps too subtle for ordinary modes of observation. It is this instinct on which his survival is based, for if he ignores it

... he becomes ... someone doomed to be unloved by fortune and destroyed by mathematics.' (*Memoir of a Gambler*, 1979.)

True gamblers go further, in deliberately ignoring probabilities in favour of their gut feelings. Is there a man so base who will not forever cherish the memory of the great Sky Masterson, nonchalant hero of Damon Runyon's story *The Idyll of Miss Sarah Brown?* 'Of all the high players this country ever sees, there is no doubt but that the guy they call The Sky is the highest. In fact, the reason he is called The Sky is because he goes so high when it comes to betting on any proposition whatever. He will bet all he has, and nobody can bet any more than this . . . and furthermore The Sky never wishes to play with any but the best of it himself, or anyway not much . . . The Sky is strictly a player . . . as far as The Sky is concerned, money is just something for him to play with and the dollars may as well be doughnuts as far as value goes with him.'

I cannot resist quoting the immortal advice given to Sky by his father when he left his home town, which stood him in such good stead in his whole life:

Son . . . no matter how far you travel, or how smart you get, always remember this: Some day, somewhere . . . a guy is going to come to you and show you a nice brand-new deck of cards on which the seal is never broken, and this guy is going to offer to bet you that the jack of spades will jump out of this deck and squirt cider in your ear. But, son . . . do not bet him, for as sure as you do you are going to get an ear full of cider.

What Sky Masterson wants is what we all want, action. Where the action is – what a compelling phrase! It promises excitement, challenge, movement . . . a tautening of the nerves . . . a subliminal hint even of hand-to-hand combat . . . Action! It expresses the whole gambling experience. The very sound of it is like cracking open the breech.

To a gambler it's irresistible, and not only to gamblers. Where the action is implies life being lived in a higher register, in a faster and more intensified form. The phrase 'where the action is' was first used in this same Damon Runyon story (1947), according to the lexicographers at the Oxford English Dictionary – 'New Orleans, and Chicago, and Los Angeles, and wherever else there is any action in the way of card-playing, or crap-shooting, or horse-racing, or betting on the baseball games, for The Sky is always moving around the country following the action.' In the mid-1960s the term 'action' was taken up in chic magazines and caught on everywhere, especially in commercials and advertising. It met the mood of the times.

Action! But what is it, where is it? 'Wherever action is found, chance-taking is sure to be,' as the late social psychologist Erwin Goffman, one of the sharpest observers of contemporary mores, has noted. In everyday life the individual takes chances, in changing his job or moving house, or if you like, in taking a wife (marriage is a lottery, my boy), but the outcome of these kinds of life-decision usually takes years to resolve. The distinctive property of games and contests is that once the bet has been made, outcome is determined and payoff awarded all in the same breath of experience. A single sharp focus of awareness is sustained at high pitch during the full span of the play.

One might start by asking: Where is the action *not* to be found? Not, ordinarily, during the week-day routine at home or at work. For here 'chance-takings tend to be organized out'. A person's activities mesh with other people's, in a regulated way – work goes on, life goes on, and one may never be aware of the risk and opportunity that in fact existed. The choices may be 'consequential' – they may have an impact in due course – but not 'problematic' – the decisions made are shared in a social framework. Or take, to make the point more clearly, the opposite situation of passing time for its own sake – a man with say half an hour to spare before leaving home: he can read a magazine until it is time to go, watch TV, do a crossword: his choice of activity may be 'problematic' – he can choose one thing or another – but it is not 'consequential' to the main course of his life. Action is both.

Action is to be found wherever the individual knowingly takes consequential chances perceived as avoidable. In his essay 'Where The Action Is' (*Interaction Ritual*, 1967), Goffman suggested that action occurs in three places: first, in commercialized competitive sport; next, in non-spectator risky sports; and third, in commercialized places of action – a light degree of action in bowling alleys, pool halls, amusement parks and arcades, a heavier degree at race tracks and casinos. The point about these activities is that they are undertaken for their own sake, as distinct from a risky occupation like being a soldier or a fireman or, say, an oil-capper. Commercialized sport is watched for fun, so it does not seem really serious, Goffman says (despite sport being a business venture), an impression reinforced by the fact that amateurs also do it, solely for the challenge.

One other type of commercialized action involving direct participation is included in his list, the social whirl of conspicuous consumption, seeing and being seen (surely the sexual chase should be included, too, but more of that in a moment), termed 'fancy milling'. Hotel casinos provide an extreme example:

Not only are money gambles made available, this type of action is overlaid with the consumption kind. A brief penetration into high living is laid on. Attendant-parked limousines are cluttered at the entrance. Beyond the entrance, the setting is luxurious. Liquor is served at the tables, often at no cost to the consumer. A quality buffet may be provided, allowing for discriminative gorging. A gratuity system is encouraged that elevates its users and provides scantily clad waitresses selected for their looks . . . Table contact is facilitated with the nationally known and with big spenders. Proximity to what some might consider the gangster element is also provided. Easy access to nationally famous entertainment is assured . . . In brief, the opportunity for ephemeral ennoblement abounds.

Certainly this sort of scene corresponds with any one of half a dozen chromium palaces on the Las Vegas strip, though I would rate its social appeal fairly low down the scale. The 'fancy milling' simply gives a shine to the action, like gloss paint. The saturation of the senses by soft lighting, alcohol, music and noise, the absence of clocks or any link with reality outside, the sexual current pulsating round the edge, the glint of violence from armed guards, all serve to disinhibit the gambler and warp players' judgement – what bets to take, how high to play, when to quit.

People will likewise gamble for high stakes in the sleaziest of dives. In gaming, the less inhibition, the more action.

The point which Goffman goes on to make is how efficient casinos are in facilitating action: you need only walk through the doors – in fact there may not even be a door to the street – and put down your stake. If the dealer is not already in play, he will immediately get moving. Shills [house players] are on hand to make up a table if needed. If you want to sit down without having to gamble, however, the only seats available (apart from in the washroom) are at the bar, where a toothsome keno [a version of bingo] girl will very likely waylay you. Play is designed to provide action not only around the (imaginary) clock, not only at all levels of betting, but for all manner of people regardless of their social status, or state of decorum (*déshabillé*, drunk, zonked out).

All this free hospitality which gamblers receive – not just in Las Vegas or Atlantic City, or London or Monte Carlo, but wherever there is high action – is immensely seductive. As all gamblers understand, there are two kinds of money – money for gambling, which is essential, and money for living, which is a marginal, even niggling affair – bills, food, hire purchase repayments, family expenses. So when the casino picks up the tab, for the hotel room, for meals, for drinks – what a joy! None of your serious gambling money is going to be 'wasted' on real goods and services. The collective extension of these acts of individual generosity is organized hospitality, known as junkets. A junket is the most inveigling of all introductions to gambling: it seems like something for nothing. The reality is a whole heap of minuses for a very little plus.

The idea started some years back when a stockholder of the Flamingo hotel-casino flew a planeload of wealthy friends from Miami to Las Vegas to show off his hotel. The hotel absorbed the cost of the round-trip charter flight and RFB (complimentary room, food and beverage, in the trade jargon). While the party was staying at the hotel, the casino recorded its biggest ever drop (total money wagered). After this experience the Flamingo, as an experiment, began inviting premium customers from a few major cities to take complimentary trips, all expenses paid.

The experiment proved so successful (as reported in *Casino Management* by Bill Friedman, 1982) that the Flamingo expanded its program and other hotels on the strip started doing the same thing. 'The sole purpose of a junket is to generate casino business,' as this manual correctly states. Consequently 'the customers' gambling losses must be greater than the hotel's expenses.' Obvious enough, even to the junketeer: so why do they fall for it?

Well, there is something extraordinarily gratifying about being the beneficiary of a junket, beyond enjoying the freebies. (I have benefited myself, not as a serious gambler, but as the friend of a genuine high roller.) The appeal lies in being treated as nobility in a dream world, a grown-ups' candy store where everything is granted as soon as you point to it. Here's a small (if slightly disgraceful) example of what I mean, which occurred at Laughlin, the new Nevada resort on the Arizona border. It's Saturday night of Memorial weekend, the line waiting outside the gourmet restaurant is 150 people long, there's no chance of a table for a couple of hours, everyone is dying on their feet for a drink. Enter the favoured high roller. Allakazam! One whisper to the Maître d' and the whole party is whisked over to a corner table and the cocktail waitress is preening her embonpoint at your side. Choose any array of dishes, any vintage (I recall another sacrilegious moment, swigging down a bottle of Château Lafite '59 with chop suey and chocolate cake), all you have to do is ask.

It's all false but the illusion of having anything you want for nothing exactly matches the gambling experience. The junketeer, air fare paid and free board at the hotel, feels that he is several hundred bucks ahead before he even gets to the tables. Anyway, maybe this is his lucky night . . . Why not? It's all in the roll of the dice.

Anyone who seeks action can find it – and not just in a casino. One can bet on anything, anywhere – the raindrops running down a window-pane if you like – as it were, constructing action out of nothing. Not mature people like you or me, of course. Or do you, by any chance, smoke? That's a bad risk which many of us take. Or eat too much cholesterol? Or drive too fast? In a sense, all life is risk. There's no safety in numbers, James Thurber once declared, there's no safety anywhere. But gamblers seek risk for its own sake. Hence the attraction in casino games of 'letting it ride' by leaving a winning bet on the table, especially at dice or blackjack, with the chance of doubling it on the next coup, and then if it wins, doubling it again, and so on (an exponential increase in action) reversing the gambler's fallacy of doubling up on losing stakes.

Where the action is – in sport, in gambling – seems to tilt rather to the masculine side of life. Like cowboy movies, the drama is always the male in action; although women may be around, they don't count in quite the same way. Yet why shouldn't women be drawn to action just as men are? No doubt about it, there are women gamblers in plenty, as any casino will show. The one field of action, however, in which men and women figure equally, or shall we say on equal terms, is elsewhere: the 'battle of the sexes'.

The sexual pursuit is surely a pre-eminent example of action. It's all there: the thrill of the challenge, the joys and entrancement of success, the pain of rejection. I am not suggesting that the delights of sex can be reduced to an equation of risk-taking: but at the same time can anyone deny the excitement-of-the-chase as an extremely powerful motive? Or that attainment of the desired objective – as with winning at gambling – also holds, within itself, the seed of a new challenge? Look at Mozart's Don Giovanni, for one.

All 'thrills', it has been suggested, consist of a mixture of fear, pleasure and hope. That is to say, some amount of conscious fear, or at least an awareness of real external danger, a voluntary and intentional exposing of oneself to this external danger and to the fears aroused by it, while having the more or less confident hope that the fear can be tolerated and mastered, the danger will pass, and that one will be able to return unharmed to safety.

This description (*Thrills and Regressions* by Michael Balint, 1959), applied specifically to fairground amusements like swings, roundabouts and switchbacks, is associated with a sense of giddiness and vertigo, leading to a loss of balance, of stability, of firm contact with the earth. The same sort of sensations come from high-speed activities such as racing, skiing, flying and so on; likewise from exposed situations like rock climbing, taming wild animals, travelling into unknown lands. Or yet again, unfamiliar or new forms of experience, new gratifications – there is an overtly sexual connotation in expressions like 'virgin peak' and 'virgin land'. Any new sexual partner is a thrill, the author adds, especially if he or she belongs to another race, colour or creed.

Certainly the three basic elements of thrills described above, a fear of danger, voluntary exposure to it, and hope that all will turn out well in the end, are present also in most sexual liaisons:

The usual pattern is that the individual is prompted – either by his own urges or by external stimulation – to abandon the safe zone of tranquil existence, expose himself more or less voluntarily to situations which inevitably increase the tension he has to bear, in the hope that his skills will enable him to enjoy these situations, release the tension by gratifying his urges, and that eventually he will be able to return unharmed to the safety of tranquil existence.

That would also seem to be an exact description of what action in gambling is all about, would it not? So to revert to Goffman's analysis, though many men shy away from involving themselves in 'making out', there are many others who are everywhere on the lookout – and equally many women too – for these opportunities, whether in the home, at work, or in other contacts. 'These chronically oriented males must be classed with those who are ready to transform any event into a betting proposition, or any task into a contest of strength, skill or knowledge.' When it comes to action, one might say, the bed is just as important as the gaming table:

> Th' expense of spirit in a waste of shame
> Is lust in action

to take an earlier, Shakespearean use of the term.

Something meaningful and peculiar seems to be involved in action, Goffman concludes: a test of character under pressure. In gambling, it is an individual's conduct when the chips are down:

qualities such as courage, 'gamble', gameness, integrity, gallantry, above all composure. To the extent that other people are watching, a person's character in this sense of the term is itself 'on the line', gambled. Action, then is not just, or not only, to be seen as impulsive or irrational conduct in taking on risks; it is also a means of showing character, of acquiring it or losing it.

One might argue one way or the other over the precise mix of qualities. Everyone recognizes 'character' when it's there – 'the right stuff' in Tom Wolfe's celebrated paean to the astronauts.

... in this fraternity, even though it was military, men were not rated by their outward rank as ensigns, lieutenants, commanders, or whatever. No, herein the world was divided into those who had it and those who did not. This quality, this *it*, was never named, however, nor was it talked about in any way.

As to just what this ineffable quality was ... well, it obviously involved bravery. But it was not bravery in the simple sense of being willing to risk your life. ... No, the idea here ... seemed to be that a man should have the ability to go up in a hurtling piece of machinery and put his hide on the line and then have the moxie, the reflexes, the experience, the coolness to pull it back in the last yawning moment – and then to go up again *the next day*, and the next day, and every next day, even if the series should prove infinite.

The Right Stuff, 1979

The crucial point about the astronauts was that they were engaged in single-handed combat. The spacecraft, the rockets, might be complex beyond belief, but the men inside them were seen as champions, possessed of the derring-do, in modern guise, of chivalric heroes. Gambling is also single combat. You can always tell, in a poker game, who's got the right stuff, because it is essentially a game of character. In all gambling games, despite the fact that the player may be taking on an inanimate object – a wheel or a pair of dice or a deck of cards – the qualities of character under pressure show up. It's what separates, as they say, the men from the boys.

In seeking where the action is, part of what one is doing, I believe, is putting one's qualities of character on trial, not for other people, but for oneself. It is a test of each individual's mettle, a test of how far a man can go in gambling, knowing that basically the chances are against him, a test of many difficult decisions – in setting a limit and sticking to it or not sticking to it, in how high, how fast and how long to play, above all when to quit. 'You gotta know when to hold 'em and know when to fold 'em', as the song says. Is it overly self-regarding to play the game as a test of one's character for oneself? The greatest advantage in gambling, in the wise words of Cardano, lies in not playing at all. So why do it? Because of the craving for action!

The argument, of course, is circular: it does not explain why people who want action should choose gambling as their outlet, as opposed to some other place where action can be found: in sport, high risk jobs, the sexual chase. The many studies that have been done on why people gamble, of what makes gamblers, produce conflicting answers. Everyone gambles one way or another in their lives: by the same token, it seems, everyone needs action.

Casino gambling offers the quickest, easiest, most clear-cut opportunity for action. It is doubly risky because in the first place the chances are against the player, and in the second place, the managements of casinos are doing their damnedest to seduce people to gamble, to lower their resistance to prudence and caution, to take even more risks. Many other people are bored by gambling. Their need for action, which I take it is part of the human condition, is satisfied in other ways – some more risky to life and limb, if less costly in monetary terms.

But what, you may object, about people who do not want to take any risk, who want a quiet life? To some extent we all get vicarious thrills from watching others taking risks, in movies, in TV serials, in sport, in detective stories and thrillers, in political and public life. There is no end to it, because action proves we are fully alive.

One of the sharpest hustlers about town, known in his day as Sal the dice man, once put it this way: If I've got action, anything is possible. If I haven't got action, nothing is possible.

III

EUROPE & AMERICA

8

MAUVAISE ÉPOQUE

Rouge perd, et noir perd, mais c'est
toujours Blanc qui gagne

It's quite an achievement to lose money running a casino, but one or two manage it. The most celebrated gaming establishment in Europe, *Le Société des Bains de Mer* in Monte Carlo lost over 12m francs on its gaming activities in 1984–5, which was well over £1m, and over 30m francs in 1985–6, which was about £3.25m. It made a small profit in 1986–87, which was wiped out by bad debts from a group of roulette players, leaving a deficit on the year of 15m francs (£1·6m).

What saved the board's face was the fortunate fact that the American-run Loews casino, just down the hill, showed a hefty profit, of which the *Société des Bains de Mer*'s 50 per cent share was worth very nearly 36m francs in 1985 (£3.8m), and 44m francs (£4.7m) in 1986 and 38m francs (£4m) in 1978. Given that the two casinos are so close together, one up the hill and one down, their results make an intriguing contrast between European and American methods of management.

In its annual report the SBM blamed the 1985 gaming loss on an increase in salaries of the casino staff by 10 per cent, while income fell by 1 per cent. It congratulated itself, overall, on 'an honourable result'. Loews income rose only marginally, so yielding a profit of around 13 per cent was, presumably, very honourable indeed. The excuse offered by the SBM for the increase in its losses on gaming in 1986 was weakness in European (single-zero) roulette exacerbated by certain difficulties in collecting bad debts. At the same time Loews had racked their profits up to 14 per cent of gaming income. I decided to take a closer look at the *Société des Bains de Mer*.

Monte Carlo today presents a very different face from the Monte Carlo of even twenty years ago, which still displayed, like the fringe of a silk petticoat, just a nuance of the great days of the *Belle Epoque*, that heady, leisurely, elegant period which extended from the *fin de siècle* 1890s down to the outbreak of the First World War in 1914. Now, between the high rise blocks and the underground parking, the strongest impression on a visitor's senses is of exhaust fumes from the traffic jams. The air in the narrow roads around the old casino, especially on windless August days, makes one choke. The port is jammed with oily cruise boats.

Nor is there any relief to be found in climbing up the steps to enter the casino itself. It is, frankly, tawdry. The one consolation – and it is worth the detour, as the Michelin Guide might put it – is its fading décor. The gaming salons, with their ceiling-high murals of dark-eyed damsels in wistful contemplation – what are they dreaming of, rouge or noir on the next spin? – revive memories of bygone days. A balm against the sweaty styleless shambles of cheap gaming all around.

What Monte Carlo has kept is the talisman of its name. It is still evocative of high life, princes and courtesans, fortunes won and lost, gold coins heaped across the tables and suicide in the gardens outside, 'the man who broke the bank at Monte Carlo', and all that. Though even he, a British engineer named Charles Wells, turned out to be a bit of a fraud. The system he used back in 1892 to break the bank (which meant emptying the table of its reserve of plaques) was based on luck; when his luck ran out, the unfortunate fellow resorted to trickery, finally landing up in prison.

Yet despite Monte Carlo having changed out of all recognition, the name of the place is still synonymous with gambling, and has been so for over a hundred years, all around the world. What a triumph of marketing! This achievement, which any modern public relations man might envy, was the inspiration of a nineteenth-century entrepreneur. His technique in promoting gaming was two or three generations ahead of his time, to be exploited more fully, like so many other ideas of the old world, when translated to America. (The doors of Bugsy Siegel's Flamingo opened with the invitation 'Come as you are to America's Monte Carlo'.)

François Blanc grew up in the countryside of south-west France and, with his brother Louis, tried his hand as a young man in a variety of jobs in the big cities. They both had a gift for cards, practised the games of the time with each other, and were smart enough to make a little money in the cheap gaming houses. Their first financial success was in that most respectable casino of finance, the Stock Exchange. From their little agency in Bordeaux they devised a method of discovering the movement of consols on the Paris bourse, via a semaphore message signalled from hill-top to hill-top (the Rothschilds could afford their own special couriers or used carrier pigeons) so as to get advance information on the way the market was going. This clever scheme finally came unstuck when the brothers were charged with corrupting a telegraph official, but not before they had made quite a lot of money.

Moving up to Paris, they quickly saw the opportunities in gaming, particularly in Germany, whose assorted duchies and principalities had no ban on gambling. They secured a concession to open a casino in Hesse-Homburg. From the start, running the little pump-room, they were successful, advertising in the French papers and attracting gamblers from other German resorts by removing the second zero from roulette (a lesson which the combined wisdom of managements in Nevada and New Jersey has still failed to apply) and reducing the bank's advantage in trente-et-quarante (the card game played in French casinos). The new casino they built, and the villas and hotels which sprang up all around, in due course served to transform what was a crumbling hilltop fortress into a fashionable spa.

'The real casino was opened with great pomp and ceremony. Over two hundred people sat down to a banquet. The walls of the large gambling salon were covered with silver-grey silk; the chairs were gleaming gilt; no expense had been spared. The effect was immediate, particularly as, in spite of their depleted bank account, the brothers continued to advertise in the leading French newspapers.' It was not just the medicinal and climatic attractions of Homburg which were advertised; their brochures claimed, for instance, that the town was 'filled with young, lovely and exquisitely dressed women, perfumed with the fragrance of flowers and animated by music and dancing.' Mm . . . mm . . . all this, and gambling too.

The story of the Blancs, and much colourful detail besides, is related in Charles Graves' *The Big Gamble* (1951). François Blanc's success in Homburg owed much to his adroit handling of the press, as Graves notes, but perhaps even more to the way in which he set out to attract gamblers and dazzle them with his opulent style. That is very modern, as was his encouragement of the French railway companies to hasten extension of their lines towards the Rhine (in our day, cheapo flights to Las Vegas). When, as sometimes happened, players had big runs of luck and huge wins, which actually threatened the financial stability of the casino, Blanc did not panic. He calmly advertised these winners' successes in the French and British press. Brilliant! At the same time, the intrepid Blanc ran newspaper campaigns in Nice and Italy to persuade local public opinion against the opening of casinos in rival resorts!

Quite an operator – so it was no surprise when he was invited by the destitute ruler of Monaco, Prince Charles III, to take over the casino there in 1862. Blanc, who had had his eye on the place for some while, drove a very hard bargain, and got what he wanted. Within 24 hours he drew up the articles of the *Société des Bains de Mer et Cercle des Étrangers*. The town was renamed Monte Carlo in honour of the ailing prince.

Blanc next proceeded to carry out on a larger scale the programme he had run in Hesse-Homburg. He chartered a steamer to ferry people over from Nice and a fleet of hackney carriages to take them by road, began rebuilding the casino – meanwhile increasing the stakes and introducing a single zero – and completing the Hotel de Paris in sumptuous style, lobbied for improved road and rail links and orchestrated newspaper publicity across the continent, stressing particularly the 'aristocratic' character of the clientele. (Some resounding names were made up for effect.)

Now in his late fifties, Blanc was as full of vigour as ever, and greatly assisted in his work by his young wife Marie, his main partner since the death of his brother some years before. A village girl, daughter of a cobbler near Hesse, Blanc at first had been taken by her extraordinarily pretty looks, but hesitated about proposing marriage; then a widower of 42, he was 27 years her senior. So, with her father's approval, he had sent the girl to Paris for four years to be educated and polished, and given a Parisian accent, to turn her into a suitable consort for the illustrious chairman of a society casino – if, when the time came, she herself should give her consent to matrimony, which she did. It proved an excellent match; they had a son and a daughter. It was Marie who thought of bringing in the Comédie Française to Homburg, to attract the customers (like the modern casino floor show), and who now persuaded Blanc to introduce the *viatique*, the hand-out for heavy losers, which became so celebrated in Monte Carlo (a version of a complimentary ticket for high rollers).

The *viatique* was not quite so free and easy under the Blancs as modern freebies, as this charming account from a little handbook *Ten Days at Monte Carlo at the Bank's Expense* by V.B. (1898) makes clear: 'If you apply to the Administration, you have first got to swear that you have lost over £300 (say £10,000 at 1980 prices); they will then take you round the Rooms like a criminal, in order that the croupiers at the tables where you have played may identify you and confirm your statement. . . .

'After this you are photographed, and once more taken round to be shown to all the doorkeepers, who are then given orders not to admit you any more. Next, you have to sign a promissory note for the amount of your travelling expenses, and instead of giving you the money, you are told that an employee of the establishment will meet you at the station at such and such an hour, and hand you a second-class ticket to your destination.'

The stories of suicides by ruined gamblers have been greatly exaggerated, Monaco's average being pretty constant year by year. The original story, supposed to be true, was of the gambler who smeared his face with tomato sauce, fired his revolver in the air, and threw himself down in a clump of bushes. The casino staff, so the story goes, stuffed his pockets with banknotes to avert any scandal that he had taken his life in despair at his losses; whereupon the dead man got up, dusted himself down and returned to the tables.

Under the dynamic management of the Blancs, Monte Carlo could hardly fail to prosper. It became in those golden days of the 1880s and 1890s the pinnacle of society at play. Thus the author of *Ten Days at Monte Carlo* arriving at Ciro's for luncheon: 'At a table in the window, the Grand Duke Michael and Countess Torby were entertaining the Duke and Duchess of Connaught and the Crown Prince and Princess of Roumania. At the next table the Lord Chief Justice and Lady Russell . . . Sloan, the little American jockey who was a most comical sight sitting next to the portly form of 'Gaiety George'. A well known Lombard Street banker had a cheery party of ladies . . . The legal and political element was very strongly represented . . . the Speaker of the House of Commons . . . the popular Conservative whip . . . the Stage [represented] by Miss Miriam Clements, 'La Belle Juniori', and Fanny Ward . . . Music by Tosti and Sir Arthur Sullivan . . . London Society was also well to the fore, and among the best-known we made out . . . Lord and Lady Wolverton, Lord and Lady 'Algy' Lennox, the Duke and Duchess of Leeds . . . If you add to all these a sprinkling of superbly dressed *demi-mondaines*, some foreign notabilities, a few barristers, City men, and stockbrokers, you will have a very fair idea of Ciro's restaurant during the Monte Carlo season.'

The meticulous V.B., who had a keen eye for value, also gives the menu on that occasion: Hors d'oeuvres variés, Oeufs pochés Grand Duc, Mostele à l'Anglaise, Volaille en Casserole à la Fermière, Patisserie, Fromage, Café, Château Carbonnieux 1891, Fine Champagne, 1846, total bill for four people 62 francs. 'After a cigar,' V.B. adds, 'we paid a visit to Smith's Bank next door, drew out our capital of £600, and then strolled across to the concert at the Casino.' Ah, those heady days! The photographs of all these long vanished notabilities, with their double-breasted suits, high collars and cravats, with their canes or yachting caps, their confident, roguish air, accompanied by their curvaceous ladies, daughters of the game, in their pearls and their ankle-length silk dresses, gives one a pang for a world forever gone.

As I walk along the Bois de Boulogne
With an independent air
You can hear the girls declare
He must be a millionaire!
You can hear them sigh and wish to die,
You can see them wink the hopeful eye
At the man who broke the bank at Monte Carlo!

The name of the Prince of Wales was kept out of the English newspapers (though not in the Tranby Croft affair, the notorious scandal over cheating at baccarat at a country house party, at which the Prince was present); he travelled under the name of Captain White (a play on the name Monsieur Blanc); to him is attributed the pretty saying that sometimes noir wins, sometimes rouge wins, but Blanc never loses. Edward's passion was baccarat. Not so his mother, Queen Victoria: she disdainfully sent back to the infernal casino a welcoming bouquet of flowers, and on a brief visit to the Rock delivered a regal snub to its ruler by ostentatiously declining to call on him.

François Blanc died in 1877, leaving a fortune of £3,600,000. Marie was still only 43. She continued the business, constructing a grand theatre which proved such a huge success – Sarah Bernhardt gave a recitation at the opening gala – that she then had to enlarge the casino. Blanc's son (by his first marriage) Camille took over as managing director on Marie's early demise a few years later. He rapidly proved as astute as his father, both in countering the anti-gambling lobbies which were continually springing up across the continent and in creating new forms of publicity to keep the name of Monte Carlo in the public eye. He commissioned new operas for the theatre and attracted musicians and actors of international renown. He knew that such artistes were not really expensive, however high their fees, because so many of them loved to gamble. Sarah Bernhardt was particularly unlucky at the tables, as was Chaliapin later on. ('I did it my way', as another entertainer of casino audiences sang a century later.)

Monte Carlo continued to thrive under Camille Blanc's direction. His success, like that of his father before him, was based on attracting the public at large, and dazzling people with shows, with luxury, with the ambience of aristocracy at play. He introduced tennis tournaments, *concours d'élégance* of motor cars, fashion parades. In those days, when the *beau monde* travelled to Monte Carlo from far and wide, it was not for a couple of nights on the town; people would stay for a month at least, often several weeks, to enjoy the season, which was of course in the winter – the Côte d'Azur did not achieve its apogee as a summer resort until the English, in their eccentric way, took to swimming and sunbathing in the 1920s. 'The casino was making a steady annual profit of a million pounds a year,' Charles Graves sums up in *The Big Gamble*, say around £20m in today's values. And so it went on, with occasional interruptions for minor wars and political mishaps, into the next century.

Camille Blanc also encouraged the publication of every sort of handbook on how to win at gambling. Roulette is the ideal game for *systemiers* or systems followers. The papers were full of arguments about one method over another, and how to win a fortune. One of the most spectacular debates was launched by Sir Hiram Maxim, inventor of the machine gun of that name; he sought to show that even after a long run of red or black, the chances of either colour turning up on the next spin were exactly the same. This drew vehement protests from the supporters of doubling up and other theories of winning. Well, the laws of probability were not so well understood in those days – and even today you can go to any casino in the world and see players at the roulette table writing down the numbers, frowning in concentration over their calculations. I've done it myself and I expect you have too.

Yet (as we all know) there is no method of beating the odds against you in roulette, either by analysing the previous spins or by ingenious staking methods. There is something about roulette, the glitter of the wheel and the magic of the spin, which seems to have hypnotized people, over the years, into believing they could find a way of mastering it. (I was solemnly assured only the other day by a television conjuror, an artist with cards, a man who had previously worked in casinos, that he knew a way of winning at roulette. How? Ah well, it was complicated, it required study, people whom he had explained it to had lacked the patience to make it work.) The problem has defeated generations of gamblers ever since Pascal's treatise on the rolling of wheels, *Histoire de la Roulette*, back in 1657, though the modern game as we know it came in a century later.

Camille had a long and successful run, nearly 50 years, continuing the tradition set by his father. But the First World War had seriously depleted the company's reserves. It was a struggle to get the casino going again. Prince Louis, himself short of money, would not abide any reduction in the annual income paid him by the SBM. He turned to another source of funds, Sir Basil Zaharoff, the international financier and arms dealer. While Camille Blanc was out of town, the wily Zaharoff placed a million pounds at the Prince's disposal; and with his connivance, seized control of the company.

Zaharoff's first step was to oust the former chairman and move in his own nominees. He also put a stop to many of the pensions the company was paying its former staff. The Bright Young Things of the twenties, who had come of age after the war, were in a mood for fun and celebration. The crowds came back, and the casino rapidly picked up, confirming its former reputation as queen of the Côte d'Azur. It was not long before Zaharoff sold his interest in the casino to a French banking consortium, realizing a million and a half pounds profit on the deal, meanwhile retaining the sumptuous Hotel de Paris for himself.

When Camille Blanc died a year or two later, in 1927, the old era, for all its new burst of energy, had less time to run than appearances suggested. The gilded style was beginning its slow fade into the glitzy colours of the Far West. Gambling was legalized in Nevada in 1931 and the focus of casino gambling gradually tilted to the new world, as new attractions and new games opened up over there. The gambling halls of the Wild West, starting slowly, gathered pace through the next decade. It was another burst of energy and gaiety, after the Second World War, which drove Americans in their millions to the tables. The lessons so ably demonstrated by the Blancs, *père et fils*, showed Las Vegas the way.

Monte Carlo, of course, continued to cast its spell, even achieving an image of Hollywood glamour thanks to the dynastic marriage of Grace Kelly (star of *High Society*) with Prince Rainier. But what would the Blancs have made of the management of their great *Société des Bains de Mer*, and the lamentable losses in its *salles des jeux* in the 1980s? It's not hard to imagine their surprise, to put it no more strongly than that.

The usual explanation when a casino loses money is that fraud is going on. After all, with the odds in the house's favour, it should be virtually impossible to lose money, in the long run. No such ugly rumours, however, disfigure Monte Carlo's reputation. Crime in the principality hardly exists, one is assured, except as a police statistic. The Mafia operates in nearby Nice, where gangland killings are a commonplace; and indeed corruption was so widespread that Nice's main surviving casino, the Ruhl, was shut down by the Ministry of the Interior in 1982.

Novelist Graham Greene has given a passionate indictment of the underworld in Nice in his polemic *J'Accuse* (1982). 'Let me issue a warning,' he began, 'to anyone who is tempted to settle for a peaceful life on what is called the Côte d'Azur. Avoid the region of Nice which is the preserve of some of the most criminal organizations in the south of France: they deal in drugs; they have attempted with the connivance of high authorities to take over the casinos in the famous 'war' which left one victim, Agnes Le Roux, the daughter of the main owner of the Palais de la Mediterranée, "missing, believed murdered". They are involved in the building industry which helps to launder their illicit gains; they have close connections with the Italian Mafia.' Mr Greene did not conceal a personal interest in the matter, in that he had befriended a French woman whose daughter was harassed by the mob, and who felt denied all chance of justice; but his allegations evidently had much substance.

The corruption in the 'milieu' was so bad that all new applications to reopen a casino – there had been a municipal casino in the Place Masséna as well as the more glittery establishment in the Hotel Ruhl – were successively turned down by the Ministry until 1987. The ban on casino gaming in Nice left a huge gap in its entertainment resources, and to that extent was a direct benefit to Monte Carlo. But to no avail. The trouble with the SBM was internal, in the management's inability, in particular, to get to grips with the privileged and extravagant conditions of life of the croupiers.

The croupiers have preserved many advantages down the years through which they enjoy an extraordinarily high standard of living. Many are earning salaries of $100,000 a year, and certainly make more money than the transient gamblers so generously tossing them tips across the table – *'Merci! Pour le personnel!'* – when they have a winning coup. The croupiers' various perks and benefits are carefully graded down the ranks, from the *directeur* to *sous-directeur* to *inspecteur* to *chef de table* to the croupier who rakes in the losers' chips. And nothing can be done to change this structure, according to the hapless management, because of the 'historical weight' of tradition. In Monte Carlo tradition is very important.

What's more, in such a tiny place, a mile square, with a Monegasque population of only 4,000, the 200 croupiers employed at the casino represent a sizeable proportion of the electorate. They have the political clout to block any changes in the structure of the SBM which might be proposed in the parliamentary assembly. On the contrary, they are in a position, year by year, to protect and improve their terms of employment. There are many little benefits jealously preserved – for instance, they like to be paid in cash, even though there is no income tax in the principality.

The management's other problem is the changing nature of the gamblers themselves. The *grand joueurs*, the big money players, demand more and more concessions in the way of 'comps' [complimentary services]. Favoured players in former days might be offered a suite at the Hotel de Paris. Now they want first class tickets and free board for a wife or mistress, perhaps a second room for children. They can get away with such demands by claiming that if Monte Carlo won't give it them, they know other casinos which will. Most of Monte Carlo's big players come from Italy. In 1986, despite stricter controls, the SBM was spending 60m francs on such services.

When the finance director complains this sum is far too high, the marketing director argues that it's the minimum required simply to maintain revenue. Bully for the gamblers! (Blanc *père et fils' viatique* was granted only after the players had gone bust.)

And what about Loews hotel-casino half a minute's stroll in the moonlight down the hill? On much the same turnover as the SBM, the casino has continued to rack up handsome profits – from 16.7m francs in 1976, the first year of its operation, to 104.8m francs in 1985. Total disbursement to the SBM by Loews casino in the decade was more than 260m francs, or around $40m. How wise Prince Rainier was (he has a reputation as a businessman) to let the Americans in!

Any casual visitor can see at once why Loews is a success. Under a high starlit dome, the whole lay-out is easy, open and classless, Western-style. No fuss, no fustian, no doors, players just step in from the hotel lobbies. The same games are played, namely double-zero roulette and blackjack (but no baccarat or trente et quarante), with the accent on slot machines. Probably the key difference from the SBM is that while the croupiers are local, they are not principally Monegasques: the 'historical weight' has been airborne up the hill.

One night I had the pleasure of dining with Monsieur Pierre Cattalano, who has spent a life-time in the Monte Carlo casino. He can recall the halcyon days, the cloche hats and flat heels and boop-de-doop of the thirties, when he first joined the casino as a trainee croupier; the dark empty salons of the war years and the Occupation. He has had personal acquaintance with a great congregation of gamblers long gone, and has spent many, many nights as a *tailleur* or baccarat dealer. He now surveys the passing scene as host to a new generation of gamblers.

'I admit it, I do feel nostalgic!' he told me. 'It is very hard for the casino to beat the gamblers these days. A man may come in for a night and win twenty thousand on the first shoe at baccarat and he will get up and leave. Maybe he is flying to New York or London tomorrow. He is not here to gamble. In the old days people played to amuse themselves. If someone like Lord Carnarvon or Lady Furness won on the first shoe, they would never dream of getting up. "I am here for the fun of it," they would say. People stayed for a month or two, not a weekend. Now . . .' M. Cattalano shrugged, 'well, look . . . you can see the difference.'

Baccarat is a tough game for the house, because runs of luck by the players can wipe out the bank. It happened in the baccarat game in Nice, before the casino was shut down. (It was a perennial risk for François Blanc in Homburg.) But it is a less dangerous game for the casino than chemin de fer – because if a big loser at chemmy bounces a cheque, the house has already paid out the winners with its own money; at baccarat, if a loser's cheque is bad, then it is a pity, but the house has only paid him in plastic chips. M. Cattalano says the baccarat bank at Monte Carlo is never closed. Around 90 coups are played in two shoes, so if thirty or forty or fifty thousand francs is bet on each coup, a lot of money is wagered over a session.

The SBM's troubles centre on the 'European' games, baccarat, trente-et-quarante and single-zero roulette. A house edge of 0.8 per cent and 1.25 per cent in the two card games, and 2.7 per cent at roulette, ought to be enough to float a battleship in the port below. But if the croupiers are taking too large a slice, and players' credit is not under control, no casino can prosper. What always amazes me, as a spectator, is seeing thousands of tourists on budget holidays splurging their money at the double-zero roulette tables, night after night . . . oblivious, apparently, of the advantage to be gained simply by walking a few steps over to the *salon privé* and playing the single-zero game.

'The most sensible advice that can be given to would-be gamblers or inventors of systems to be used at Monte Carlo,' François Blanc once observed, 'is – don't!' He was speaking of roulette, the *systemier's* game *par excellence*. Roulette, much as we might like to think otherwise, cannot be beaten, no matter what system you may try. It is mathematically impossible.

But . . . but what, after all, if there is a way, a way that no one has ever thought of before? Not by ancient alchemy but modern technology. Obviously anyone who could devise it would have to be, if not a genius, at least pretty imaginative. I was alerted to the possibility of such a system by a throwaway line in Ed Thorp's first study of blackjack (see chapter 1) *Beat The Dealer*. 'There are also several people (including myself) who possess a method for beating roulette,' he declared. Since Professor Thorp is not a TV conjuror but a highly original mathematician, I was half-way impressed.

'I played roulette on a regulation wheel in the basement lab of a world-famous scientist,' Thorp wrote. 'We used the method and steadily averaged 44 per cent profit. In an hour's run, betting no more than $25 per number, we won a fictional $8,000!'

The scientist was Claude Shannon, whose many-sided contributions to mathematical theory include the foundations of information theory. It was in his basement that the roulette experiment was set up, which Thorp had perceived, in an intuitive flash, as a graduate student some years before. Shannon's basement, as Thorp described it, was a gadgeteer's paradise. It was kitted up with $100,000 worth of electronic, electrical and mechanical devices. With a regulation roulette wheel ordered from Reno, set on a billiards table, they set about measuring the position and velocity of the roulette ball, in order to predict where it would land up on the wheel.

It is possible to predict the movement of the planets, so why not a roulette ball? The answer is that a roulette ball, being subject to several variable factors in the force of the croupier's throw, the point of entry of the ball, the speed of rotation of the wheel, the ball's impact on the rotor in the centre, then contact with a number of deflectors, and finally on ridges between the pockets, is very difficult to predict. The account of the experiment given in Thorp's *The Mathematics of Gambling* (1984) is rather technical and for a layman difficult to follow, but they cracked the problem, to the extent of devising concealed mini-computers (with toe-operated switches) to test the method in a casino. 'The few times I have used it to turn two or three dimes into a pile of silver dollars has caused enormous excitement,' Thorp wrote in *Beat The Dealer*; but certain electronic problems prevented the system from being used on a large scale.

What happened was that Thorp and Shannon, accompanied

by their wives, spent a week at the Riviera in Las Vegas, trying out the technique with an analog computer the size of a cigarette pack, including a radio transmitter to maintain contact at the table. The computer received data on successive revolutions of the rotor and ball in front of a fixed point, in order to calculate the section on the wheel that the ball was likely to land in; the radio then informed the man doing the betting which numbers to back. The trouble was the wires of the hearing aid carrying the radio signal kept breaking. Getting wired up was all rather a hassle. Over the years they tried to debug the system – which was conceptually very simple – but eventually gave it up. Thorp added that the basic reason he never persevered was the system's Achilles heel – all the casino had to do to nullify the whole operation would be to bar bets once the ball was set in motion.

It was the invention of the microprocessor which led to the breakthrough. A group of computer hackers, physicists and assorted enthusiasts chasing the good life in California at the end of the seventies hit on the idea of devising a system for predicting the movement of the ball in roulette, and set up a sort of social-technological collective to do it. The point was that the microcomputer is digital, it works on numbers as distinct from electrical analogs; so instead of relying on linear approximations, as with an analog computer, the team was able to develop an algorithm for solving the equations of motion that govern the game of roulette. The account of their ups and downs given in *The Eudaemonic Pie* by Thomas Bass (1985) is absorbing. It represents, perhaps, the last word in roulette, because it is now illegal for players to use a computer in Nevadan casinos.

Eudaemonic is a Greek word meaning conducive to happiness – the pie was supposed to be the share-out of gambling profits. The essence of the group's technique was that the computer could work out in microseconds a game that in real life takes a million times longer. That is, while the ball was making its first couple of spins around the wheel the computer would signal where it was likely to land up twenty seconds later – in plenty of time for a bettor to place his money on the key numbers.

'The program – a set of mathematical equations similar to those used by NASA for landing spaceships on the moon –

tracks a ball in orbit around a spinning disk of numbers. During the ten to twenty seconds in which the game is played from beginning to end, the computer calculates coefficients of friction and drag, adjusts for changes in velocity, plots relative positions and trajectories, and then announces where in this heavenly cosmos a roulette ball will likely come to rest on a still-spinning rotor ... information gathered while the game is in play ... is supplied by a data taker clicking two passes of the rotor in front of a fixed reference point on the frame of the wheel, and two or more passes of the ball in front of the same point. It is now an easy matter for a computer to calculate ... its final collapse onto the spinning disk of numbers.'

And you thought roulette was a difficult game, didn't you?

The system worked all right – in a physics lab. The trouble was putting it into practice in a casino. Obviously the equipment had to be concealed. In the first phase the team concealed the equipment about their persons – the men employed sacroiliac belts slung across the chest and worn like holsters for hidden weapons. One belt held the computer nestling under the left armpit; another held the batteries under the right. The women wore their computers and batteries snapped into leotards with pockets that fitted under the bosom. Coils of antenna wire were worn as a yoke round the shoulders in T-shirts. Everyone wore a solenoid plate on the stomach. And, not surprisingly, a thousand glitches upset the process when it came to the real thing – loose wires, bad connections, shocks, clamping solenoids, drifting signals.

Even so, the system cleared several thousand dollars betting in dimes and quarters. But to make big money it needed upgrading. In the second phase of the project the team set about building a computer small enough to fit inside a shoe, and strong enough to be walked on. It was an incredibly complex task of miniaturization, but eventually it was done – a computer sandwich two by four inches wide, half an inch deep.

It took a long time, more than a year in fact, causing the Eudaemons to draw down their last reserves of will and patience, let alone $15,000 in expenses. By now the collective obsession to beat roulette in a big way had taken over from the claims of ordinary life, like working, teaching, completing PhD theses. Their state of mind can be gauged by a dream one of the team described: 'I was inside a casino ... But it was also a church, with candles and incense burning. ... There were nuns and priests officiating at what looked like a roomful of altars. ... But then when you got up close you saw that the nuns had bare legs. The priests were really croupiers, and the worshippers at these altars were blackjack and roulette players taking the Holy Sacrament in the form of casino chips and Bloody Marys.'

Finally the new equipment was invisibly stitched into the soles and heels of two pairs of leather Oxford shoes. Thomas Bass, chronicler of the story, was assigned the role of high-stakes bettor. The team hit Las Vegas. And ... you guessed it. 'I notice something strange about the computer's signals. There seems to be a problem with the solenoids. Every few seconds, apparently at random, they pop with different vibrations. I start to place a bet with one signal and then switch midway on getting another. Or I wait for a buzz and get nothing ...

'The computer underfoot tinks and whirs from one prediction to the next. Extraneous buzzes pop off when the ball isn't even in motion. They follow rapid-fire, one on top of another ... With more and more buzzes coming out of nowhere, my foot feels like a foot massager run amuck. I'm getting a ten-week course in acupuncture all in one night.'

The problem was random noise. Noise is the electronics term for a signal with no function. It probably came from the surveillance system of 'the eye in the sky' which is nothing but a giant TV installation. It's like the Russians jamming the Voice of America. So many signals were beaming across the casino that only garbage could get through.

That experience proved to be the end of the line. To go back to the former system, by taking the computer out of the shoe, strapping it to the leg and redesigning the whole process, was too much. The Eudaemonic Pie, involving so many cooks, baked for so long, never got eaten; it got thinner and thinner and disappeared into the Californian moonshine.

The team could certainly claim a statistical victory; they had proved they could beat the game; and then they quit. A fitting epitaph on the affair was taken from Dostoyevsky: 'However comical it may be that I should expect to get so much out of roulette, the routine opinion, accepted by everybody, that it is absurd and silly to expect anything at all from gambling seems to me even funnier.'

One day another team will try to beat roulette. I believe they'll do it.

9

MAKING CRIME PAY

They're always looking to lock up
the loopholes. And we're always
looking to find ways to open them
up.

Mafia boss

Crooks and cheats are drawn to gambling like maggots to blue
cheese. So it was in the beginning, as the loaded dice found in
prehistoric graves around the world attest; so it is now, as newspaper reports of criminal involvement in gambling the world
over so frequently show; and so it always will be, until human
nature changes.

It's not that gambling is all that different from other human
activities, simply that the cash is more accessible. It's the stuff
which gambling is made of, a cornucopia of ready money. Everyone knows that corruption can occur in politics, or in
government administration, as indeed it can in business or
banking or the stock market; or, sad to relate, in little matters
affecting our personal lives, like filling in one's tax return; corruption may come to light in the police force itself, in the very
office of the attorney-general, even in the White House. So why
should gambling be exempt? There are many honest and
honourable men and women in gambling, of course, just as there
are in the government, in business, and the law. But you know
what I mean.

The temptations in gambling are more open. They invite
chicanery. It is no use lamenting human nature: it is as it is, like
the laws of probability are as they are. So it is not really surprising when the criminal element in gambling is exposed to
view from time to time. All that changes is the style and the
method.

One of the interesting characteristics of fraud in gambling is that it occurs all the way through the operation. It comes in at the 'top' end, in organized crime. Down the years, since gambling was legalized in Nevada, there has been a plethora of gangsters involved in running the casinos, or behind the casinos, with their hands in the till. It was one of them, Bugsy Siegel, who, right at the start, staked out in the desert sands the mighty money machine which became modern Las Vegas – more productive by many billions of dollars than the turbines of the Hoover dam which provide the power the city runs on.

Crime comes in at the bottom end of the social scale too – all the nameless little cheats and deceits practiced by the public who are constantly dreaming up new ways of turning a fast buck; the compulsive gamblers, driven in desperation to 'borrow', steal or embezzle funds; the croupiers and dealers who defraud the players or their employers. Dishonesty of one kind or another occurs at all levels, all the time, and it can no more be 'cleaned up' than you can stop burglary.

Nostalgia and cute musicals should not be allowed to romanticize the fact that it was one of the nastiest men who ever lived who founded modern Las Vegas. Bugsy Siegel opened the Flamingo in 1946. It lost for the first two weeks and he had to close down. But once it got going properly the joint began to coin money; Bugsy, however, didn't live long enough to enjoy the rewards of his labours. He was gunned down one dark night at his home in Beverly Hills.

Bugsy was as precocious in crime as some boys are in music, art or science. 'By the age of 21,' according to Ed Reid and Ovid Demaris in their classic account of the early days of Las Vegas, *Green Felt Jungle* (1965), 'Siegel had committed every heinous crime in the gangster's handbook: mayhem, white slavery, dope pushing, bootlegging, hijacking, robbery, rape, burglary, bookmaking, numbers racket, extortion and numerous vicious murders.' The Flamingo, with its eye-popping combination of gambling, glitter and girls, became the model for every casino on the strip, and far beyond. Such shapes! Such colours! Such signs! as Tom Wolfe enthused in his surreal reportage on Las Vegas: 'Two cylinders rose at either end of the Flamingo – eight stories high and covered from top to bottom with neon rings in the shape of bubbles that fizzed all eight stories up into the desert sky all night long like an illuminated whisky-soda tumbler filled to the brim with pink champagne.'

Twenty minutes after Bugsy was bumped off, and long before the police got to the scene of the crime, his heirs and successors were meeting at the Flamingo, cutting themselves into a new deal. The show must go on. There ought to be a statue of Bugsy Siegel at the start of the Las Vegas strip. A strong fictional account of his life and times is given in the novel *Las Vegas Strip* by Morris Renek – 'I've got this great idea for a fantastic money machine. You'll get a hernia carrying your share. And no one – no one – can hold us up for ransom again. We're free men and we're rich. Because what we're going to do is on the side of the law.'

But all those gangster goings-on that gave the green felt jungle its reputation happened a while ago. Nowadays, the visitors bureau will tell you, things are different – corporate management, business-school execs, computer accounting, to say nothing of a network of state-run supervisory and law enforcement agencies. Maybe so, but twenty years after his exposure of Las Vegas, Demaris produced an even thicker tome on the new resort of Atlantic City, which he called *The Boardwalk Jungle* (1986). Not a lot appears to have changed. One Mafia boss summed it up acutely in a long discussion about 'skimming' in Vegas, which was wire-tapped by the FBI: 'I believe that in time everyone out there, the fishes out there get corrupted. They can't help it. You know they live right in the midst of it.'

Exactly, it's in the air, in the water. The connection between crime and gambling is, in one way, quite productive. I believe it explains why everybody in Las Vegas and Atlantic City works so hard. The pit bosses, the dealers, the cashiers, the keno girls, the waitresses, the bus boys are all of them dead tired. Beneath their tans, they are exhausted. The reason they work so hard is fear of losing their jobs. In towns where people are desperate for jobs, where there is no recognized system of employment and no unions to speak of, in an industry where the dollar in your hand is the only measure of performance, everybody down the line has to produce results – or they're out. It's not the Protestant work ethic, it's the fear of 'the man' upstairs – the figure in the background who demands results. It doesn't make much difference if the people up on the top floor are legitimate button-down businessmen, or if they are (as it so often has turned out) subject to other shadowy operators at a distance: the sense of money-power radiating all the way down to the ever-open doors at the casino entrance has the same concentrating effect. One step, literally, beyond the door you can see what happened to the poor guys who didn't understand, who didn't make it – the bums on the sidewalk, panhandling for quarters.

'The prosperity of the desert resort after World War II was remarkable. In 1945 Las Vegans feared that the conditions that created rapid wartime growth would disappear, but the decline never fully materialized,' notes historian John Findlay of Pennsylvania State University in *People of Chance* (1986). The number of visitors grew steadily: in 1957 people employed in hotels and gaming in Clark County totalled 10,800 and gross gaming revenues $79,551,000; by 1972 employment had risen to 35,300 and revenues to $476,126,000. By 1985 the totals had leaped to 76,600 and $2,232,793,000. (University of Nevada, Reno, Bureau of Business and Economic Research.) How's that for productivity? And this despite the rival attraction of Atlantic City gaming.

How has it been possible? Many reasons, obviously, but above all its reputation for excitement. Las Vegas far outshone Reno, whose claim to be 'the biggest little city in the world' came to seem small-time. Las Vegas was big time. Even today its name spells a kind of dangerous glamour, beamed out to every home by James Bond movies and myriad TV thrillers. This dangerous image has been aided and abetted, unconsciously perhaps, by the sinister side of gambling, the unsavoury reputation of the characters who were known to be running the operation or calling the shots behind the operation.

The odds saw to it that Vegas casinos made money 'legitimately'. For not only were their doors open round the clock for the benefit of free-wheelers on a three-night package, but the resort also succeeded in extending its racy appeal to conventioneers and business groups, while on the 'illegitimate' side there was the attraction, as Findlay suggests, of rubbing shoulders with gangsters. In bygone days a taste for low life was known as 'nostalgie de la boue'; in Vegas it is the other way round. The thrill comes from the crudity and crime which lie just behind the surface of high life.

'Suckers love to see tough guys just like they like to see big-name entertainers,' a Mafia chieftain has explained. 'They love to walk into a casino or a card room, spot you, and whisper in someone's ear: "Hey, Joe, do you know who that guy is?" If a place gets a name that mob people come in regularly, suckers will flock there just to gape at mob people like they were movie stars and to get next to a table to watch how you gamble . . . Before you know it, they're into the game themselves, and they're dropping a bundle.' Gambling may be legal but it still carries for most people a risqué moral nuance, manifested in the criminal glint at the edges. Every visitor senses it, in the hard eyes and bulging holsters of the security men emptying the strong boxes; it's not a town where you step out of line.

If one individual could be said to embody the high-low spirit of Las Vegas, it is Frank Sinatra. For three decades he has made it his kind of town. No other cabaret performer packs in the audiences as he does. When Sinatra comes to town everybody lives it up. The crowds come in, not just his own hangers-on, the show biz set, the fans of his singing, but all the people drawn to action and excitement. Mr Sinatra's reputation down the years has achieved an extra celebrity by the company he keeps (see the Doonesbury cartoon strip overleaf) and there have been numerous stories of his rows at the tables and beyond. He is a man who lives gambling, who likes to play high, who mingles with the big boys behind the scenes, and has made no secret of the fact that he owns part of their action and they own part of him. 'Let the chips fall where they may,' has been Sinatra's attitude, and Vegas has taken him to its neon heart.

Stories of his rows at the table are legion. Here he is, to take a fine example both of his bad temper and his cool, at the baccarat table at Caesar's. They were playing high after the show with Sinatra on a limit of $8,000 a hand, but demanding to double it. He kept holding up the game, insisting on betting $16,000, but

Doonesbury   BY GARRY TRUDEAU

Universal Press
Syndicate © 1985
G. B. Trudeau

the house instructions were firm (the story comes from Lyle Stuart's *Casino Gambling For the Winner*, 1978). He was not to be dealt cards unless he committed himself.

'Mr Sinatra, are you "shilling" or going for the money?'

He balked at answering: too often he had got up and said he

was 'only fooling' or 'just being a shill for you', and refused to make good his losses.

Over the course of a few weeks Sinatra and a real estate broker friend had won nearly a million, and collected every cent. Now Sinatra was in the process of losing it back, but instead of cash he was papering the cage with markers.

On the night instructions were to cut off his credit when his losing run hit $400,000. He still had a handful of white ($500 chips) but kept insisting on another $25,000. The croupier called over the casino manager, Sandy Waterman. He told the star: 'Frank, you owe us four hundred big ones. If you want more you've got to pay off something. The boys want their money.'

Sinatra stood up from the table. He flung his chips into Waterman's face, at the same time smacking him on the forehead with the palm of his hand. According to this account, Waterman turned and ran to his room. Minutes later he returned with a loaded gun in his hand. He pointed it at Sinatra. 'Listen you! If you ever lay a hand on me again I'll put a bullet through your head.'

'Aw, come on,' Sinatra drawled, with a disparaging gesture, 'that gun stuff went out with Humphrey Bogart!'

Disconcerted by Sinatra's nonchalant approach, Waterman's arm lowered just enough for one of Sinatra's gofers to strike it. The gun fell to the floor. Waterman knew he was in trouble. He turned and sprinted to the cage, with Sinatra and his pack in hot pursuit.

Sinatra's left arm was in a sling, the result of some surgery on his veins. The cashier's door opened. As Waterman tried to close it behind him, Sinatra clung to it. The door smashed against his bad arm. Blood spurted upward. Everyone stood appalled. The drama was suddenly over. Sinatra hurried back up to his suite and a gofer ran to call a doctor.

I was in Vegas at the time and heard rumours of the row, which got little play in the press. These are the sort of incidents which both damage and enhance Las Vegas' image. Under the new style of corporate management of casinos, of course, such things could never happen these days!

Sinatra has never lost his drawing power, as was shown when

Steve Wynn of the Golden Nugget hired him to headline his new venture in Atlantic City. The deal was worth $10m to Sinatra, plus enormous perks, spread over three years. Sinatra's first appearance of a four-day engagement reportedly brought in $20m in revenue. But once again trouble was not slow in coming, as *The Boardwalk Jungle* noted. Sinatra created chaos at the blackjack table when he insisted that the dealer, an oriental girl, deal from a single deck of cards held in her hand rather than out of a dealing shoe holding six decks. When she protested that this was against the rules, Sinatra told her, 'You don't want to play one deck, you go back to China,' and threatened not to perform at the casino unless his demand was accepted. Terrified, the pit boss gave in.

In the ensuing investigations, the staff involved were suspended and the Golden Nugget fined. Sinatra and Dean Martin, who was with him, after apologizing and pleading ignorance of the local rules, were absolved of any responsibility. They were 'just out to have a little fun', said Steve Wynn. But the gaming commissioner termed Sinatra an 'obnoxious bully'. The charge continued to rankle him. Finally Sinatra decided that he wasn't going to sing in a State which used him as a 'punching bag', as his attorney put it. He cancelled all future engagements. None of Steve Wynn's blandishments could persuade him to change his mind.

It took a week-long series of Doonesbury cartoon-strips by Gary Trudeau, that most brilliant satirist of American mores, mocking Sinatra's alleged links with organized crime, to resolve the issue. The gaming commissioner said the cartoons had gone too far and that Sinatra should not cast himself into exile because of one late-night confrontation on the casino floor. Taking this as putting things in their proper perspective, Sinatra relented. He would sing in Atlantic City again. Indeed, his regular appearances at the Golden Nugget in Vegas helped Wynn transform this downtown dive into one of the classiest joints in town. That's show business.

It is significant that Sinatra greatly admired Bugsy Siegel. The two men shared certain qualities, as Kitty Kelley acutely noted in her massive 'unauthorized' biography of Sinatra (*His Way*,

1986). 'Both were notorious womanizers who took flamboyant lovers but always returned home to their long-suffering wives. Both travelled with entourages, possessed ferocious tempers, and had grandiose visions of empire-building. Bugsy dreamed of a gambling metropolis in the Las Vegas desert while Frank envisioned himself the kingpin of a million-dollar resort hotel two miles outside of Las Vegas. Bugsy's dream flourished . . . Frank's luxury resort . . . was never completed.' But he was cut in for a slice of the Sands back in the 1950s, thus obtaining a lucrative foothold in Vegas. The avowed motive of the mob's generosity was to tie him to performing there.

Vegas has never inquired too closely who owns what. The city fathers – sons and daughters too, if the high rate of juvenile crime is a reliable indicator – do not care to look too closely at these things, provided the business itself is creating jobs and making money. The community has expanded from a frontier township of 8,422 in 1940 to 64,405 in 1960 to a city of 300,000 in 1986. An editorial in the *Las Vegas Review-Journal*, seeking to explain away various criminal conspiracies that had been going on back in the sixties, gallantly declared: 'We do not think it is fair to imply the worst simply because someone has entered into a business transaction with a person in the gaming industry. Just in case anyone has forgotten, gambling in Nevada is a legitimate business conducted by responsible businessmen.' Quoting this fine sentiment at the end of their exposé in *Green Felt Jungle*, the authors note that the 'legitimate and responsible' businessmen tune never varies, whether sung by politicians, newspapers or gambling interests. Or as a State Governor once put it, 'Our attitude to life, save under the most urgent provocation, is relaxed, tolerant, and mindful that if others are allowed to go on their way unmolested, a man stands a chance of getting through the world himself with a minimum of irritation.'

Or as the same sentiment was expressed in *eo le o Chan e*, in more academic language: 'The industry benefited from the tolerance of state officials, who were generally reluctant to interfere with the business unless operators appeared to be injuring either themselves or the image of Nevada gambling . . . ermissiveness was most widely publicized in the matter of licensing casino operators who had either criminal records or alleged connections to organized crime.' Quite so: not to mention the fact that the tolerance of state officials was often eased by bribery. But who else was there, in those early days? The dividing line was bound to be a bit smudgy between the legitimate operators and the mobsters who had always been involved in the numbers racket, illegal bookmaking, loan sharking and kindred neighbourhood social works. After Bugsy Siegel showed the way, though he did not survive long enough to enjoy the gold rush in the desert, the gambling scene was wide open.

The sort of thing that went on, which the public never knew about until long afterwards, can be illustrated by the scandal exposed at the Stardust. (My favourite casino in those days. I spent many agreeable hours in its poker room until various malpractices came up; I also liked the exterior which boasts the prettiest signboard in town, radiating blue, red and gold stars.) What happened, as revealed by an investigator of the Gaming Control Board, was that every day all the takings from the slots were being weighed out in specially rigged scales in a back room, so as to skim off a quarter of the total casino win, without anyone on the security side being any the wiser. The money was then shipped off to Mafia families in places like Detroit and St Louis. It was all very precisely done.

The following vignette comes from a six-hour conversation at a 'business conference' in Kansas City, taped by the FBI in 1978, quoted in extenso in *The Boardwalk Jungle*. The speaker, one Carl Thomas, then owner of a couple of small-time joints in Vegas, was acting as a technical adviser to the family:

'You can feed the computers the wrong weight on the scales. You can snatch some money off, then you've got the guy in slots that's a hundred per cent he'll do business with you. What we did at Argent (the corporation which previously owned the Stardust and the Fremont), and I think we'll set it up again, is set up a separate bank and a separate count for the slots. A little room with its own vault, everything separate from the tables. With that scale, I think we can beat it. I got the designs already on paper, space wise.

'. . . You skim off forty thousand a week in coins and grab

forty thousand in C-notes and nobody knows that. My concept of this place is these guys hit the slots one month and the drop boxes the next. Never set a pattern . . .

'. . . The guy that reads the scales is your guy. I bought one of them (scales) myself, it cost me fifteen thousand, but my guy reads it . . . You pay this guy off anywhere from five hundred to a thousand a month, he's your guy. He knows something is going on but he don't know what or what magnitude or anything. These guys want to make a living, too . . .'

Another member of the group remarked at one point that he thought they had devised a system for the Stardust where they could skim a million dollars a year, or a million and a half.

Kansas City Mafia boss Nick Civella gave a laugh: 'The way you're making it sound is like you think that's a lot of money.'

Most of the men involved in these scams were convicted in due course. Civella died of cancer a few weeks before the trial in Kansas City. How widely their elaborate systems of skimming were applied in other casinos, by other people, can only be guessed at. The point is that a casino might still be run properly, from the management's point of view, with checks and audits every step of the way, but the boll weevils are already in the woodwork. The larceny at the Stardust and associated goings-on in Las Vegas were certainly applicable elsewhere; the investigation had a direct bearing, in fact, on the proposed ownership of new casinos in Atlantic City.

Atlantic City started out with the best of intentions. Such ventures always do. Casino gaming was the open sesame to rejuvenate a dying city – it would boost employment, broaden the tax base, cut welfare rolls, stimulate tourism. To persuade the people of New Jersey that gambling would be a good thing, an enormous campaign was mounted by the proponents of gambling. Well, they were entitled to lobby their cause. The only snag was that the supporters of gambling always have a lot more money to play with than their opponents. More than that, some of the supporters of gambling in Atlantic City came from very shady backgrounds.

Like the Mary Carter Paint Company – what a sweet name. This was a little paint manufacturer and retailer, down in

Florida, which was transformed one fine day into the mighty casino empire of Resorts International. The Mary Carter Company was brought in to turn Paradise Island in the Bahamas into a profitable enterprise. Resorts got things done: a bridge was built from Nassau to Paradise (formerly Hog) Island, a licence obtained and a casino opened. All this, obviously, required the right contacts and Resorts had them. It was used to dealing with politicians down there, it had connections, some open, some more dubious, down Miami way. The name of Meyer Lansky, 'mogul of the mob', and others cropped up in gamblers' gossip.

Nothing was ever proved: what was certain, whoever was behind it, was that Resorts had the driving force to get things moving in Atlantic City. It aimed to be the first casino to establish itself when casino gambling was approved. The first step was to secure public and legislative backing. Resorts saw the way the tide of opinion was running. It bought an option on 55 acres of land on the boardwalk, it acquired the massive pile of the old Chalfonte-Haddon Hall hotel, to be converted into a casino, it launched a PR campaign under the title 'The Committee to Rebuild Atlantic City'. Riding the tide from the shoreline up to city hall, it promised the transformation of a crumbling old seaside resort into an economic marvel. The campaign was hard but rewarding. Resorts succeeded in winning a temporary licence to operate its casino; then, overcoming all objections to its past and present conduct, a permanent licence, a year ahead of all its rivals.

The principle that a man is innocent until proven guilty is reversed under New Jersey casino law: a company has to prove it is worthy of a licence. A long list of sharp dealings, shady connections, questionable practices, was raised about Resorts during the run-in and the civic hearings. The questions, as reporter Gigi Mahon showed in her exposé, *The Company That Bought The Boardwalk* (1980), remained largely unanswered. In the end terms like innocent or guilty hardly seemed to matter. Who cared about all the question marks, the allegations of corruption in high places, the occasional stretching of the rules? The point was that Resorts was in there.

Even Al Merck, the gaming commissioner who attracted some public notice because of his outspoken reservations on licensing Resorts (he made no secret of his voting No in the referendum on casino gambling for New Jersey), finally acquiesced in approving Resorts' licence. There was too much going, too much money invested, to turn the company down. An engagingly witty and cultivated man, who entered public service out of a sense of duty (he is the elder scion of the family pharmaceutical company), Merck told me that he believes organized crime is not involved in the casino industry directly these days; it is in there, certainly, but primarily in the ancillary services – 'Did you know that every restaurant in New York City gets its linen from the Mafia?'

Atlantic City itself has not profited from the arrival of casinos. It is a cliché, that can easily be verified on a bus trip into town, that Atlantic City is a dump, or, more precisely, a string of high-rise casinos in a wasteland of non-development. Who cares if the Mafia do provide the linen, one might say, if they keep the place clean? The night Resorts opened its doors, people hit the tables and the slots like a swarm of locusts. 'The tables were jammed ten and twenty deep. You couldn't move through the aisles. The smoke was so thick, it was as if the place was on fire.' The fire was in the gamblers' pockets – Resorts' great faith was justified. The operation started off making close to a million bucks a day. Wall Street got the news, and casino stocks took off like rockets.

Ten years later there are ten or eleven casinos along the boardwalk, but nothing else – really nothing – to show for it all, apart from a rising crime rate. The employees who staff the casinos mostly come in from out of town: they have to because there is no new housing, no schools, no amenities of any kind. And these people, the dealers and dicemen and other employees down the line, are all doing their job very efficiently, earning their pay the hard way – no one is questioning their probity. By the summer of 1982, the average monthly take per casino was $15 million. Resorts passed the $1 billion mark in total revenues in February, 1983.

Where did the money go? Who did get rich? And what happened to all the millions paid out in state taxes? The question has been addressed in a study called *The Atlantic City Gamble* (1983) by two experts in urban studies at Rutgers University, George Sternlieb and James W. Hughes. Their conclusion is that casino gambling is not the be-all and end-all of urban renewal, the kind of 'magic bullet' it was cracked up to be.

'Nothing of consequence has been done to improve the poor housing conditions that predate legislation . . . nothing has been done to relieve the hardships that displacement causes . . . The situation for minority groups is even worse . . . the projected bonanza to Atlantic City . . . has been largely offset by the stresses on the municipal treasury that the casinos have brought in their wake . . . particularly public safety . . . Perhaps most detrimental is the vast potential for corruption . . . to buy political influence and patronage.'

It's not all bad. A lot of people have made money and a lot more have had a good time losing it. It's the old story in a new setting. Authors Sternlieb and Hughes do not take an admonitory line at all: their concern is to point up the lessons of Atlantic City, so that other jurisdictions thinking of bringing in casino gambling will benefit from the experience. There is certainly a lot of experience to learn from. The civic administration in Atlantic City was ludicrously under-powered to do the job.

By 1986 the casinos were lobbying for round-the-clock gaming as in Las Vegas. Their restricted hours of opening, 10 a.m. to 4 a.m., 6 a.m. on weekends and holidays, prevented them from making an adequate return, they complained. If casino gambling comes to Florida or New Orleans or one of the other places that have been pondering the pros and cons, will things turn out any better? Atlantic City, one is tempted to say, can only improve.

I used to know a French journalist, a good colleague, who personified to a high degree the chauvinism of the French. Everything was bigger or better or more logical in France. One day, when I was telling him about a terrible murder case that was being reported in the British press, he interrupted me: 'But you know, we 'ave much bigger murdairs in France!'

It is in a distinctly cautionary spirit, therefore, that I say there is much less crime in England than in America so far as gambling is concerned. The British have their own gangsters and con men in plenty, there have been cases of bribery and corruption and skimming in the past, and there will no doubt be others in the future. One operator of a popular London casino had the nerve to write a book on casino management, before deciding to skip to sunnier climes with most of the takings, and has not been heard from since. But the British have been successful in keeping the Mafia out. The reason (see chapter 3) is that the whole structure of gaming is different.

Typically, in Britain, the offences in gaming are 'technical'. They involve minor infringements of the network of rules laid down by the Gaming Board, not the lurid excesses of organized crime. Such technical offences are nonetheless taken very seriously indeed by the regulatory authorities, leading on occasion to multi-million-pound casino groups being shut down and put out of business. Comic rather than tragic, and wonderfully revealing of national character, as the most spectacular case of all demonstrated.

It involved the rivalry between the British bookmaker Cyril Stein and playboy extraordinary Victor Lownes. The casino industry in London, which accounts for over 70 per cent of the country, had benefited wonderfully from the new Gaming Act at the end of the 'swinging sixties'. The rules were restrictive, yes; but provided the management kept to the rules, they had – in a famous phrase applied to television franchises – a licence to print money. The casinos clustered around the bottom of Park Lane, which was the focal point of gambling in London – a kind of Mayfair 'strip' – could hardly go wrong. The public at large was able to indulge its habitual craving for gambling anew. The big tourist hotels were crammed with Americans still searching out swinging London. And above all, there were the Arabs. The oil boom, followed by successive upheavals in the Middle East, notably the collapse of Lebanon and the fall of the Shah of Iran, had caused an influx of Middle East money to London.

Where else could these oil-rich exiles disport themselves, in a town where the bars shut at 11 p.m., but at the casinos? And how they gambled! They dropped not tens of thousands but hundreds of thousands: collectively millions. The stories of the largesse of the Arabs were legion – of the doorman who, when he respectfully held out his palm, on ushering a winning punter into his limousine, was casually tipped a five hundred pound chip – or was it five thousand?

The casino managements understandably fell over themselves to attract and hold on to these high rollers. But if the desire to gamble is deeply rooted in human nature, greed goes even deeper. In their rivalry, the casinos' avarice far outstripped their judgement of the risks.

The dilemma the big operators faced in catering to the Arabian high rollers was that, under the Gaming Board's regulations, they could not offer them anything very showy in return. Effusive greetings on arrival, naturally; dinner on the house, of course; a car to carry the sated punter back to his hotel at the end of the night, obviously. But not much else. (The Gaming Board's annual report for 1984 spoke solemnly of diaries and pens as acceptable gifts.) In Vegas, by contrast, a high roller is taken care of like a prize pig – his every whim and wish is indulged in an environment that is enclosed and totally self-sufficient. He need never leave Caesar's or the Nugget or the Sands (while his credit lasts). It's a town where anything the favoured customer wants goes – as a casino manager once put it to me: 'If a guy says he wants six ladies in black suspender belts and red garters let down from the chandelier – okay, he's got it.'

Every night in London the big clubs had the same awful worry – that Abdullah or Ibrahim or Mohammed – all on first name terms in that jokey-deferential way the English have – might stroll a few yards down Park Lane or Curzon Street and be ushered through another set of swing doors. Gamblers are always changing over according to whether they feel lucky in one place or unlucky in another. And when one of the Middle Easterners crossed the street, there went maybe half a million quid's worth of profit.

Besides, all the little regulations were irksome. The rule that a player had to write out a cheque each time he wanted credit in the course of the evening, instead of just consolidating the total amount on one cheque; the rule that a player should never get new credit if his previous cheques had not been cleared. With Middle Eastern banks no one had ever seen or heard of, who in hell knew what was going on? And with a man dropping half a million over a weekend, it didn't seem prudent to inquire too closely. These were 'technical' issues.

The casinos got careless as well as greedy. That was how the 'casino wars' began, though even so, the in-fighting would not have got out of hand had the principal personalities involved not been, personally, so antipathetic: Cyril Stein and Victor Lownes.

Stein had built up the Ladbroke's bookmaking business to become the biggest and most successful group in the country. He came from a shrill, street-wise London background, and on the way up had acquired all the skill and hard graft associated with the bookmaking business. (Another side of his life, which few knew about, was his total dedication to Zionist fund-raising – which prompted the quip that, thanks to Stein, the Israeli economy was being fuelled on Arab petro-dollars lost at the tables.) His casinos were a new venture and immensely successful. Lownes, by contrast, was the playboy of the western world, Hugh Hefner's man in London. He led a free-wheeling, fast-talking life, hosting celebrations every weekend at his 'school' for Playboy bunnies down at his elegant country house in Hertfordshire. The thriving British gaming operation had turned out to be a financial life-saver for the then ailing Playboy group.

The falling out of the two men came over the pursuit of the high rollers. The story, as revealed in the satirical magazine *Private Eye*, was sensational: Ladbroke's was said to be running an undercover operation to note down the registration numbers of all cars taking gamblers to rival clubs like the Playboy and the Clermont, and then paying 50p a time to an illicit contact working on the police national computer in Nottingham for each number to be checked out, so as to trace the name and address of the owner of the vehicle. The punters, having been identified, could then be wooed across by personal invitations to wine and dine at the Ladbroke club.

The story was news to Lownes too. He confronted Stein head on. He had already warned Ladbroke's that Playboy was going to support the police in their objections to this sort of thing, which was a very big step to take against a business rival – in effect a move to drive the casino division of Ladbroke's, then ringing up £25m a year in profits, right out of business. The dispute came into the open at a meeting of the Association of British Casinos in May, 1979.

Lownes, according to his own account (*Playboy Extraordinary*, 1982) figured that not to protest was another way of saying 'Oh, well. We're all at it.' He did not intend to help the police directly. 'But I wanted to go formally on record as raising an objection. And if Stein had behaved differently at the meeting instead of threatening me as he did, that is all I most probably would have done. Only after he threatened me did I bring in our lawyers and get really involved.'

Stein made a statement, according to Lownes, which directly challenged everything Lownes stood for. 'He wanted, he said, to draw the Association's notice to the fact that Playboy was objecting to renewal of his licences. His words were: "I'd like to say that if Playboy doesn't withdraw its objections, the mud's really going to fly. And it's not just going to be Playboy."' Lownes' reaction, scribbled on a note to a colleague sitting next to him, was typical: 'Fuck 'em.'

By this date, the bloom had gone off the casino industry. The flow of petro-dollars was drying up. True, the clubs were still coining money hand over fist. But there was a nasty smell in the air over Mayfair, the slick smell of corruption. There had been too much money around, too much temptation. Skimming and other malpractices were coming to light in dark corners. In November 1979 the Coral Group, a household name in British bookmaking, was disgraced. Its top casino executive, it transpired, had been nicking five thousand quid a week, just like that, over a period of 18 months – there had been an elaborate abuse of the credit regulations for certain Arab high rollers. The clubs were shut down. Old Joe Coral was a broken man and his son Bernard departed to run a luncheon club off Fleet Street.

The Gaming Board at the national level and Magistrates Courts locally were reacting severely. Amid all the public scandal and litigation, several clubs lost their licences, including the Victoria, a chromium temple of middle-class gaming in the Edgware Road.

In one of his most spectacular coups, Lownes bid for the place, later winning back its licence on appeal. It was a famous victory but it did not endear him to prim officialdom. Overall, there was a suspicion that the casinos were getting out of hand and, in consequence, a growing sense of public unease.

Lownes was really beginning to relish English life. The go-go Playboy and upmarket Clermont were the two best clubs in town. With his movie-star salary, his riding to hounds, his swinging parties, his clutch of toothsome bunny girls waving him on – Lownes had it all. (Could anything be more revealing of the way the English run things than the fact that Lord Allen of Abbeyfield, the then chairman of the Gaming Board, was paid a part-time salary of around £60 a week, while Lownes was the highest paid executive in the whole country?) The only thing Lownes had to do to stay on top was run his gaming operation according to the book.

And the ebullient Victor took the book to heart. He began going around making speeches extolling the virtues of the British gaming industry. Riding the wave of his own propaganda, like his bay hunter taking the fences, he cast himself as Mr Clean. His opposition to the renewal of Stein's licences was not, in his view, a gigantic bit of *chutzpah*, but motivated by the desire to clean up the industry etc. etc. He informed Stein that he was in favour of full disclosure of all the facts and figures, as a basis for reform of the tax system of casinos. Stein, narrow-eyed, would have none of it.

After Stein repeated his threat, that the mud would fly, Lownes thought he had better run a check over his own clubs' operating procedures. Everything was fine. Lownes' staff assured him the business was a hundred per cent clean. Well they would, wouldn't they? Lownes went right on partying and hunting and starring in the gossip columns, unaware of the cardinal but unwritten rule of English social life: you can live how you like, and do what you like, but you must never, ever, flaunt it.

What schemes were smouldering in Cyril Stein's breast were not revealed. For one thing, he did not commit his thoughts to the media; for another, his own secretary claimed that senior executives had ordered vast quantities of documents at

Ladbroke's to be shredded, ahead of the police investigations –
which did not give Stein as chairman (though he denied the
charge) quite the Boy Scout image his shareholders might have
wished. In any case, it required little imagination to guess the
form of Ladbroke's revenge; for it rapidly emerged that in their
mania to scoop up all the 'mud' they could find on Playboy's
operations, the company was actually paying out substantial
sums to its former employees. (*Bunny*, by Russell Miller, 1984,
details the whole story.)

In due course the hearings of the case against the renewal of
Ladbroke's licences came up. Stein, in the witness box, got grilled.
The defence was as full of holes as a Gruyère cheese. And it was
no surprise when Ladbroke's three top clubs in London were
ordered to be shut down. Soon after, Stein sold the rest of the
group's casino interests, while there was still something left to
sell. It had been a total débâcle. Victorious Victor was left with
the field of the cloth of gold virtually to himself.

Nemesis was not long in striking the victorious playboy down,
physically as well as financially. On an icy day out hunting, his
favourite horse lost its footing and Lownes was thrown, sustaining severe concussion. While he was still in hospital, the
police launched a mass raid on the Clermont and the Playboy
clubs. Scores of officers went in, names and addresses of everyone
present were taken, all the papers and records were seized.
Whether mud from Ladbroke's had stuck or not was beside the
point; this time it was clear that the police were out to get
Playboy. Lownes professed to be amazed; he put it down to the
police wanting to show they were getting busy with all the clubs
on principle.

He was right in one way and wrong in another. There was no
bribery and corruption, no fraud, no cheating of customers, nor
any other criminal offences at his clubs. What was uncovered
were 'technical' offences against the Gaming Act – muddles over
cheques and the granting of credit: cheques had been drawn on
non-existent bank accounts by some of the Arab players, new
credit had been extended when previous cheques had not yet
been cleared, and so on. It was in fact a 'grey area' of the law,
but one which the authorities now chose to interpret strictly. In

another incident (which Lownes himself had put a stop to) hotel porters had been given honorary membership of clubs to enable them to introduce new players. And one of the directors, Liberal MP Clement Freud, had been foolish enough to gamble on the premises, which was likewise against the rules.

Over in Chicago the top brass in the Playboy organization, who had been scheming for months to get rid of the free-wheeling Victor, finally saw their chance. While the casinos in London were in effect funding the entire Playboy operation, Lownes had been untouchable. The police raids gave them a golden opportunity to persuade Hefner to give his old friend and fellow swashbuckler the chop. His dismissal, which came as a thunderbolt to Victor, was front page news. New management under a retired British admiral (whose previous job had been running car parks) was hurriedly installed, on a pledge of strict compliance with the law. Unfortunately all this served only to confirm the authorities' basic objection that real control of the company was vested in Chicago not London.

Lord Allen and the Gaming Board, stung by many pricks, opposed renewal of Playboy's licences. A phalanx of lawyers, hired by each side, prepared for a long and juicy argument. The Playboy people, however, chose to defend their record without calling on Lownes as a witness, and to answer the charge – the ultimate condemnation in British gaming law – that they were 'not fit and proper persons to run a casino', off their own bat. They were probably bound to lose, and lose they did. There were long faces up in the boardroom, and even longer transatlantic calls to the Playboy mansion in Chicago.

Faced with the cost and uncertainty of going to appeal, the boys in Chicago (the group was already running onto the rocks in applying for a licence in Atlantic City) lost their nerve. Just a year and a half after Ladbroke's ignominious withdrawal, Playboy followed suit. All its golden gaming interests in London, lock, stock and limousines – Lownes had a fleet of them for ferrying customers around town – were sold off in a desperate liquidation to the first buyer it could find, a provincial company operating a TV franchise. (The new owners parlayed their £14m investment seven-fold in four years, selling out for over £100m.)

Lownes, insouciant as ever, flew off for a vacation and talked of opening a night club. I was not the only one who felt he had brought a much needed note of gaiety to the British gaming scene, which has become very dull and (understandably) cautious since he left it.

The case showed that mere 'technical offences' concerned with credit and clearing cheques, minor matters of procedure, with no suggestion of criminality, could bring down a big company, notwithstanding the fact that it was earning foreign currency, paying big taxes and providing thousands of jobs. But that's the British way. I am not suggesting it's better than the American way, just different.

10

MORALS: WRONG WAY UP

*I have sworn before the Rabbis David
Bensusan and Moses de Castro, and
in the presence of the sons of Rabbi
Israel Ohab, that I will never play
any game in the world.*
Oath sworn in Ferrara, 1535.

Hardly anyone worries about the old arguments over whether gambling is immoral nowadays. The debate has been overtaken by more practical concerns. But these, too, raise moral issues.

Gambling, which used to be seen in the mediaeval times as a sin, came to be regarded by society in the last century as a vice, then in our own day as a form of entertainment (albeit in its compulsive form a mental illness) and a useful revenue earner for the state, especially in lotteries. How views can change!

Surprisingly the Bible, from which Western religious attitudes derive their ultimate authority, does not mention gambling as such. There are several references to drawing lots, for example the division of the land among the tribes of Israel. But a nice distinction may be noted here between drawing lots and lotteries: the device of drawing lots was to make a broad but fair division, and thus avoid disputes, rather than, as in a lottery, to win a prize. By contrast the most celebrated instance of a gamble in the Bible, when the Roman soldiers cast lots for the garments of Jesus, stands condemned by its context. Overall, there cannot be any doubt that the spirit of Biblical teachings in both Old and New Testaments is opposed to gambling, even though there is no specific prohibition: 'Thou shalt not gamble.'

That came in with the State, which often had social or economic reasons for reinforcing ecclesiastical authority, as in Henry VIII's prohibition of 1541 against games of chance. The prime motive of this legislation was to halt the neglect of archery.

Even as recently as 200 years ago gambling was considered a sin, a topic which could not be considered in polite society, observes Nelson Rose (*A New Deal For Problem Gamblers*, 1987). It was not until the 19th century that religious feeling began to die down and gambling came to be seen not as a sin but (like prostitution) merely a vice. It could at least now be discussed (though not presumably in front of wives or servants). The view of gambling as a vice is still the dominant view in the law of the United States, adds Professor Rose (author of the invaluable *Gambling and the Law*, 1986). In Britain, gambling is viewed rather as an unfortunate weakness of human nature, for which a proper outlet needs to be provided.

But attitudes are changing fast. During the eighties, aside from the expansion of Las Vegas, several American states gave serious consideration to following the example of Atlantic City and introducing casino gambling. Nearly 30 states set up their own lotteries. It was as if almost everyone wanted, as they say, a piece of the action. And why not? In a society where the pursuit of pleasure is sanctioned by every kind of analyst and therapist, where sexual freedom is upheld almost as a political right, where religious leaders themselves are grappling with previously undreamed-of moral issues – AIDS, gay clergy, women priests – gambling no longer seemed such a big deal.

Interestingly enough, while Christianity and Judaism might waver, Islam has had no doubts. Gambling is strictly forbidden according to Islamic law. The prohibition goes back to the Koran. 'For all we know,' states the *Encyclopedia of Islam*, 'the Moslem ban on gambling has existed since the time of the Prophet in the same form as later on, and has remained in force throughout.'

> They ask thee
> About wine and gambling.
> Say: 'In them is great sin,
> And some use, for a few;
> But the sin far exceeds
> their benefits.'
>
> Sura 11, Ayat 219 (based on various translations)

The only other reference to gambling in the Koran condemns gambling and drinking, together with making images and divination of the future, as evil occupations – Satan's handiwork. The sin of gambling is underlined by its being mentioned in the same breath as idolatry, according to the commentators.

Gambling was conceived as a transaction in which property changed hands arbitrarily and unproductively, something falling also under the injunction of the Koran against frivolous and worthless business transactions. Universal and reckless gambling was evidently endemic in pre-Islamic Arabia. It probably occurred in a variety of pastimes, notably archery, horse and camel racing, also pigeon racing; in sports such as athletics, swimming and wrestling; and in board games, above all (as can be seen all over the Middle East) backgammon. Gambling seems to have flourished 'everywhere and always' in the Moslem world, the *Encyclopedia* sums up, in spite of its being prohibited.

In the modern world, it may be noted, insurance against risk has been interpreted in Islamic law not as a gamble, if conducted on business principles. Risk here is calculated on the basis of statistics on a large scale, from which chance is so to speak eliminated.

So if gambling is strictly forbidden, what about all those punters from the Middle East, the spillover from the oil boom, not just playboys, but princes, politicians, diplomats, bankers and businessmen, who gambled their heads off in London in the seventies – and their worldly successors who are still to be seen thronging the tables? Perhaps they had in mind another, rather useful, precept of conduct adumbrated by one Hanafi Kadikhan of Calcutta, in 1835. The suggestion of this sage was that a Moslem could legally gamble with non-Moslems in non-Moslem territory.

The most important fact about gambling was that its relationship to the spiritual realm, beyond material concerns, was clearly perceived and strongly felt, concludes Franz Rosenthal in *Gambling in Islam* (1975). This seems to have exercised a greater influence upon the actual practice of gambling in Moslem civilization than all the guardians of law and tradition. 'Gambling aroused a deep-seated feeling of metaphysical guilt which tended to inhibit the natural instinct for it, although it was unable to suppress it.'

Jewish tradition has been more flexible in not directly opposing gambling, but expressing a strong animus against it. Objections to gambling do not appear until the time of the Mishnah, the codification of oral law, around 200 AD. Evidently the people of biblical times were not tainted by gambling, notes an American rabbi with unconscious irony – otherwise it certainly would have been mentioned as a prohibited sin (*Current Reform Respona*, Solomon B. Freehof, 1969). The Mishnah, in a famous ruling, states that those who play with dice and those who race pigeons are ineligible to testify in the courts. The Talmud takes this up by explaining that gamblers do not participate as they should in constructive social efforts. (A similar censure applied to chess players.)

A commentary on Psalm xxvi opposing gambling speaks in a vivid phrase of 'those that play at dice, who calculate with their left hand, and press with their right, and rob and wrong one another.' Maimonides objected to gambling as a form of robbery. But since it was not actual robbery, money lost in games of chance could not be collected in the courts of justice, despite rabbinical prohibitions against gambling.

In mediaeval Europe, dice, lotteries, betting, cards and other games were common pursuits of the Jews (who were of course disqualified from most of the regular entertainments and sports of gentile society) and many communal decrees were passed against gambling. 'The large amount of legal discussion which the literature contains is itself an evidence of how widespread the habit of gambling became,' Freehof adds.

So widespread were these games, says the *Jewish Encyclopedia*, that even scholars and prominent leaders of the synagogue were seized with an uncontrollable passion for them. One such case was Leon Modena, a learned man and scientific thinker who taught and preached in Venice towards the close of the 16th century. His passion was for cards. He was unable to resist the fascination of gambling, says Israel Abrahams in *Jewish Life in the Middle Ages* (1896), because of his fatalism. The belief that all his actions were predestined evidently undermined any resolution he might make to stop gambling.

He was fully aware of the evils of gambling, for at the precocious age of 14 he wrote against it a diatribe in dialogue, which has been translated into several languages. Though he often resolved to abandon the vice, of which he was deeply ashamed, he never succeeded in doing so, even in his old age. The Rabbis of Venice published an order excommunicating any member of the congregation who played cards within a period of six years from the date of the promulgation of the decree . . ., probably directed against him; at all events, he successfully summoned all his learning and force to defeat this attempt to fetter his freedom.

Punishment was strict, yet there were many occasions on which the prohibitions were lifted, such as new moons, weddings, week days of festivals, and especially during Chanukkah, 'when even pious and scholarly men indulged in card playing'. (Almost as if, like wine, gambling maketh glad the heart of man.)

An important point – similar to the dispensation for Moslems, mentioned above – was that local prohibitions did not apply to immigrants and visitors. A Jewish visitor who lived in a town where games of chance were permitted continued to enjoy the same licence when staying in a place where gaming was banned: but he was only allowed to play in private. Overall, Jewish regulations drew a distinction between gambling as a pastime and gambling as a profession. The complaint that games were a waste of time failed to influence the people, concludes the *Encyclopedia* (which goes to show, one might say, that on such issues the people showed more wisdom than their spiritual leaders).

In Christian tradition, the contrast between Catholic indulgence and Protestant severity has led to a sharp division of views on the ethics of gambling. According to Catholic teaching, there is nothing immoral in gambling, provided it is kept within bounds: gambling is an acceptable contract, so long as the parties understand the nature of it and faithfully carry it out. Excessive or fraudulent gambling is sinful, but such abuses are not considered inherent in the act of gambling itself.

By contrast, the typical Protestant approach – with its high focus on the 'work ethic' – holds that gambling violates a number of moral imperatives as well as being harmful to society. Thus, the California Church Council, which lobbied against every bill to legalize gambling, argued that 'gambling creates no new wealth ... depresses legitimate business ... increases welfare costs ... increases crime ... corrupts government ... is a sophisticated form of legalized stealing ... produces the wrong attitudes towards work ... contradicts social responsibility ... violates all the sound, standard theories of taxation'. In sum: 'Gambling is socially disintegrating, politically corrupting, and morally dangerous. Gambling is bad business, bad politics and bad morals.'

This energetic campaign did not, however, succeed in dissuading California from introducing a state lottery (prizes up to $30m) in 1985.

A more colourful, and perhaps better reasoned, opposition was offered by the Southern Baptist Convention in a paperback called *Gambling: A Deadly Game* (1985), the cover of which displayed a pair of dice marked with a skull and crossbones.

It begins: 'A horror story unfolding in the United States is being ignored by the majority of citizens and politicians. We stand at the precipice of a monumental transformation of American society which will dramatically affect our nation, our families, and our churches. No social institution will be isolated from the outcome.' (The author of this diatribe, Dr Larry Braidfoot, hails from Nashville, where they have a way with words.)

His message is that the gambling industry is engaged in a frontal assault on every state in the union, the only region to resist being the South. 'Money has become the power that fuels the gambling engine. The issue of legalized gambling is no longer about small groups of individuals who simply want to have their brand of fun and enjoyment. It is about corporations and syndicates which stand to make tens of millions of dollars by changing state laws and community life.' Dr Braidfoot might be right at that, but he was sounding the trumpet far too late. (He also defended, in passing, the resolution of the Southern Baptist Convention to hold its annual meeting in, of all places, Las Vegas in 1989. It would be an opportunity, he declared, to have 'an evangelistic impact' on that city, so much in need of evangelism.)

The British, too, from time to time, agonize over the morality of gambling: perhaps the last set piece was the debate prior to the introduction of Premium Bonds, back in 1956. This scheme is a sort of government-run lottery designed to encourage saving by the public, rather than speculation (no money is lost by the participants, other than the interest they might have earned on the bonds if invested in a normal savings account).

Thus the then Archbishop of Canterbury, Dr Fisher, an outstanding holder of that ancient see, told the House of Lords: 'A nation depends for its health upon the constructive spirit of its people. A constructive spirit is occupied positively with the good to be achieved, and the spirit of a people is to be found in the nature of their ordinary activities and their constant ways of thinking; it is to be found also in the incentives to which they most readily respond. Anything which to a serious degree debases what I will call this spiritual coinage of a people is dangerous and debilitating.'

He was opposing a Bill about small lotteries, not so much in itself but as the prelude to Premium Bonds. 'The Government know, as well as the rest of us, that we can regain stability and strength only by unremitting exercise all through the nation of the old-fashioned but essential virtues: integrity of character, strict honesty, the duty of honest work honestly rewarded . . .' etc., etc. The Bill establishing Premium Bonds was passed in 1956 and since then a grand total of 30 million winners have been paid out prize money of £1.74 billion.

Yes, gambling is here to stay, with the full support and in many instances encouragement of the State. The moral issue has changed. It should be formulated, one might suggest, under the heading: What should be done to protect the gambler? We, the gamblers, are the people who make it all happen, who pay for the industry and its profits. It is our interests which should be at the centre of social and moral concern.

I take one instance, a crucial one, of a practical sort, the granting of credit. Credit is the propane of gambling. All players depend on it to get lift-off, not just high rollers. But it is very dangerous stuff. 'The casino's motivation for granting credit is to increase the volume of play, and ultimately, the profitability of the operation. Credit can increase the total volume of wagering, especially when it is given on the casino floor at times when a player has run out of money and wishes to continue playing. This availability,' says Professor William Eadington, of the University of Nevada, Reno, 'creates gambling behaviour analagous to impulse shopping, and can cause many players to lose more than they had initially intended' (*Credit Play and Casinos*, 1986). Or as Albert Merck, one of the original casino control commissioners in New Jersey, put it, 'Without credit a gambler can be hurt; with credit, losses can bury him.'

Credit granted for gambling is different – wouldn't everyone agree? – from credit granted for commercial activities or via credit cards. It is likely, Eadington says, that many players underestimate their risk of loss because of their optimism (self-deception, rather) and thus get more credit than they would on a rational evaluation of the risks. In British casinos, gambling on credit is not allowed: chips are issued only against a cheque which has to be processed through the gambler's account in two banking days – the idea being to meet the demand for gambling in a regulated way, not to stimulate it.

In Nevada, gamblers' credit is strictly a business decision on the part of casino operators. If the guy looks like he will pay, no matter how far he is in the hole, how dazed or how drunk, then the chips keep on coming. Nevada regulations make no explicit reference to credit policy. 'Customers who go overboard and gamble more than they can afford are the backbone of the gaming industry,' declares Friedman in *Casino Management*. In Atlantic City, too, when markers were 'rolled over' (like third world debt) credit policy was in effect open-ended.

At one extreme (but I would suspect probably the common practice), casinos strive to relieve a player of all his cash and financial assets as rapidly as possible, fearing that otherwise the player will simply go and blow his stack at some rival establishment down the street. At the other end of the scale, reining in this maximalist approach, casinos naturally try to determine a player's psychological and financial limit on any given visit. If a player goes over the edge, he may shift his custom anyway, quite apart from the casino's longer-range problem of debt collection. So some restraint on credit is a matter of self-interest.

Credit policy, therefore, is 'one of the most important philosophic and moral questions . . . in examining the effect of casino gambling on society', Eadington notes. Should a casino industry be allowed systematically to extract the entire accumulated wealth of some individuals, due to their weakness and lax credit policy? Safeguards on credit could easily be devised – possibly on the British model – but their adoption would depend largely on the extent of 'negative economic impacts' on the industry. Or, as one might irreverently put it: Can the sharks be persuaded to stop biting?

Well, yes. One or two debtors have hit back at the industry for exploiting customers. In the past few years there has been a 'quiet explosion of litigation' involving disputes between casinos and compulsive gamblers, Nelson Rose reports. Significantly, very few of these cases have been reported in the press: usually they were settled with pledges of secrecy imposed on all parties – for obvious reasons. I don't think any Nevada or Atlantic City casino would want it known it had ever given any money back!

This litigation follows the growing acceptance by the courts of the American Psychiatric Association's definition of compulsive gambling as a disease (see Chapter 4). Three main issues have come up: a casino sues for unpaid gambling debts and the player raises, as a defence or counter-claim, that he is a compulsive gambler; a casino is sued by a third party, usually the player's employer, for the player's embezzlements; a casino is sued by a player in tort for contributing to damages caused by his excessive gambling, including emotional distress and even suicide.

The cases with the greatest potential impact on the gambling industry, Rose adds, are those in which a gambler argues that he is not liable for his gambling debts because he is a compulsive gambler. 'The legal gambling industry would suffer a terrible financial blow if this doctrine were accepted: casinos would be unable to collect many large debts, would be forced to write off smaller debts or spend great amounts of time and money on those debts they did eventually collect, and might have to curtail their liberal credit policies.'

So casinos now face a new kind of dilemma, when both high and low rollers can raise the defence of being compulsive gamblers. Thus to cite just one case, a player sued Resorts International in New Jersey seeking to void a $170,000 casino debt and for the return of an additional $750,000 he lost over the previous five years. The complaint alleged that Resorts had 'recklessly and negligently extended credit to the player, and had plied him with free alcohol in an 'elaborate scheme ... designed to ensnare compulsive gamblers and to encourage them to gamble recklessly and to continually incur debts to Resorts'.

The case was settled with all parties agreeing to keep the terms of the settlement confidential. In other cases, the gambler's claims have been dismissed. It has taken a little time for casinos, prosecuting debtors, to grasp the significance of the APA classification of compulsive gambling as a disease. Their lawyers are now finding ways of countering this defence. Indeed the courts themselves are often divided.

Casinos' greatest fear, says Rose, is losing a case and creating a binding precedent preventing debt collection. Their next greatest fear is winning a case, because that might create a public outcry to ban such limited powers of collection as they have. In short, the law is evolving, and the industry reacting, in the wake of changing public attitudes to gambling – that is, to changing perceptions of the morality of gambling.

Among many groups which are drawn to gambling, the Jews are a prime example. It appears, from observation and hearsay, that a high proportion of Jewish people is involved in gambling; and while this is no more than a personal impression, it is reinforced by the experience of clinicians like Dr Custer who recall that a third of the patients who sought help in the Veterans' Association program for compulsive gamblers were Jewish. That is a very high percentage, given the tiny proportion of Jews in the American services. In Britain, Jewish entrepreneurs have had a dominant role in both bookmaking and casinos. Other ethnic groups may enjoy gambling too – the Chinese have their own reputation – but the Jewish involvement seems worth examining.

One man who knows something about it from personal experience is the director of the Council on Compulsive Gambling in New Jersey, a reformed gambler himself, Arnold Wexler. 'When I was a kid,' Wexler recalls, 'my grandmother used to give me $7 every week to go to Hebrew school. The $7 was for the rabbi. By the time I was ten, I was working on my fifth rabbi ... I had figured out that if I didn't give the money to the rabbi, I could keep it and use it for gambling.' When his first child was born, after a long labour, Arnie did not ask the doctor how his wife and baby daughter were doing; he asked how much the baby weighed. Seven pounds one ounce. He rushed to the phone and bet on horse 701.

In the greater Philadelphia area, where Wexler grew up, more than half the compulsive gamblers who seek help are Jewish. The high correlation between Jews and gambling may be because so many successful Jewish businessmen fit the profile of the typical compulsive gambler, he believes. That is, a bright, hard-working youngster, who has done well at school, is energetic and successful in his job: after gambling lightly, getting a taste for winning, he starts losing and gets in deeper; deluded by the hope of a big win to recoup, he cashes in his assets and borrows all over town; finally the point is reached when he makes a partial confession to someone in the family, who responds by doing what Dr Custer says is precisely the wrong thing – bailing the gambler out.

The trouble is that this fresh start is very much like the big win the gambler was looking for. 'It may be the strength of the Jewish family structure, the willingness of loving parents and friends to help the gambler who is in trouble, that contributes to the high number of Jewish compulsive gamblers seeking help,' Custer suggests. In other words, there may not necessarily be more Jewish compulsive gamblers than people of other groups, simply that Jewish gamblers are more likely to seek help. The same goes for gamblers of Italian family background, who were also at the top of the Veterans' treatment program.

Wexler went through it all and came out with the zeal of the convert. He switched the high-octane energy of his compulsive gambling into a night and day commitment to supporting GA and helping gamblers nationally, and made a career for himself in beating the habit.

A colleague of Wexler (a former lawyer disbarred for embezzling his clients' funds, who pleaded the new defence of being a compulsive gambler) points to one of the traits about gambling which attract Jews. 'It fits the Jewish image. I got the royal treatment, called by my first name everywhere. You see the big shot with the big cigar, the Cadillac, the yacht . . . It's not like being an alcoholic, where the stereotype is of the guy laying in the gutter.' Wexler recalls a compulsive gambling friend whose son's bar mitzvah was 'comped' in its entirety by an Atlantic City casino, plus 47 free rooms for his guests. (What a wonderful deal for the casino, if you think about it!)

'The Jewish gambler plays, he plays well, and he'll teach his son to play and bring his wife . . . and she'll play too,' according to one Atlantic City executive. The marketing men rank the Jewish player at the top of the range of target groups, along with the Italians and Chinese.

Reaching out to the Jewish customers takes many forms. One of the basic is the 'Jewish host', who provides the premium player with red carpet treatment, issues him (or her) with a line of credit and, no doubt, takes care of any little personal needs. Other casinos cater to a Jewish clientele by featuring entertainers who draw a Jewish crowd, by running a kosher-style delicatessen, or offering package deals like Passover specials. This sort of marketing strategy – obvious enough, given Atlantic City's proximity to New York and other big cities – goes right to the heart of Jewish life.

Thus, one casino staged a seder (the Passover meal and service, which celebrates the deliverance from Egypt) for its Jewish patrons. 'What we're saying to the Jewish community is that we'd like to have you here for your Passover seder,' the marketing director explained, stressing that the seder and the activities that took place in the casino were totally separate (but giving a new meaning to the age-old Passover question, 'Why is this night different from all other nights?'). The turn-out for the High Holidays (known as 'The days of awe') made the casino look like a peak summer weekend, it was reported.

Another casino executive explained the success of such marketing strategies in terms of Judaism itself. 'There are life-based religions versus faith-based religions. In a life-based religion like Judaism, the rewards are supposed to be in the here and now. Lead a good life and you'll be rewarded in this life. Reward yourself with a mink coat, a new car, or good times. In a faith-based religion you're supposed to get your reward in the future.' (To enhance this strategy, might one suggest a slot machine in the shape of a golden calf?) The same casino is just as likely to run a big St Patrick's Day promotion because of its wide appeal to the Irish. 'If I thought that would translate to a Purim promotion, I'd try that too.'

Wexler's group is not prohibitionist, it focuses on education. He has recommended, for instance, that all advertisements for gambling in New Jersey should close with the statement: 'If you or someone you know has a gambling problem call 1–800–Gambler' (the gambler's hotline). Beyond this, he believes the message should be displayed on lottery machines and racetrack programs, in casino rooms, on markers and chips, and in public telephones in casinos.

The subjective impression that 'Jews like gambling' may be set alongside another ready-to-wear piece of popular wisdom, which is 'Jews don't drink'. The apparent dearth of alcoholism among European and American Jews has been widely noted in sociological studies; yet this relative sobriety is not associated with a restrictive attitude to drinking. Drinking and gambling are linked, as social activities, and in cases of excess by psychological factors. So if Jewish people go in for gambling, how come (it might be asked) they don't have a reputation as drinkers?

A tentative answer is that gambling offers the same kind of satisfaction as drinking, but in a form which better suits Jewish cultural attitudes. A study of Jewish families in the East End of

London, for instance, indicated that an excess of gambling may counterbalance a relative dearth of alcoholism (*Alcoholism and Gambling: the Case of the Jews*, S. J. M. Fernando, 1982).

'The question then arises,' this paper says, 'whether excessive gambling is actually promoted by Jewish cultural factors – just as alcoholism is discouraged.' It might seem so. 'Jews perceive drinking as a means of social practicability and ritualism, as opposed to the Irish who look to drink as a source of excitement and conviviality,' another study concludes. Sobriety among Jews arises from an attitude of mind which sees the function of drink as an instrument – a means to an end – rather than a source of excitement – an end in itself.

Immigrants might turn to gambling out of desperation, as a report in a Yiddish newspaper set the scene in Leeds, in 1884. As soon as they were paid, the men ran straight to the pub and bet on the horses. 'Everyone's miserable wage was squandered away.' Thus the lot of the immigrant and his family was made even harder. One Morris Winchevsky, a Jewish socialist and poet of the time, describing the exploited and miserable life of the East End immigrant, wrote evocatively that when a man heard his wife and children crying out 'Tutte! Broit!' (Father! Bread!) he could be excused for going off gambling and drinking.

Certainly in modern Jewish life cultural factors tend towards gambling. The drive to get on, to be successful, the work ethic of the successful immigrant, is clearly imbued in Jewish life, as is the fondness for cards and games. It is an instinct which finds instant expression in gambling, especially the immediate satisfaction of being looked up to by others as a big gambler – and therefore a popular and successful individual in society at large. The rewards of gambling look like a short cut to worldly success, meretricious as such recognition may be.

Heavy drinking is the reverse of all that. It is, rather, a way of opting out, of escaping from troubles of one sort or another, granted it has its convivial side too. I am not, of course, drawing hard and fast distinctions: in some groups – another study cites the American Irish – gambling and alcoholism may well go together. The point made in the survey of East End Jews is that gambling can serve as an alternative to alcoholism, or other addictions – drugs being the most destructive.

Is gambling, for cultural reasons, an addiction to which Jews are particularly susceptible? Maybe not, but I wouldn't bet on it.

11

CONCLUSION: THE GAME OF LIFE

> Everything that happens in our
> world resembles a vast game in
> which nothing is determined in
> advance but the rules.
> Manfred Eigen and Ruthild
> Winkler, *Laws of the Game*

As we approach the end of the twentieth century, the worldwide appeal of gambling is stronger than ever. Every year sees new resorts opening up to allow casino gaming, more jurisdictions setting up lotteries. The common motive among licensing authorities is to find a new and painless way of raising revenue. New it may be, but painless it is not – in the sense that gambling is bound to alter the economic and social balance in any community. For every plus there is a minus. Among the gaming operators the common motive is to make a fast profit. 'Twas ever thus, you might say.

Most interesting, to my mind, is that gambling has retained all of its fascination, in so many different societies and cultures, around the world. Despite all the distractions that our modern times have to offer – the plethora of entertainment available at the flick of a switch, all the leisure activities which ease of travel, technological innovation and economy of production have made available – gambling has kept its hold on people. That should not really be a cause for surprise. As this book shows, the urge to gamble is a basic instinct of human nature. Does human nature change from one generation to the next?

A decade ago some 75 countries were offering gambling in one form or another. The total has certainly risen since, and the opportunities for gambling within these countries – headed by the United States – have in many cases been expanding. I was amused to see an advertisement for the American magazine

Gambling Times at the front of an international gambling directory, posing the question:

'How much money will you bet in your lifetime? $1,000 . . . $10,000 . . . $100,000?'

Nice question. The answer is over $1,000,000! The average couple visiting Las Vegas or Atlantic City drops about $300 a trip, the ad says, but, to do that, they will have bet something like $12,000, betting their basic bankroll, plus winnings, over and over again in successive small wagers. If this vacationing couple makes two trips to the bright lights a year, that means $24,000 wagered: and over 40 years the total amount bet is close to the million dollar mark (and well above it if occasional visits to the racetrack and so on are included.) That, of course, is how the casinos make their profits, slicing a small edge from a limited sum over and over and over. Note that while the couple in question may have bet nearly $1m, their net loss was only $300 × 80, or $24,000. (A small price for a lot of entertainment, as the casinos would say.)

I don't see any reason why the trend to gambling should not continue in the twenty-first century. As daily life becomes more automated, as leisure assumes a greater proportion of people's time (at least in the more affluent countries) and as a way of relieving people's feeling of being hemmed in – the sense that one's individual choice is more and more constricted by routine in overcrowded societies – gambling offers a ready outlet. One day, during the next century, life will probably be discovered on another planet, beyond our solar system. (The chances are not too bad: it is estimated that there are about 10 billion galaxies in the universe and, maybe, 100 billion billion planets where the kind of conditions exist that produced life on earth.) It will be interesting to see what role chance plays in that other life.

This is not a wholly idle speculation on my part, because the operation of chance plays an integral and crucial role in our own form of life here on Earth, as both quantum physics and molecular biology have shown. In the beginning, so we are told by the cosmologists, was the big bang, and out of that almighty and still continuing explosion, our Earth was formed. Its creation was a product of chance, one chance in unimaginably large odds;

matter itself, physics has revealed, is subject to the laws not of providence but of probability. That is, the physical laws which determine the way the Earth is are not hard and fast: the discoveries of quantum mechanics demonstrated that they operate in an altogether different way, through probabilities. As everybody knows, without quite understanding what it signifies, quanta 'jump', they behave in peculiar ways which go against all the established laws of classical physics.

Einstein could not bring himself to accept the extraordinary weirdness, as it has been described, of the behaviour of atomic particles. 'I cannot believe that God plays dice,' was his celebrated dictum. He grew up to believe, as most of us do, that the universe is governed by immutable laws, which were susceptible of mathematical explanation. What quantum physics showed was that fundamental atomic processes occur at random. The 'rules' governing microscopic particles are statistical. More than that, human intention influences the outcome of experiments. So God does play dice with the universe. Einstein, in that particular sense, was wrong, or rather, he allowed his life-long belief in the order of nature to take precedence over the evidence to the contrary of quantum physics.

The process of chance in ordinary life is well established, for instance in the way insurance companies predict life expectancy. The actuaries who write your policy do not know how long you will survive to enjoy it, and they don't even think about that question: what they know is how long many thousands of people of the same age and social group will live on average. The working of probability in the behaviour of atomic particles is similar.

There is no way of predicting exactly when a particular atom of a radioactive substance will decay: but experiments have shown that out of a large number of radioactive atoms of the same element a certain proportion will always decay in a certain time. Every radioactive element has a half-life, during which exactly half of the atoms in a sample decay. Radium has a half-life of 1,600 years, carbon–14 a half-life of a little under 6,000 years (which makes it so useful in archaeological dating). Without knowing what makes one atom in a vast array of atoms disintegrate while others do not, statistical tables enable physicists to predict the rate of decay in the same way that insurance companies predict life expectancy (as science writer John Gribbin explains in his entertaining account of quantum physics *In Search of Schrödinger's Cat*, 1984).

In physics nothing is real until it is observed – the atomic world does not exist in a definite state until an apparatus is set up to measure it; and in so doing the experimenter affects the behaviour of the phenomena observed. When I first came across this weird postulation – which is the central mystery of quantum physics – it occurred to me that in gambling nothing is real until the bet is on. In experiments to track electrons, as long as the observer is not actually looking at an electron, its behaviour is that of a wave of probability (like the numbers waiting to be spun on the wheel); the moment the observer looks at an electron it becomes a particle (the number is called). The wheel goes round, the numbers come up one after the other – but unless you are actually betting on the result (measuring the electron), the sequence has no significance, you certainly don't get an emotional charge from what's happening. (That is why it's not much fun watching other people, or standing around making 'mental' bets.)

I'm not seeking to press the analogy, but it is no accident that the examples of cards or dice come up so often in illustrating the workings of probability. How are we supposed to think about this atomic world of the quanta? physicist Heinz Pagels asked in his popularizing account of modern physics (*The Cosmic Code*, 1982). He chose a pack of cards to illustrate the answer:

Imagine that an individual atom is a deck of cards and a specific energy level of that atom corresponds to a specific poker hand dealt from the deck. Poker hands have probabilities that can be calculated – using the theory of card playing it is possible to determine precisely the possibility of a given hand's being obtained from the dealer. The theory does not predict the outcome of a particular deal. Demanding this latter kind of determinism requires looking into the deck – cheating. . . . The theory does not say whether in a particular single measurement the atom will in fact be found in a specific energy level, just as the theory of card playing can't predict the outcome of a specific deal. . . . The new quantum theory denies that such individual events can be determined . . . it is only the probability distribution of events that is causally determined by quantum theory, not the outcome of specific events.

Probability, instead of being merely a way of calculating chances in gambling – as was the popular view of it, going back to Pascal's original calculations about dicing – is at the very basis of physics. In fact the study of probability, from its beginnings as a science, was concerned with two separate things: on one side, for what it could reveal about games of chance, and on the other, with assessment of general propositions (like Pascal's wager on the existence of God) in a non-statistical way. In the early days, as *The Emergence of Probability* by Ian Hacking (1975) explains, the relation between the two was not perceived. It still seems a little quaint, even to us, that such a great thinker as Pascal should be troubled by his friends with 'low' questions about dice; but these puzzles about odds are directly related to the 'high' side of the science.

It's an interesting linkage, which dignifies the whole process of gambling, doesn't it? I mean if this is how the world is made . . . nothing is determined, it's all probabilities. The inclination which our species has to take risks, in particular to gamble, can be seen as a human metaphor, in microcosm, for the chanciness of the created world itself. 'Life is a gamble', as we all know, but in the sense that the very principles of nature operate through chance, life is a game in an infinitely profounder sense.

Life arose (according to the molecular biology theory of evolution) by the inter-action of the elements on the earth – hydrogen, carbon dioxide, ammonia, methane ('the primeval soup'), subjected to ultra-violet rays from the sun – reacting through an infinity of combinations and recombinations, over hundreds of millions of years, to produce the earliest microscopic life in the form of organic molecules, which evolved, in more familiar terms, into the building blocks of life, DNA and RNA.

This process in the evolution of living organisms can be likened to an endless game, in which chance was the determining factor, chance operating, that is, within chemical laws, by natural selection. Not 'blind' chance, as Richard Dawkins explains in his racy defence of Darwinian evolution *The Blind Watchmaker* (1986), but cumulative chance, which means a long, long series of small chance events, over aeons of time. The spontaneous arising of life was a long shot, admittedly – it might occur only once in a billion years. But that is not such a long shot as we might suppose.

Our human perception of probability is itself a limited one, as it were commensurate with our physical size and longevity. Dawkins makes the good point that just as our range of vision is a narrow band in the middle of a much broader spectrum of electromagnetic frequencies, so our ability to cope with probability lies in a fairly narrow band at the bottom of the scale, from familiar chances, such as throwing a double six with two dice (1 in 36), up to, say, getting a hole-in-one at golf, which is rare but not too improbable; but falls well short of, say, grasping the chance of getting four perfect hands dealt at bridge, which is 2,236,197,406,895,366,368,301,559,999, to 1!

The element of chance in the creation of life, which seems so extraordinary to us, might not do so to a creature from another planet, which had a lifetime of a million centuries, because its sense of probability would be very different from ours. In its experience of life, many long shots would happen as a matter of course. To it, even a perfect deal at bridge might seem quite plausible.

Chance and rules, if you think about it, are the basic elements of all games. Whether you are involved in organized sport on green fields or play two-handed on green baize, there is a set of rules within which chance – the unpredictable performance of the players, the run of the ball, the turn of the cards – decides the outcome. That is the whole interest of play: without the unknown and unpredictable element of chance (poker with all the cards open) all such games would be utterly boring. Obviously the degree to which chance affects different games may be more or less, but it is always there (in chess it is provided by the incalculable immensity of moves possible). Chance and rules, likewise, are the basic elements of nature: within physical laws, the behaviour of the atoms and molecules is random. That is why biologists can claim: 'Everything that happens in the world resembles a vast game in which nothing is determined in advance but the rules.' The 'play' is what matters.

Chance usually gets a bad press. The sheer uncontrollableness of chance runs against human desire for certainty, for being sure of what we are doing. ('Security,' warned the witches in Macbeth, 'is mortal's chiefest enemy.') Moreover, the prevalence of chance undercuts the feeling, shared by almost all peoples since mankind first evolved, that there must be a purpose to life, that our existence is in some way determined. Maybe it is so, maybe not. In either case chance is at the very core of things, both in the operation of physical laws in matter and in the formation of protein molecules in the creation of life.

The instinct of play – by which I mean here the pleasurable challenge of exploiting chance in games – was for generations past underrated or neglected and even today tends to be looked down on as a secondary matter. 'It's only a game' is a way of saying something is relatively unimportant. But it is very important!

All our capabilities arise from play. First there is the play of limbs and muscles. The aimless grasping and kicking of an infant develop into carefully coordinated movements. Then there is the play of our senses. Playful curiosity sends us in search of profound knowledge. From play with colours, shapes and sounds emerge immortal works of art. The first expressions of love take the form of play: the secret exchange of glances, dancing, the interplay of thoughts and emotions, the yielding of partners to each other. In Sanskrit, the union of lovers is called *kridaratnam*, 'the jewel of games'.

Thus Eigen and Winkler in *Laws of the Game* (1975), a study of the interplay between chance and natural law, who go so far (following Hermann Hesse) as to devise bead games, played with dice, which simulate the basic statistical processes of life itself – games which symbolize population growth, natural selection, life and death. The point which such bead games illustrate is how the random throw of the dice – within the rules of the game – determines the pattern of beads on the board, just as chance –

operating within natural law (God playing dice) – determines evolutionary processes.

As I said at the start of this book I am not a gambler, in any serious way, and that is true, but I sometimes feel that I could be – to throw money, caution, sense, to the wind and let go! I gratify my gambling instincts in a weekly poker game: this particular game is a game of high skill, but with a large gambling element in it. No doubt that is its attraction for all the players in the school, week in week out. During an extended period when I could not play in the game, I found it necessary to assuage my gambling instincts directly, by casino gaming. Because I happen to be very disciplined in my approach to gambling (a habit instilled from poker) I never got over my head, or anywhere near it, and could more or less regulate this gambling outlet like an emotional tap. Quite convenient, and not unduly costly. Sometimes I got lucky, sometimes not: luck is a neutral concept, on which every player imposes his individual valuation.

I think this sort of need to find an outlet in taking risks – in my own case in playing high stakes poker – goes deep in everyone, goes right back down the DNA chain, spanning thousands of millions of years, to the origins of life itself.

INDEX